41

41

A PORTRAIT OF MY FATHER

by

GEORGE W. BUSH

RANDOM HOUSE
LARGE PRINT

To Mother and Dad with love

CONTENTS

Author's Note   xi

BEGINNINGS   1

WAR   28

HEADING WEST   50

HAT IN THE RING   87

MAN OF THE HOUSE   120

DIPLOMACY   138

RUNNER-UP   180

WITHIN A HEARTBEAT   208

THE ROAD TO THE WHITE HOUSE   235

NUMBER 41   277

THE HARDEST YEAR   324

THE AFTERLIFE   373

Acknowledgments   415

Index   421

AUTHOR'S NOTE

A FEW MONTHS AFTER we left the White House, Laura and I invited Tim Lawson and his wife, Dorie McCullough Lawson, to our ranch in Crawford, Texas. I had commissioned Tim—a real artist, not an amateur like me—to paint some scenes of the landscape we love. As Tim observed the native prairie grasses and live oaks on the property, Dorie and I talked about her father, David McCullough. I told her that a highlight of my presidency had been meeting her dad, the fine historian and Pulitzer Prize–winning biographer of John Adams.

After updating me on her father's health and projects, Dorie said, "You should know that one of my father's great regrets in studying John Adams is there was no serious account of him by his son John Quincy Adams."

She knew, of course, my connection to John Quincy: We are the only sons of Presidents who have served as Presidents ourselves. "For history's sake," she said, "I think you should write a book about your father."

At the time, I was working on a memoir of my own presidency. But Dorie's idea planted a seed. Eventually, it sprouted into this book.

Over the years, I suspect there will be many books analyzing George Herbert Walker Bush, the man and his presidency. Some of those works may be objective. This one is not. This book is a love story—a personal portrait of the extraordinary man who I am blessed to call my dad. I don't purport to cover every aspect of his life or his years of public service. I do hope to show you why George H.W. Bush is a great President and an even better father.

I loved writing this book; I hope you enjoy reading it.

BEGINNINGS

IN LATE MAY 2014, I received a phone call from Jean Becker, my father's longtime chief of staff. She got straight to the point.

"Your dad wants to make a parachute jump on his ninetieth birthday. What do you think?"

About eighteen months earlier, Jean had called to review the funeral arrangements for my father. He had spent nearly a month in the hospital with pneumonia, and many feared that this good man was headed toward eternity. He could not walk, and he tired easily. In my phone calls to Dad, he never complained. Self-pity is not in George Bush's DNA. Now he was hoping to complete another parachute jump—the eighth of his life, counting the one he made after his torpedo bomber was struck

1

by Japanese anti-aircraft fire over the Pacific in 1944.

"Are you sure this is what he wants?" I asked.

"Absolutely," she said.

"What do the doctors say?"

"Some say yes, some say no."

"What about Mother?"

"She is concerned. She knows that he wants to do it. But she's worried that the jump will tire him out and he won't be able to enjoy the birthday party that she's planning for that night."

After some thought, I said, "I think he ought to do it."

"Why?"

"Because it will make him feel younger."

The truth is that my opinion didn't matter much. After a parachute jump on his eighty-fifth birthday, my father had announced that he would make another jump on his ninetieth birthday. And George H.W. Bush is a man of his word.

A few weeks later, Laura and I arrived for the birthday celebration in Kennebunkport, Maine. The jump logistics were complete, the party was planned, and Mother was now on board. The afternoon before the jump, I sat next to Dad on the porch of his beloved home at Walker's Point, perched on a rocky outcropping over the Atlantic. I had been painting an ocean scene and was wearing cargo pants stained with oil paint. For a few peaceful minutes, we stared quietly at the sea.

"What are you thinking about, Dad?" I asked.

"It's just beautiful," he said, still looking out at the ocean. It seemed that he had said all that he wanted to say.

We sat quietly for a few more minutes. Was he reflecting on the jump? His life? God's grace? I did not want to interrupt.

Then he spoke. "Do those pants come in clean?"

I laughed, something I have been doing with my father all my life. His quip was typical. He was not nervous about his jump or his life. He was at peace. And he was sharing his joy with others.

The morning of Dad's birthday, June 12, dawned chilly and gray. There was a modest breeze, about fifteen miles per hour. At first, we feared that the clouds might force a change in plans. Fortunately, the veteran paratroopers coordinating the jump, known as the All Veteran Group, determined that the visibility was sufficient. The mission was a go.

The crew fired up the Bell 429 helicopter that was parked on the lush green lawn outside the two-story wooden cabin that served as Dad's office at Walker's Point. Dad was clad in a custom-fitted black flight suit with a patch that read "41@90." His preflight routine included a final weather clearance, a harness check, and an interview with my daughter Jenna, a correspondent for the **TODAY** show. Even with his jump looming, he was willing to share his time to help his granddaughter.

"What's your birthday wish on your ninetieth birthday?" Jenna asked.

"For happiness for my grandkids," he replied. "I hope they have the same kind of life I have for ninety years—full of joy."

He did have one more wish: "Make sure the parachute opens."

Family and friends gathered at the landing zone: the lawn of my parents' church, St. Ann's, the same place where Dad had landed five years earlier and where his parents had been married ninety-three years earlier. (As Mother put it, if the jump did not succeed, at least we wouldn't have to travel far for the burial.) At about ten forty-five a.m., one of the members of the jump team approached me.

"Mr. President," he said, "your father is airborne."

A few minutes later, we spotted a small speck in the sky—the chopper at 6,500 feet. After the helicopter made a circle around the church, we saw several chutes pop open. Two belonged to the video jumpers tasked with chronicling the leap. The other was a large red, white, and blue chute carrying Dad and master jumper Mike Elliott, who was making his third jump with Dad and his 10,227th jump overall. The crowd cheered as the tandem headed our way.

"They sure are coming in hot," my brother Marvin said, with a touch of worry.

He was right. The wind had taken the chute off course. Mike corrected with a hard turn in the final descent. Dad slammed into the ground, skidded for a few feet, and then face-planted into the grass.

The crowd went silent. Would he get up? Was he hurt? No one moved until the ground crew lifted him into his wheelchair. The grandkids struck up a chorus of "Happy Birthday" to camouflage their anxiety.

Finally the sea of uniforms parted. George H.W. Bush had a smile on his face.

I grabbed Mother, and we walked toward Dad. She leaned over and gave him a kiss. I followed with a handshake and a hug.

"How did it feel?" I asked.

"Cold," he said.

"I'm sure proud of you, Dad," I said. "That was an awesome jump."

He pointed to his partner. "Mike did all the work," he said.

The scene captured the character of George Bush. He was daring and courageous, always seeking new adventures and new challenges. He was humble and quick to share credit. He deflected attention from himself and refused to brag about his accomplishments. He trusted others and inspired their loyalty. And above all, he found joy in his family and his faith. Nothing made him happier than being surrounded by his wife, children, and grandchildren in a place where he had so many wonderful memories.

After the jump, Dad returned to Walker's

Point to eat, take a nap, and prepare for the 250 family members, friends, and Bush administration alumni attending the birthday party that night. He rewarded himself with a Bloody Mary over lunch. Then he received a call from his friend Arnold Schwarzenegger, the movie star and former Governor of California.

"Happy birthday," Arnold said, "to the most badass ninety-year-old I know."

I agreed with Arnold's assessment. George H.W. Bush set an example for many people in many ways. He is determined to live his life to the fullest—to the very end.

WALKER'S POINT, the site of my father's ninetieth-birthday parachute jump, is a fitting place to begin the story of George Herbert Walker Bush. The stunning eleven acres consist of a rugged promontory jutting into the Atlantic Ocean off the southeast coast of Maine close to the town of Kennebunkport. The land was purchased around the turn of the twentieth century by my father's grandfather and namesake, George Herbert Walker. Known to his family and friends as Bert, G.H.

Walker was a fierce competitor in all aspects of life. In his younger years, he played competitive polo and briefly held the title of Missouri heavyweight boxing champion. Later he was an accomplished golfer who founded the Walker Cup competition between American and British amateurs.

Bert Walker's competitive drive extended into the world of business, where he earned a reputation as a hard-charging entrepreneur. He started his own investment firm in his hometown of St. Louis at age twenty-five. After a few flush years, he moved his operation to a larger stage, New York City. There he joined forces with another savvy investor, William Averell Harriman, and became President of W.A. Harriman & Company. Bert Walker wasn't afraid to risk money, and he sure wasn't afraid to spend it. He owned a yacht, Rolls-Royces, and homes up and down the East Coast—including Walker's Point, the only one that remains in our family.

As a father, Bert Walker doled out tough love to his sons. His youngest son, Lou, once showed up drunk for a mixed doubles championship at the tennis club in Kennebunkport. The whole family was gathered for the match. When Bert

Walker, standing courtside clad in a tie, discovered his son's debauchery, he pulled him off the court. Back at Walker's Point, Lou was summoned into his father's office. Bert Walker told him that his drunken performance had stained the family reputation. Then he imposed the sentence: Instead of returning for his next semester at Yale, Lou would spend a year working in the Pennsylvania coal mines. To show up drunk for tennis was rude and disrespectful, and those qualities were not tolerated in Bert Walker's boys.

In sharp contrast to the way he treated his sons, Bert Walker showered his two daughters with affection. He showed particular warmth toward his younger daughter, Dorothy, who was born in Kennebunkport in 1901. In return, Dorothy Walker adored her father. And somehow she managed to inherit his best qualities while sanding off his rough edges. Eventually she passed those traits on to her son George Herbert Walker Bush.

Like her father, my grandmother had an insatiable competitive streak. My mother once dubbed her "the most competitive living human," a title she earned in pursuits from tennis (she was a nationally prominent player in the small world of women's amateur tennis) to tiddlywinks. She once challenged a friend to swim from Walker's Point to the Kennebunk River Club, over a mile away. Thinking she was joking, the friend quit after a few hundred yards. My grandmother swam the full distance in the frigid Atlantic waters. In her most legendary feat, she played in a family softball game while nine months pregnant, swatted a home run in her final at bat, and then announced that she had started labor as she crossed the plate.

My grandmother tempered her zeal to win with genuine humility, and she demanded that all her children do the same. She expected grace in victory, good sportsmanship in defeat, and a commitment to "do your best" at all times. She instructed her children to downplay personal accomplishments and share credit with others. And her cardinal rule was that one must never brag. In her view, arrogance was unattractive, and a person with true self-confidence did not need to gloat. "No one likes a braggadocio," she liked to say.

When my father was a child in Greenwich,

Connecticut, my grandmother asked him how one of his baseball games had gone.

"It was great," he replied. "I hit a home run."

"That's nice, George," she responded.

Then she stuck in the dagger. "But how did **the team** do?"

Another time, Dad explained that he'd lost a tennis match because he'd been off his game.

"You don't have a game," his mother shot back. "If you work harder, maybe you'll get one."

His mother's early lessons in humility stayed with my father his entire life. During his 1988 presidential campaign, I accompanied him to the National Press Club in Washington, DC. He was there to share his knowledge of world affairs and answer questions from the audience. George Bush knew the policy issues cold. His handling of questions on Soviet relations and Central America was a tour de force. As a light-hearted finale, the moderator asked, "Why are you wearing a red tie?"

The question caught him off guard. From my chair next to the podium, I could see him struggling for an answer. I stage-whispered, "Because I spilled gravy on my blue one."

Dad grabbed the verbal lifeline, and the room erupted in laughter at his self-deprecating quip. Then he ruined the moment by blurting out, "That's what you have a son for." That was typical of my father. Proper attribution of the gravy line made no difference to me; I just wanted him to look good. But George Bush was just too humble to fake it.

Dorothy Walker Bush was a woman of strong faith. She read Bible verses to her children over breakfast every morning. One of her favorite passages was Proverbs 27:2: "Let another man praise thee, and not thine own mouth." Every Sunday, she expected the family to go to church, usually Christ Church in Greenwich or St. Ann's in Kennebunkport.

While religion played a central role in her life, she never used her beliefs to judge others harshly. Her faith was solid and enduring, and it gave her an enormous capacity to love. When I think of her, the words **angelic** and **saintly** come to mind. One of my favorite memories is of visiting her and my grandfather in Greenwich when I was little. She would tickle my back as we knelt down to say prayers before bed: "Now I lay me down to sleep."

My grandmother reserved a special kind of love for my dad. As his brother Jonathan once told me, "Mum loved us all, but she loved your father more." He continued, "The amazing thing is, none of us resented that. We loved him too." It says a lot about my grandmother and my father that their family felt that way. When Dorothy Walker Bush died at age ninety-one, Dad called her "the beacon of the family . . . the candle around which all the moths fluttered." Of all the influences in his life, nobody did more to mold his character than his mother.

IN THE FALL of 1919, shortly after she celebrated her eighteenth birthday, Dorothy Walker met Prescott Bush in her hometown of St. Louis. He stood six foot four and weighed well over two hundred pounds, without a trace of flab. He had dark black hair, a deep baritone voice, and a big, bright smile. He had come to my grandmother's house to visit her older sister, Nancy, whom he had recently met at a St. Louis social club. When he saw Dottie Walker stride into the room from an afternoon tennis match, he was smitten. Before long, so was she.

Like Dorothy Walker, Prescott Bush had grown up in the Midwest. His father, S.P. Bush, ran a manufacturing company in Columbus, Ohio, called Buckeye Steel. An avid sportsman, S.P. had helped organize a local baseball league, served as an assistant coach on the Ohio State football team, and cofounded Scioto Country Club, which featured a Donald Ross–designed golf course where Bobby Jones won the U.S. Open in 1926 and a young Jack Nicklaus learned to play.

After spending his childhood in Columbus, Prescott Bush went east to Rhode Island for boarding school at St. George's. He excelled in the classroom and, like his father, was a fine athlete. His best sports were baseball and golf. While my grandfather wasn't exactly the Golden Bear, he remains the best golfer ever to tee it up in our family. He held a scratch handicap for most of his life, competed in the U.S. Senior Open, and more than once shot his age.

For college, Prescott Bush went to Yale. (His grandfather James Smith Bush had started the family tradition of attending Yale.) A star first baseman on the baseball team, he was also such a solid golfer that the golf team recruited him for their toughest matches. On some spring days he would hit the links in the morning and the ballpark in the afternoon. He also had a great voice. He sang with the Yale Glee Club and the Whiffenpoofs. While we inherited some of Prescott Bush's traits, my father's branch of the Bush tree did not acquire his vocal talents.

In 1916, just before he began his senior year, my grandfather was one of a handful of Yale students to volunteer for active duty with the Connecticut National Guard. When America entered World War I, Lieutenant Bush shipped off to France as a field artillery officer. He spent ten weeks on the front lines under the command of General John "Black Jack" Pershing. When Germany surrendered, he served as part of the occupation force before returning home with the rank of captain. His decision to volunteer made a profound impression on my father, who would face a similar choice a generation later.

After the war, Prescott Bush took an assistant manager job with Simmons Hardware in St. Louis, where he soon met Dorothy Walker. They married in August 1921 at St. Ann's in

Kennebunkport. (At the time, I doubt they could have envisioned the parachute jump there ninety-three years later.) As a present for the new couple, Bert Walker built them a bungalow on the grounds of Walker's Point. The house still exists and is now occupied by my sister Dorothy, who is named for our grandmother.

My grandparents spent their early married years on the move. Prescott Bush took on business assignments in St. Louis; Kingsport, Tennessee; and Columbus, Ohio. Eventually he accepted an executive position with a rubber company called Stedman Products in South Braintree, Massachusetts. My grandparents found a house in Milton, Massachusetts, on Adams Street, named for the political family that produced Presidents John and John Quincy Adams. There, on June 12, 1924, George Herbert Walker Bush entered the world.

It wasn't long before Prescott Bush was on the move again. In 1925, he accepted a new job at the U.S. Rubber Company in New York City. He moved his family to Greenwich, Connecticut, about thirty-five miles northeast of Manhattan. Greenwich was the town where my father would grow up and my grandparents would live for the rest of their lives.

ONE OF THE lessons that my father and I learned from Prescott Bush was the value of making and keeping friends. During his time at Yale, Pres Bush had befriended Roland Harriman, known as Bunny. (I have never understood how a man got the nickname "Bunny.") Shortly after my grandfather arrived in New York, Bunny floated the idea of his joining him at the W.A. Harriman investment house, which his older brother, Averell, had founded and Bert Walker had joined as President. My grandfather accepted the offer. His trust of Bunny overcame any reluctance that he might have felt about working for his father-in-law. A well-tended friendship thus opened the door to my grandfather's thirty-year career in investment banking. Eventually he became one of the leading partners at the firm, which merged with Brown Brothers to become Brown Brothers Harriman, one of the most respected and successful firms on Wall Street. The firm was also bipartisan. Averell Harriman, a Democrat,

later became Governor of New York and a leading member of the Roosevelt and Truman ad-
ministrations, while Prescott Bush and his son
and grandsons became active on the Republican side of the aisle.

Prescott Bush taught his children that the
measure of a meaningful life was not money
but character. He stressed that financial success came with an obligation to serve the community and the nation that made prosperity
possible. Although he was busy with his Wall
Street career, he always made time to serve
causes that mattered to him. He was an early
leader and prolific fund-raiser for the USO,
which supports our military and veterans. He
served as an official in the United States Golf
Association, eventually becoming its President
(a position that his father-in-law, Bert Walker,
also held), and he was a strong supporter of the
United Negro College Fund. For two decades
he served as moderator of the Greenwich Representative Town Meeting, a position that paid
nothing and required huge amounts of time.
While his friends were out at dinner parties or
playing cards, he was on the phone trying to
persuade homeowners to grant easements for

the Merritt Parkway, an important highway that connects Connecticut and New York. A devotion to serving others was one of the most important values that Prescott Bush instilled in his children—and that my father passed along to my siblings and me.

Prescott Bush adhered to the creed that when you give your word, you keep it. In 1963, Nelson Rockefeller divorced his wife and married a former campaign volunteer who had left her husband and children to be with him. Even though he and Rockefeller shared a political party, my grandfather denounced him in a speech at a Greenwich girls' school that **Time** magazine described as "one of the most wrathful public lashings in memory." My grandfather asked whether the country had "come to the point in our life as a nation where the Governor of a great state—one who perhaps aspires to the nomination for President of the United States—can desert a good wife, [the] mother of his grown children, divorce her, then persuade a young mother of four youngsters to abandon her husband and their four children and marry the Governor." Clearly Prescott Bush was not afraid to express his beliefs. I can only imagine

what he would say if he saw what our society
looks like today.

While my grandfather held strict views on
moral issues, he had a lighthearted side as well.
He loved to sing, and some of his happiest times
came at family sing-alongs or rehearsals with
the quartets he organized. He had a booming
laugh and loved a good joke, although it had
to be a clean one. More than once, he stormed
out of a room when he was offended by someone's attempt at off-color humor. In 1959, my
grandfather was nominated as the "presidential candidate" of the Alfalfa Club, a fixture of
the Washington social scene. His acceptance
speech brought down the house.

"Of my staff I have demanded the same devotion to duty that I have shown," he said. "In-
deed, everyone in my office shoots under eighty.
Carrying on the great tradition of Thomas Jefferson, we have endeavored to prove the axiom
that the government that governs best governs
least." When he talked about the sacrifices that
my grandmother had made to move to Washington, he paraphrased Nathan Hale in lamenting, "I regret that I have but one wife to give for
my country." Years later, my father, my brother

Jeb, and I all followed in his footsteps as Alfalfa Club presidential nominees.

Dad idolized his father. In many ways, he patterned his own life after Prescott Bush's: volunteering for the war, excelling in business, and then serving his fellow citizens. I remember the look of pride that would light up Dad's face when he told his friends that his father was a United States Senator. I suspect one of his first thoughts after he took the oath of office as President in 1989 was how much he wished he could have shared the moment with his father. That made it all the sweeter for me to embrace my dad at my presidential inaugurations in 2001 and 2005.

AS A LITTLE BOY, Dad loved to share with his older brother, Pres (Prescott Bush Jr., named after my grandfather). Any time he received a gift or a toy, my father would run after Pres, offer up the item, and say, "Have half." When he got a new bike, he tried to give half of it to Pres by letting him push one of the pedals. My grandfather took to calling him "Have half."

Prescott and Dorothy Bush insisted on a rigorous education for their children. Dad spent his first eight school years at Greenwich Country Day School, a private school founded by local families. His early schooling experience stood in stark contrast to mine. At Greenwich Country Day, many kids arrived in a car driven by the family chauffeur. At Sam Houston Elementary in Midland, Texas, most kids walked or rode their bikes.

For high school, Prescott and Dorothy Bush sent their two oldest sons to Phillips Academy in Andover, Massachusetts. My grandparents chose the school because of its academic excellence and because they wanted their sons to get to know boys from different parts of the country.

Andover proved to be a valuable experience, as it did for me when I attended the school a generation later. Both my father and I benefited from the discipline and challenge of the academics. And we both learned important lessons outside the classroom. As teenagers on our own for the first time, we both learned to be independent, to work hard, and to make friends.

At Andover, Dad displayed a natural leadership ability. People gravitated to him and wanted to follow him. His teammates chose him as captain of the baseball and soccer teams and playing manager of the basketball team. He headed up the school chapel's fund-raising efforts and was elected President of the senior class.

Even though my father was a so-called big man on campus, he didn't let his reputation go to his head. One day a younger student named Bruce Gelb was getting hazed by some upperclassmen, possibly because he was one of the school's few Jewish students. When Dad saw the upperclassmen picking on him, he told them to knock it off. They listened. George Bush went on his way and never thought much of it. Bruce Gelb did. He always remembered that one of the most popular boys on campus didn't turn a blind eye to his suffering. He became a strong supporter of Dad's throughout his life, and my father later appointed him to several important government positions, including Ambassador to Belgium and Director of the United States Information Agency.

ANDOVER LIKED TO stress its motto, "The end depends on the beginning." George Bush was blessed with a good beginning. His family loved him, provided him with a great education, and instilled in him good character traits. He had made a large group of friends, impressed his teachers, and excelled in sports. He had also lined up his next step. He had been accepted to Yale, where he would follow in his father's footsteps.

Then, on Sunday, December 7, 1941, everything changed. Dad and some classmates were walking across the Andover campus near the chapel when they learned that the Japanese had attacked Pearl Harbor. The next day, long lines of volunteers formed outside recruiting stations across the country.

Every boy my father's age faced the same choice: enlist for the war, or continue with life as planned. The advice Dad received all pointed in the same direction. Andover's commencement speaker his senior year was Henry Stimson, President Roosevelt's secretary of war and an Andover alumnus. He urged the graduates to go to college, assuring them that they would have their opportunity to join the military later. Prescott Bush strongly agreed. He told Dad to go to Yale and find his own way to serve from there.

There was another reason for my father to stay close to home. During Christmas vacation of his senior year in high school, he attended a dance at a country club in Greenwich. While chatting with friends, he was struck by the beauty of a girl across the room. Barbara Pierce was sixteen; he was seventeen. He wanted to ask her to dance, but there was a problem: He couldn't waltz. So they sat out the dance and just talked. He learned that she was from Rye, New York, and that she was home from a boarding school in South Carolina. They hit it off and agreed to meet the following day at a Christmas party at the Apawamis Club in Rye.

That night, the band did not play a waltz, and George H.W. Bush got Barbara onto the dance floor. There was instant affection, and they agreed to stay in touch. They saw each other again at the Andover senior prom, after which he gave her a good-night kiss. (She insists it was her first.) Neither of my parents can recall much of what they talked about in those early days, but they remember making each other laugh. Before long, they had fallen in love.

One thing they discussed was his decision to join the military. As my father described to

Mother, he was outraged by the attack on Pearl Harbor. The murder of more than 2,400 innocent people created in him the same sense of righteous indignation that many Americans— including me—experienced after the terrorist attacks of September 11, 2001. He also felt a sense of obligation. His father had always stressed that the comforts they enjoyed came with a responsibility to give back. In the words of the Bible, "To whom much is given, much is required." George Bush recognized that he had been given a lot. He was physically able to serve, and he felt a duty to do so. He told my mother that he had decided to join the Navy as an aviator.

To that point in his life, George Bush had not faced many tough decisions. He had never defied his father. But Dad had made up his mind, and he did not waver. After his high school commencement, he looked his father in the eye and said, "I'm going in." My grandfather shook his hand. He respected the decision, and from that point on he gave his complete support.

George H.W. Bush enlisted on June 12, 1942, his eighteenth birthday. Two months later, his father accompanied him to Penn Station in

New York, where he would board a train to North Carolina to commence his training. As my father stood on the platform, the stern and imposing Prescott Bush wrapped his son in a hug. For the first time in his life, Dad saw his father cry.

WAR

EVERY PILOT REMEMBERS his first flight. For me, it was in a Cessna 172 at Moody Air Force Base in Valdosta, Georgia, in 1968. For my father, it was in an open-cockpit Stearman N2S-3 at Wold-Chamberlain Naval Air Base in Minneapolis in 1942. The cadets called the plane the "Yellow Peril," because it was painted yellow and could prove perilous to fly. Its other nickname was the "Washing Machine," a reference to the number of cadets who washed out of pilot training.

My dad described his first solo flight as "one of the biggest thrills" of his life. I know exactly what he meant. It's an exhilarating feeling to sit in the cockpit, accelerate down the runway, and lift off into the air. The plane doesn't care where you came from, where you went to school, or who your parents are. All that matters is whether you have the skill to fly—"the right stuff," as Tom Wolfe called it. Ensign George Bush flew almost every day through the bitter Minnesota winter. He grew comfortable in the air and excelled at landing on snow and ice—a valuable skill, but not one that would prove useful in the South Pacific.

Pilots say that learning to fly makes you feel taller. In my father's case that was certainly true. By the time his commanding officer pinned on his gold flight wings at Corpus Christi Naval Air Station in June 1943, he had grown two inches since his enlistment, topping out at six feet, two inches. He was not quite nineteen years old, making him the youngest pilot in the United States Navy.

After flight school, Dad had a brief period of leave before moving on to his next assignment. He spent it with his family in Maine, and his mother generously invited a special guest: Barbara Pierce, who was on summer break from Smith College. For two weeks in Maine, my parents were together constantly. By the end of the trip, they had decided to secretly get engaged.

The secret didn't last long. In December 1943, shortly before a commissioning ceremony for the aircraft carrier USS **San Jacinto,** which would carry my father into battle, my parents decided to inform their families of their plans to marry. To their amazement, everybody knew the secret. Their love for each other was obvious. As my father wrote to my mother, "I love you, precious, with all my heart and to know that you love me means my life. How often I have thought about the immeasurable joy that will be ours some day. How lucky our children will be to have a mother like you." (That is one of their only remaining wartime letters; the rest were lost during one of my parents' many moves.) After the carrier commissioning ceremony, my grandmother slipped my father an engagement ring—a star sapphire that came from her sister, Nancy. Later that day, he presented it to Barbara. She still wears it today (although apparently she still has her suspicions that it might actually be blue glass).

IN JANUARY 1944, after completing the intensive year and a half of training, Ensign Bush reported for duty aboard the USS **San Jacinto**. The **San Jac** was named for the battle in which General Sam Houston defeated the Mexican caudillo Santa Anna. In a glimpse of Dad's life to come, the carrier flew both the Stars and Stripes and the Lone Star flag.

The young Navy pilot joined a group of fliers that would form squadron VT-51. Jack Guy came from rural Georgia and had left his job as a bank teller to join the Navy. Lou Grab grew up in Sacramento, California, where his father owned a gas station. Stan Butchart was a native of Spokane, Washington, who had always wanted to be a pilot. The squadron mates had little in common. At Andover, George Bush had learned that he could relate to fellow students from different parts of the country. In the military, he learned that he could relate to people from different walks of life.

My father had a knack for making people laugh. He came up with nicknames for everyone. (Sound familiar?) Stan Butchart was "Butch." Jack Guy was "Jackoguy," based on his middle initial. My father acquired a distinctive moniker of his own. During a training run near the Maryland coast, he was flying low over the beach when he saw a circus setting up below. Apparently the animals didn't have much experience with naval aviation, because the roar of the plane sent one of the elephants into a stampede through town. From that point on, Dad's buddies dubbed him "Ellie the Elephant." He responded with an elephant-screech imitation that he honed throughout the war. I never heard him unleash the elephant call, although it might have come in handy when he was Chairman of the Republican National Committee.

The plane that alarmed the circus elephant was the TBF/TBM Avenger, a torpedo bomber. The Avenger was the Navy's largest single-engine, carrier-based plane. It held one pilot, two crewmen, and four five-hundred-pound bombs. To accommodate the ton of ordnance, the plane had a bulging belly, earning it the affectionate nickname "Pregnant Turkey."

The Avenger was a heavy aircraft that was challenging to fly. The toughest task was landing on the narrow, bobbing deck of an aircraft carrier. A proper landing demanded concentration, precision, and teamwork. A pilot had to approach at the correct angle, follow the flag signals of a landing officer, and then catch one of the carrier's tail hooks to avoid skidding off the deck. When I was President, I was a passenger for a landing in an S-3B Viking jet aboard the USS **Abraham Lincoln**. I had grown up with great respect for carrier pilots, but after that landing my respect doubled.

By the spring of 1944, the **San Jac** was bound for the Pacific. My father was in the cockpit of his Avenger for the first catapult shot off the new carrier. As he wrote to his mother, he was "mighty glad the machine worked." By April 20, 1944, the carrier had traveled from Norfolk, Virginia, through the Panama Canal, and out to Pearl Harbor in the middle of the Pacific. The crew saw the charred remains of the USS **Utah** and **Arizona,** a fresh reminder of the reason they were at war—and of the enemy they were about to confront.

The months after Pearl Harbor had been grim, as the Japanese war machine expanded its reach throughout the Pacific. By the spring of 1942, only Australia and New Zealand remained as allied bulwarks. The tide began to turn in May of that year, when American and Australian naval forces stopped the Japanese advance at the Battle of Coral Sea. A month later, the United States won its first major victory at Midway. The Navy then began an island-hopping campaign to liberate Japanese-occupied territories one by one, with the ultimate objective of attacking Japan.

The **San Jac**'s first assignment was to strike Japanese installations on Wake Island. The mission was successful, but the reality of combat quickly hit home. On a patrol flight, Dad's roommate and closest friend on the carrier, Jim Wykes, dropped off the radar screen. Search parties could not locate him. He and his two crewmen were listed as missing. Soon it was clear they were not coming back. My father ached for his friend. He understood that death was part of war, but this loss was personal.

A few days later, he wrote a heartfelt letter to Jim's mother. "I know your son well and have long considered myself fortunate to be one of his intimate friends," he wrote. "His kindly nature and all around goodness have won for him the friendship and respect of every officer and enlisted man in the squadron." He continued, "You have lost a loving son; we have lost a beloved friend."

That was the first of many such letters that my father would write to the families of fallen comrades during the war. Decades later, he would write similar letters as President. So would I. Of course, nothing you say in such a letter can ever make up for the loss of a loved one. But the simple act of writing the note—of showing that you care—can help ease a grieving family's pain.

After the engagement at Wake Island, the **San Jac** continued toward Saipan. In mid-June, the carrier came under sudden attack by Japanese planes. As the catapult launched my father's Avenger into the air, the oil pressure suddenly dropped. The engine was failing. The only option was a water landing. Ensign Bush guided the plane into the ocean, touching down with the tail and skidding across the water. He and his crew climbed out onto the wing, inflated the life raft, and paddled away as the Avenger's bombs exploded underwater. An American destroyer, the **C.K. Bronson**, scooped them up with a cargo net. It would not be the last time that George Bush gave thanks for a life raft.

Flying was dangerous, but so was life on the ship. One night my father was on duty on the

carrier deck when a plane approached for landing. The pilot misjudged the distance, failed
to grab a tail hook, and smashed into a gun
mount. The pilot, crew, and several bystand-
ers were killed. Dad saw the pilot's severed leg
twitching on the deck until a petty officer or-
dered the sailors to clean up the mess and get
ready for more landings.

Those experiences must have deeply affected
a twenty-year-old kid. The more I have learned
about the horrors of World War II, the more
my admiration has grown for George Bush and
the many others in his generation who served.

OF ALL THE harrowing days that George H.W.
Bush endured, none was more dramatic than
September 2, 1944. The pilots in the squadron were up early for a briefing on their mission to take out the radio tower on the heavily
fortified island of Chichi Jima. The structure
was the most important communications node
in the Bonin Islands, a key element in protect-
ing the heart of the Japanese empire.

My father almost always flew with the same
two crewmen, gunner Leo Nadeau and radio-

man John Delaney. But that day Lieutenant Junior Grade Ted White asked if he could serve as the gunner. White, the squadron's ordnance officer and a Yale alum, wanted to see the weapons system in action. Dad warned that it might be a rough trip. They had taken heavy fire over Chichi Jima the day before. White insisted, my father agreed, and the skipper, Lieutenant Don Melvin, approved.

Around seven fifteen a.m., four Avengers lifted off the **San Jac** and flew in formation toward Chichi Jima. Hellcat fighters covered them from above. My father's plane, with White as gunner and Delaney manning the radio, was third in line to dive toward the target. As they began their descent, Japanese anti-aircraft guns on the island let loose. Tracer fire crossed the sky, and exploding shells filled the air with black smoke. All of a sudden, the Avenger shook hard and lurched forward. The plane had been hit. Smoke poured into the cockpit, and fire ran along the wings toward the fuel tanks.

Dad was determined to complete the mission. He continued his two-hundred-mile-per-hour dive, dropped his bombs, hit the target, and banked hard away from the island. He had hoped to make a water landing, but the plane was on fire and he was out of time. The only option was to bail out.

"Hit the silk!" he shouted to his crewmen through the intercom.

Then he turned the plane slightly to reduce pressure on the crew door. He assumed that Delaney and White had jumped. With seconds left, he unbuckled his harnesses, dove out of the cockpit, and pulled the rip cord on his parachute.

The jump did not go as planned. My father gashed his head and tore his parachute on the tail of the plane. He hit the water hard and submerged. When he surfaced, his head was bleeding, he was vomiting from swallowing seawater, and he had been stung by a Portuguese man-of-war. He swam furiously away from the island, which was only a few miles away.

Then he saw Doug West, one of his fellow Avenger pilots, tip his wings at an object in the water. It was an inflatable yellow life raft. One of the pilots had dropped it after they watched the plane crash. He climbed in and started paddling with his hands. Overhead, American pilots laid down withering fire to drive away a convoy of small boats that the Japanese had deployed to capture the downed flier.

For the next three hours, under the baking summer sun, he paddled against the current and prayed for rescue. Somehow he found the strength to keep going. I'll never know for sure what went through his mind. I think he must have thought back to the lessons his parents taught him—to try as hard as he could, never give up, and have faith that God would find a way to protect him.

Weary from paddling, he finally saw a black spot in the water. At first he thought he had imagined it, but eventually he could make out a periscope. His next fear was that it was a Japanese sub. As it got closer to him and surfaced, he recognized the U.S. Navy logo. The USS **Finback** rescued my father a few minutes before noon. Two sailors grabbed his arms and pulled him out of the life raft and onto the ship. "Welcome aboard, sir," one of the enlisted men said. "Happy to be aboard," he said, clearly an understatement.

In a remarkable twist of history, Ensign Bill Edwards captured my father's arrival on the

Finback using a handheld Kodak movie camera. Decades later, a national audience would see the footage of that morning in the Pacific: American sailors saving the life of a twenty-year-old pilot who would go on to be the President of the United States and the father of another.

IN THE DAYS after the shoot-down, my father thought constantly about his crewmen Delaney and White. Neither of them had been found. Aboard the **Finback,** he had nightmares about the crash. He would wake up wondering if he could have done more for his men. The day after his rescue, he wrote a letter to his parents saying that he felt "so terribly responsible for their fate." Eventually he would learn that witnesses to the crash had seen one of the crewmen bail out of the plane and fall to his death when his parachute failed to open. The other had almost certainly been killed aboard the plane.

My father wrote letters to the families of Delaney and White. He extended his sympathy and told them that he wished he could have done more. Del's sister Mary Jane wrote back. "You mention in your letter that you would like to help me in some way," she said. "There is a way, and that is to stop thinking you are in any way responsible for your plane accident and what has happened to your men. I might have thought you were if my brother Jack had not always spoken of you as the best pilot in the squadron."

Despite her words, Dad continued to feel a sense of responsibility for his crewmen's deaths. He stayed in touch with both of their families for decades. When he was elected President more than forty years after the crash, he invited Delaney's and White's sisters for a private visit in the White House. During Dad's interview with Jenna on his ninetieth birthday, almost seventy years after the shoot-down, she asked whether he still thought about his crewmates.

"I think about them all the time," he said.

MY FATHER SPENT about a month on the **Finback** before rejoining his squadron. Even though he had few official responsibilities, he threw himself into submarine life. He befriended the crew and learned as much as he could about the operation of the sub. Among other tasks, he volunteered to censor outgoing mail to prevent the release of classified information. He read letters from farm boys asking about the latest harvest and from lonely sailors professing their love for a sweetheart back home. The military was providing him with an education that was not available at Andover or Yale.

He volunteered to sit watch on the **Finback**, including the overnight shift. Years later, he would remember those quiet times alone on the submarine deck, underneath the pitch-black sky in the middle of the Pacific, as important moments of clarity in his life. He thought a lot about how grateful he was for his family. He thanked God for answering his prayers when he needed it most. And he dreamed about Barbara, the girl he loved and planned to marry.

After his time on the **Finback**, my father had the option to go home on leave. Although I am sure he would have loved to see Barbara and his family, he felt a duty to return to his squadron. He reunited with the **San Jac** in early November. In December, the men received a month of leave.

Lieutenant Bush arrived at the train station in

Rye, New York, on Christmas Eve 1944. As he stepped onto the platform, he saw the woman he had pictured so often during those long months at sea. Mother and Dad had planned to get married after the war. But during their months apart, they had agreed to have the wedding as soon as he returned home. Given the short notice, they had to handwrite the date on the invitation: January 6, 1945.

When asked on his ninetieth birthday what the happiest moment of his life had been, Dad said that it was the day that he married my mother. My parents had a classic wartime wedding: Dad in his Navy blues and Mother in her white dress with a veil borrowed from Dorothy Walker Bush. Several of my father's Navy pals, along with his younger brother Jonathan, served as ushers. His older brother, Pres, who had just gotten married a week earlier, acted as best man. My father agreed to a first dance but warned Mother it would be the last time he danced in public. Obviously he never dreamed that he would one day have to dance at twelve inaugural balls.

* * *

AFTER A BRIEF honeymoon in Sea Island, Georgia, my father returned to duty. His assignment was to prepare for the final stage of the war, the invasion of mainland Japan. The Japanese had defended their home islands ferociously, and the operation promised to be bloody. As he trained at an air base in Maine on April 12, 1945, he heard on the radio that President Roosevelt had died. My dad had disagreed with some of Roosevelt's domestic policies that dramatically expanded the reach of the federal government, but he respected his Commander-in-Chief and he mourned the loss of the nation's leader in such a perilous time.

Vice President Harry Truman took the oath of office that day. Having sat behind the same desk that he did, it's hard for me to imagine how overwhelming it must have been to take over unexpectedly in the midst of two major military campaigns, and then to be briefed for the first time on the secret program that had developed a nuclear weapon. Within months, Truman faced one of the most agonizing decisions any President has ever confronted. When the massive firebombing of Tokyo failed to break Japan's resistance, he gave the order to drop atomic bombs on Hiroshima and Nagasaki. He knew the human costs would be devastating. The introduction of a new and horrifying weapon destroyed the enemy's will to fight and spared many American lives, possibly my dad's. My father always defended Harry Truman's decision as courageous and right.

Mother and Dad had moved to Virginia Beach, where he was stationed before an expected deployment. There they heard the news of the Japanese surrender. They raced into the streets with his fellow pilots and their families to celebrate. Then they went to church, where they gave thanks to God.

On September 2, 1945, a year to the day after the shoot-down over Chichi Jima, the Japanese delegation arrived aboard the USS **Missouri** to sign the formal declaration of surrender. All told, my father logged a little over 1,200 hours in the air for the Navy, flying 58 combat missions and making 126 successful carrier landings. But it was a different flight that his family remembered most. To celebrate the end of the war, he buzzed over Walker's Point in his Avenger. His family cheered and wept below. On September 18, 1945, three years and three months after enlisting on his eighteenth birthday, George H.W. Bush was honorably discharged from the Navy. He had given his all to the war. He had survived. And America had won.

LIKE MOST VETERANS, my father didn't spend a lot of time talking about the war. He did not want to relive the grisly details of combat, and he did not consider himself a hero. In his mind, he had done his duty and wanted to move on with his life. He also believed that his service paled in comparison to that of those who had given their lives. To regale his friends and family with stories of his own experiences seemed like dishonoring those who had made the ultimate sacrifice.

Mother was more than willing to share Dad's experiences. She and I would sit on the floor and page through the scrapbooks she made of his years in the Navy. There were snapshots of his buddies aboard the **San Jac,** seashells that he collected for her on the beautiful Pacific islands, and a piece of the rubber life raft that saved his life. I would ask him to tell me stories, but he did not oblige. It took years for me to understand the impact the war had on his life.

The war meant that my father, like many in his generation, grew up in a hurry. By the age of twenty-one, he had served in combat and seen friends die. He had risked his life and almost lost it. He knew he could handle pressure and risk. And he discovered the satisfaction that came from selflessly serving others, a cause that drove him for the rest of his life.

In 2002, my father took a trip back to the site of his shoot-down with CNN anchor Paula Zahn and historian James Bradley—the author of **Flyboys,** a fine book about American pilots shot down over Chichi Jima. As he approached the island, the seventy-eight-year-old man who was once the youngest pilot in the Navy laid two wreaths in the ocean to honor his crewmen Delaney and White. When he arrived on Chichi Jima, two thousand inhabitants of the island turned out to welcome him.

On the island he met a man who had defended Chichi Jima as a member of the Japanese military on the day Dad was shot down. The man had personally observed the torture, execution, and cannibalism of captured American pilots. His brother had been killed in the atomic bomb attack on Hiroshima. Yet he held no malice for the United States. To the contrary, the actions of the Japanese government during the war had so enraged him that he had taken the name of one of the Marines executed on Chichi Jima. He had gone on to work in the American embassy in Tokyo, helping to improve relations between the two countries.

As the two former enemies stood together, their heads topped with gray hair, the man told my father more about the day he had been shot down. He confirmed that the Japanese had sent boats out to capture the downed pilot and that my father would likely have suffered the same horrific fate as the other American prisoners. He described how the boats turned back when Avenger pilots strafed them from above. As the **Finback** exposed itself to enemy fire to pull my father aboard, one of the Japanese man's fellow soldiers expressed his astonishment that the Americans would divert so many resources to save one pilot. One thing was for sure, the man said: Their own government would never have done that for them. How different from our nation. America has an honored tradition of never leaving its soldiers on the battlefield—and we never should.

From his earliest days, George Bush was a man who valued courage, loyalty, and service. Those were the traits that his mother and father had instilled in him. And the United States of America, especially its citizens in uniform, embodied those ideals. That was the country that Dad risked everything to defend. And that was the country he would one day lead.

HEADING WEST

I ONCE ASKED MY MOTHER how she and my father managed to stay happily married for almost seventy years. "Both of us have always been willing to go three-quarters of the way," she said. She meant that each of them was more committed to their marriage than they were to themselves. They were both willing to alter their own needs in order to satisfy the other's.

Throughout my life, Mother and Dad exhibited that selfless love. In their early married years, Mother showed it most. After all, she was willing to go three-quarters of the way across the country.

The decision to move from New Haven, Connecticut, where my father graduated from Yale in 1948, to West Texas shaped my parents' life.

By driving his red Studebaker away from the opportunities waiting on Wall Street, George H.W. Bush defied convention, took a risk, and followed his independent instincts. My parents learned that they could survive and thrive amid a harsh climate and unfamiliar people. They took to a competitive industry notorious for its booms and busts. They laid the foundation for a strong marriage—a lasting, lifelong partnership that endured profound trials, produced great joys, and set an inspiring example for my siblings and me. They gave me another gift. All my life, I have been grateful to George and Barbara Bush for raising me in West Texas.

IN NOVEMBER 1945, George H.W. Bush stepped out of uniform and enrolled at Yale. Like many of his generation, college had been delayed by the war. Many incoming freshmen were parents. Mother and Dad joined their ranks on July 6, 1946, when I was born at Grace–New Haven Hospital. They named me George Walker Bush, after my father and great-grandfather—minus the Herbert. I recall asking Mother why I wasn't a Junior. "Son, most forms don't have room for five names," she said. I took my time to arrive, entering the world only after my grandmother Dorothy Walker Bush administered a healthy dose of castor oil to Mother. (It was my first taste of the oil business.)

Mother and Dad lived less than an hour from his parents in Greenwich, but life in New Haven must have felt worlds away from Prescott and Dorothy Bush's house on Grove Lane. My parents first rented a tiny apartment on Chapel Street with their black standard poodle, Turbo. When I arrived, they had to move out because the landlord allowed dogs but not babies. They found a place on Edwards Street, where the owner allowed babies but not dogs. Fortunately, I made the cut and Turbo went to live at Grove Lane. In their final year in New Haven, my parents moved to a large house on Hillhouse Avenue occupied by about a dozen families with children. Mother still laughs about hanging my diapers out on the clothesline in plain view of the Yale President, who lived next door.

My parents enjoyed their New Haven years. Any stresses of college paled in comparison to what my father had endured during the war.

That's not to say that Dad took it easy. As usual, George Bush threw himself fully into the task. He worked hard in the classroom, earning Phi Beta Kappa academic distinction and graduating in two and a half years. He was a member of the Delta Kappa Epsilon fraternity. He was very outgoing and made a lot of friends. On their first Thanksgiving at Yale, Dad learned that some of his classmates could not travel home to be with their families. So he invited ten friends over for dinner. Mother reminded him that they did not have a dining room. That did not matter. My parents and their friends sat on the couches and the floor and enjoyed the first Thanksgiving turkey that Mother had ever prepared. That impromptu meal was a preview of things to come. Throughout the years, my parents' many homes were open to family and friends. While Mother occasionally complained about the endless stream of visitors, she was always a gracious hostess.

Not only did my father make friends, he kept them. Decades later, he was in regular contact with his college friends. One of his friends was Lud Ashley from Toledo, Ohio. Like Dad, Lud eventually went into politics. Unlike Dad, Lud was a liberal Democrat. In Washington, they were on the opposite sides of some of the most heated political questions of their times. That did not affect their relationship. They spent time together and shared laughs just like they had at Yale in the 1940s. Once you were a friend of George Bush's, you had that status for life.

My father's favorite collegiate pursuit took place on spring afternoons at Yale Field. As he later put it, he majored in economics and minored in baseball. He was captain of the team and, like his father, played first base. Mother and I attended nearly all his home games. During her pregnancy, she sat in an extra-wide seat designed for former Yale law professor William Howard Taft. She loved to keep score, and one of my favorite things to do as a little guy in Texas was to read her box scores of Dad's games. The Yale team reached the College World Series in 1947 and 1948. They finished second to the University of California–Berkeley the first year and to the University of Southern California the next year. (For true baseball aficionados, the Cal Bears were led by Jackie Jensen, the American League MVP in 1958, and the

USC Trojans were managed by the legendary Rod Dedeaux.)

My father's most famous moment as a college ballplayer took place on the pitcher's mound. There he met Babe Ruth during the spring of his senior year to receive a signed copy of Babe's autobiography for the Yale library. A photographer snapped a picture that would later become iconic: one great man near the end of his life, another embarking on his.

It's hard to imagine how Dad managed to do it all—to be a top student, a star athlete, a man with a huge group of friends, and a devoted husband and father. As Mother put it with characteristic bluntness, "He worked hard." That's true. George Bush did not waste time. He filled every minute of every day with activity.

WHILE DAD'S MOST famous moment on the diamond featured Babe Ruth, his baseball hero was Lou Gehrig. Dad admired Gehrig's ability, consistency, and modesty. He dreamed of following in Gehrig's footsteps as a major league ballplayer. After one Yale game, a few interested scouts reached out. While my father's fielding was excellent, he didn't have a big enough bat to make the major leagues. His coach, Ethan Allen, described Dad with classic managerial brevity: "Good field, no hit."

My father ruled out other options as well. In June 1948, he received a surprising letter from a childhood friend, Gerry Bemiss. Evidently, Bemiss had heard that Dad was entering the ministry. While my father was always a religious man, he did not envision a career in the clergy. "I have never even thought about the cloth—only a tablecloth or a loincloth," he wrote.

One option was to go work for his uncle George Herbert Walker Jr., known as Herbie. Herbie adored my father. In later years, I sensed that the attention he showered upon Dad came at the expense of the love he gave to his own sons. He assured my father that he would have a prominent place at his Wall Street firm. Similarly, executives at Brown Brothers Harriman, Prescott Bush's firm, made a serious recruiting pitch for my father.

It was not surprising that George H.W. Bush was in high demand. Few could claim the trifecta of war hero, Phi Beta Kappa, and captain of the baseball team. Dad took the Wall Street job offers seriously. He respected the work that his father did, and he wanted to put his economics degree to use. Plus, a job in finance would likely ensure he could earn a solid living for Mother and me.

Yet something pushed my father in a different direction. Wall Street represented the conventional path. After flying bomber planes, landing on aircraft carriers, and working next to people from all walks of life, the idea of boarding a commuter train from Connecticut and sitting behind a desk in New York had limited appeal. Rather than trade paper, he wanted to build something. He wanted to do something different with his life. And he wasn't afraid to take a risk.

Dad also wanted to prove that he could succeed without help from his family. That independent streak ran in his blood. His great-great-grandfather Obadiah Bush had traveled west with the forty-niners during the Gold Rush. His grandfather G.H. Walker had broken away from the family business in St. Louis to strike out on his own in New York. His father, Prescott Bush, was proud that he hadn't taken a dime from his parents.

That still left the question of exactly what to do. My parents had read the book **The Farm** by Louis Bromfield, which touted the classic American experience of tending your own land. They flirted with the idea for a while but ultimately decided the lifestyle wasn't for them. I could just imagine Mother milking a cow.

In February 1948, Dad's grandfather S.P. Bush died. My father joined family and friends on a flight to Columbus for the funeral. On the way he spoke to Neil Mallon, a close friend of Prescott Bush's from Yale. Neil ran a company called Dresser Industries that sold drilling equipment and supplies to oil operators. Neil mentioned that Dad should consider working for Dresser. He could learn how a business operates from the ground up: managing inventory, making sales, and getting products to market. He could see firsthand a fascinating industry, the oil business. There was one caveat: He would have to move to the oil fields of the Permian Basin—an isolated, dusty, scorching-hot patch of West Texas populated mostly by ranchers and roughnecks, and full of oil.

The opportunity intrigued Dad. He had read articles about the Texas oil boom, where colorful entrepreneurs like H.L. Hunt and Clint Murchison were making fortunes. He had enjoyed his brief stint in Corpus Christi during his Navy flight training. And one thing was for certain: He would be on his own. Prescott Bush and G.H. Walker cast a long shadow, but it didn't reach Odessa, Texas.

Shortly after graduation, Neil offered Dad a job with a Dresser subsidiary called Ideco, the International Derrick and Equipment Company. He accepted. There's no doubt that my father got the position because of his family's connections. I benefited from connections in my own life. I was fortunate that generous family members and friends helped create opportunities for me. But there's a limit to the power of connections. While they can open doors, they cannot guarantee success.

In my father's case, Neil Mallon opened the door to a job as an equipment clerk at an Ideco warehouse in Odessa with a salary of 375 dollars a month. A clerk's duties included sweeping floors, arranging inventory, and painting pump jacks. He would meet interesting characters and figure out whether he liked the oil business. Beyond that, there were no guarantees.

For the second time in his young life, George H.W. Bush made a bold and life-changing decision. As a high school senior, he had given up the safety of college to serve in the war. Now he would leave behind the comforts of Greenwich, Connecticut, and move his young bride and infant son to West Texas.

GEORGE BUSH DID not make the decision alone. Barbara Bush made it too. Moving to West Texas was not a natural step for Mother. She had grown up in a relatively affluent family in Westchester County, New York. Her father, Marvin Pierce, came from Ohio, where he had been a star athlete at Miami University. He was a big, burly guy who used his fierce work ethic and Midwestern charm to build a successful career as President of the McCall Corporation, at that time one of the largest publishing companies in America.

Her mother, Pauline Robinson Pierce, descended from James E. Robinson, a Justice of the Ohio Supreme Court. She relished her family's position in the social hierarchy and spent money lavishly on life's "finer things." She supervised her children closely; she bought all of Mother's clothes and decided where she would go to high school and college. She doted on Mother's older sister, Martha, a model who appeared in **Vogue** magazine. Mrs. Pierce believed in what might be called the refined life. I can only imagine her horror at the idea of her daughter living out in West Texas, where the only thing refined was oil.

Fortunately, my father didn't need to persuade Pauline Pierce. He only needed to convince Mother. That was not a hard sell. As she later told me, "I was young and in love. I would have gone anywhere your father wanted."

I think there was more to her willingness to move than her devotion to Dad. "Christmas was a nightmare," she told me. "We would spend Christmas Eve in Greenwich with the Bushes. Then Christmas morning with my parents in Rye. Then back to Greenwich for Christmas lunch." Moving west would free her from the pressures of competing families.

Although she may not have realized it at the time, Mother too had an independent streak.

Otherwise, she would not have been a willing partner in seeking new adventures. I can only guess how Dad's life would have turned out if his wife had been less open to change. History might have been different.

One of my favorite family stories occurred shortly after my parents got married. Mother lit up a cigarette, and my grandfather Prescott Bush asked jokingly, "Did I give you permission to smoke?"

Before she could catch herself, Mother shot back, "Well I didn't marry you, did I?"

Usually nobody spoke to my grandfather that way. The sharp rejoinder just popped out. Fortunately, he responded with a big laugh. One thing was for sure: Barbara Bush was willing to speak her mind. That was something she did quite frequently in later years. Mother's quick wit and self-deprecating humor endeared her to millions of Americans. Her willingness to speak her mind stood in contrast to some tightly scripted political spouses. As a result of her wide following, she helped many Americans understand and love her husband. Many people told me that anyone who married Barbara Bush had to be a good man.

* * *

IN THE SUMMER of 1948, George H.W. Bush had two immediate tasks: start his job, and find a place for Mother and me to live. While he scouted for housing in Odessa, Texas, we stayed with my great-grandfather G.H. Walker at his summer house in Kennebunkport, Maine.

Life was a lot more comfortable on Walker's Point than in West Texas. In those days, Odessa was a town of under thirty thousand people located twenty miles from its sister city of Midland and more than three hundred fifty miles from the nearest major airport in Dallas. Most streets were unpaved. Few buildings were taller than one story; the skyline consisted of oil derricks dotting the horizon. Summer temperatures routinely hit triple digits, sometimes before noon, and long droughts were common. The flat terrain offered no relief, nor was there any natural shade, since West Texas had no native trees. And the wind howled, often carrying with it punishing waves of dirt.

Odessa took its name from the Ukrainian city bordering the Black Sea, and at first it must have felt like a foreign country to my father. He didn't know a single person when he arrived. People he met were more like the folks in the Navy than those he knew back home. Odessa was a blue-collar town, home to oil field laborers: mechanics who fixed the equipment and roughnecks who worked on the rigs. One of my father's coworkers once asked him whether he'd gone to college. As a matter of fact, Dad replied, he had just graduated from Yale. The fellow thought for a second and said, "Never heard of it." The fashion in West Texas was different too. Dad once walked out of the house wearing Bermuda shorts. After several truck drivers honked at him, he went back home and packed away the Bermuda shorts for good. Even the food was unfamiliar. My father always remembered the first time he saw someone order a West Texas delicacy: chicken-fried steak.

Dad found a house on East Seventh Street. The good news was that it had a bathroom, unlike most residences on the street, which had outhouses. The bad news was that we had to share the bathroom with two women who lived on the other side of the duplex—a mother-daughter pair who made their living by entertaining male clients throughout the night. The thirteen-family house next to the Yale President didn't seem so bad by comparison.

Life in West Texas required other adjustments. Shortly after Mother and I joined Dad in Odessa, she woke up during the night to the smell of gas. Thinking the house was at risk of explosion, she grabbed me and hustled out onto the curb. A neighbor who witnessed the evacuation kindly explained that a shift in the winds had brought the scent of the oil fields wafting in. Nothing was wrong. We could all go back to sleep. Mother's experience confirmed a truth about West Texas: Life revolved around oil. It was in the ground below, the air above, and the minds of everyone who called the place home.

The key to my parents' successful transition to their new surroundings was their attitude. They didn't approach life in West Texas as a hardship to be endured; they embraced it as an adventure—their first of many as a couple. They took an interest in people and made friends. In the process, they realized that they didn't need chauffeurs and French maids to enjoy life. They had each other. And they could make the most of any situation.

The three of us spent Christmas 1948 in

Odessa. On Christmas Eve, Dad's company held a party for its customers. He volunteered to mix drinks. To show his holiday spirit, he raised a glass of his own for almost every cocktail he poured. By the end of the evening, the jolly bartender was helped into the back of a company pickup truck. One of his coworkers drove him home, eased down the tailgate, and rolled him onto the front lawn. The Bushes were fitting in just fine in West Texas.

THE STORY OF the Odessa Christmas party, which Mother never let Dad forget, typified my father's approach to work: When he committed to doing something, he did it all out. If George Bush was assigned to sweep the warehouse, the manager would find the cleanest floor he'd ever seen. If he had to paint rigs, he would come in Saturday morning to slap on an extra coat so that the job got done right. My father enjoyed working hard, and he liked to see the result of his efforts. The lessons his mother had instilled had taken hold: Do your best. Don't be arrogant. Never complain.

After a while, his supervisors recognized that

their trainee was capable of bigger things. So in 1949, when I was three years old, Dad was transferred to California. There he worked seven days a week in an oil pump factory and then as a traveling salesman for Dresser subsidiaries, hawking drill bits and other equipment. We lived in four different cities that year: Whittier, Ventura, Bakersfield, and Compton. In Whittier and Ventura, we rented rooms in local hotels for extended stays. In Bakersfield, we lived for a few months in a rented 950-square-foot white frame house. In Compton, we lived in an apartment in the Santa Fe Gardens complex. (Sadly, the complex was condemned many years later after being overtaken by drugs and violence.)

Our transient lifestyle in California was tough on Mother, who was constantly packing, unpacking, and taking care of me. On top of that, she was pregnant with my younger sister Robin, who was due around Christmas 1949. We were living in Compton at the time. Mother wanted to be sure that someone would be available to watch me when she went to the hospital, so she asked our next-door neighbor, with whom she had become friends. The neighbor agreed. Not long before Mother went into labor, she learned that the neighbor had fled with her children after her abusive husband came home drunk one too many times. So much for my babysitter. Somehow Mother found somebody to take care of me (nobody can remember who), and my sister Robin was born on December 20, 1949.

Robin was named after my grandmother Pauline Robinson Pierce, who had died in a car accident three months earlier. My grandfather refused to let Mother travel to the funeral for fear that the trip would endanger the baby. It was tough on Mother to be so far from her dad—whom she adored—in his time of grief.

The year in California was not easy for my father, either. He was on the road almost all the time. He estimated that he put about a thousand miles a week on his car. He was not a fast-talking pitchman, but he developed a sales approach that proved effective. He would forge personal relationships, just like he had in school and the military. Over time, he offered his customers something more than drill bits: He earned their trust.

In the spring of 1950, my father received the

news that Dresser had transferred him back to West Texas. He could live in either Odessa or Midland. As a twenty-five-year-old father of two, he wanted to settle down. He and Mother chose Midland, which was then home to 215 oil companies and about 21,000 people. We would call Midland home for the next nine years. It is the first city that I remember living in, and it will always be the place I consider my hometown.

MIDLAND, TEXAS, took its name from its location halfway between Fort Worth and El Paso on the Texas and Pacific Railway. Like Odessa, Midland gave you the feeling of life on the edge. I remember my father going into the backyard of our house in Midland and confronting a huge tarantula on the porch with a broom. The hairy critter took a big hop, and it took all of Dad's skill as a first baseman to keep it from slipping past him into the house.

While Midland and Odessa had similar topography, they had different demographics. Most people in Odessa worked in the oil fields; most people in Midland worked in offices. Like

Odessa, Midland was a boomtown, and it was hard to find housing. We lived briefly at a hotel and then moved into a new 847-square-foot house on the outskirts of town. The neighborhood was called Easter Egg Row, because the developer had chosen vibrant paint colors to help residents tell the houses apart. Our Easter egg at 405 East Maple was bright blue.

Midland in the 1950s featured an equally colorful cast of characters. There were people who were broke one day and rich the next. There were old ranch families who had lived on the land before the oil strikes. There were Texans from other parts of the state, especially graduates of the University of Texas and Texas A&M. My father was part of a small contingent of Ivy League graduates who had turned down opportunities on the East Coast so that they could scratch an entrepreneurial itch in the oil patch. There were professionals who provided support services for the oil industry: doctors, bankers, lawyers, teachers, and homebuilders, including a kind man named Harold Welch whose only daughter, Laura Lane, I would marry years later at Midland's First United Methodist Church.

Midland was a competitive place. Oilmen hustled to beat their neighbors to precious leases and royalties. The uncertainty of the business had a leveling effect. Anyone could hit it big; anyone could drill a dry hole. For all the hard work and science that went into the business, every oilman would have traded it all for good luck. Yet Midland also fostered a sense of community. People banded together in the harsh and isolated environment.

Life in West Texas was simple, like the names of the towns along its dusty roads: Big Lake (barely a lake), Big Spring (just a little water), and Notrees (not even one). My pals and I spent our days outside, playing baseball or football. On Fridays in the fall, people packed into Midland Memorial Stadium to watch the Midland High Bulldogs. One of my favorite Midland players was Wahoo McDaniel, who later starred for the Oklahoma Sooners, the New York Jets, and the professional wrestling circuit. On Sunday mornings, most people went to church. Looking back now, I can see why my parents liked Midland so much. The mixture of competition and community reflected my father's upbringing. He had taken the values that he learned at home and plopped them down in the middle of the Texas desert.

A few months after we arrived in Midland, my father received an unexpected letter from Tom McCance, an executive at Brown Brothers Harriman. The firm had renewed its offer. Dad's knowledge of the Texas oil business would be valuable on Wall Street. The offer could have provided a perfect escape hatch. My parents could say that they had enjoyed living in West Texas, had learned something new, and were ready to return to their roots. That's not what they did. My father thanked Mr. McCance for his generosity, but he declined. He had staked his claim in West Texas.

SOME OF MY warmest memories of our Midland years are of the time I spent with Dad. He was busy building his business and traveling. He was active in the community, teaching Sunday school at First Presbyterian Church and leading fund-raising drives for the United Way and the YMCA. Yet I never felt his absence. He always made it a point to spend as much time with his children as he could. As my brother Jeb put it, George H.W. Bush invented "quality time." He would come home from work, pull out a mitt, and toss the baseball with me in the yard of our home at 1412 West Ohio Avenue, where we moved in 1951. That house is now the George W. Bush Childhood Home. (I've always wondered why the museum isn't called the George H.W. Bush Home Where George W. Bush Lived as a Child.)

On some weekends, Dad and his friends would take me dove hunting—a ritual for many in West Texas. I carried the .410 that he gave me for Christmas after he was convinced that I had mastered gun safety lessons. We would congregate around a water hole in the middle of the dry land, cooking burgers on a portable grill and waiting till sundown in hopes that the doves would fly in to quench their thirst. He also took me out to the oil fields, where I saw the rigs and pumping units up close. Those trips helped spark an interest in the oil business that I would later pursue by becoming an independent oilman in the mid-1970s.

Our house was a hub of activity. One day he brought home an engineer from Yugoslavia whom he'd met through his oil business. He stayed with us for a week, and my father showed him around the West Texas oil fields. During one of our summers in Midland, my father's younger brother Bucky, fourteen years his junior, and Bucky's college pal Fay Vincent—who later became Commissioner of Major League Baseball—came to live with us while they roughnecked on the oil rigs.

My parents were constantly inviting their neighbors over for backyard barbecues or cocktails. I remember one Christmas when I received a horn as a gift. I blew the horn a few too many times, and my father took it away from me and broke it. A few days later, one of our neighbors acquired the same model horn, called the house until my father answered, and then blew the horn into the phone. Another time, my father played a prank on his good friend and fellow Yale graduate Earle Craig, who was known to bite into the pearl onion that floated in his martini with a grand flourish. One night Dad mixed the drink with a rubber onion. When the Earle of Craig (as he was known to some) dramatically bit into the faux onion, the circle of friends (likely a few martinis deep) had a good chuckle. Earle knew it was all done in fun. Life in Midland was friendly and carefree.

I don't remember a lot about our conversations from those years, but it's safe to say that we spent most of our time talking about school or sports. My father was not the kind of man who gave us lectures on politics or philosophy. He believed in leading by example. If I had a question, he was there to answer it. He always gave good advice.

When I was about six years old, I went with some friends to a general store in Midland. I saw a couple of plastic toy soldiers in a jar on the shelf. I decided to put them in my pocket and walk out of the store without paying. Later that day, my father noticed me playing with the pilfered soldiers in the front yard.

"Hi, son," he said. "What are you doing out here?"

"Playing soldiers," I said.

"Where did you get those?" he asked.

I hesitated. He asked the question again.

After a little soul-searching, I confessed. "I took them from the store," I said.

"Come with me," he said. We got in his car and drove to the store. He instructed me to walk into the store alone, return the soldiers, and apologize to the manager for stealing them. I did what he asked and felt genuine remorse. When I got back in the car, Dad didn't say another word. He knew he had made his point.

Most of the day-to-day work of raising my siblings and me fell to Mother. She drove me to baseball practice and kept score at my games, just like she had for Dad. She was the den mother who took our Cub Scout troop to Carlsbad Caverns and the Monahans Sand-hills. Mother always welcomed my friends for lunch or dinner between marathon sessions of baseball or football. She administered the discipline when necessary. Unlike my father, she did not believe in subtlety. One of her favorite tactics when I was young was to wash my mouth out with soap when I said or did something "smutty," like the time she caught me urinating in the hedges in our yard. For the most part, though, she gave me the slack to have fun and be a free-spirited boy.

My parents' approach to raising their children reflected the attitude of their generation. My father spent more time with us than his father had with him, but dads in those days were not as involved as they are today. Most weren't as emotional, either. In our early years, my father was not a hugger, nor did he say "I love you." But he didn't need to. We always knew that he loved us unconditionally.

We knew that my parents loved each other, too. In the sixty-nine years that I have observed my parents' marriage, I have never once heard them exchange harsh words. Sure, there's a little needling here and a good-natured disagreement there. But I have never sensed anger or frustration. Their solid, loving bond was a source of stability for me when I was a child—and a source of inspiration for me when I married Laura.

At the time, my siblings and I didn't fully appreciate how lucky we were. Others did. At Laura's fiftieth high school reunion, my boyhood friend Mike Proctor pulled me aside for a chat. Mike had lived across the street from us when we were growing up. We were the same age and in the same grade. Mike spent a lot of time at our house. We rode bikes together, played football together, and were part of the same Cub Scout troop. Unbeknownst to me, Mike's family had some serious problems at home.

At the reunion, Mike said, "There's something that I've been meaning to tell you for a long time. I need you to do me a favor."

"Sure thing, Mike," I said. "What is it?"

"Tell your mother that I said thanks."

He continued, "Back then, you probably didn't realize how dysfunctional my family was. Because of your mother's kindness, I saw how a real family works."

The next day I called my mother and told her what Mike had said. I could tell that the expression of gratitude touched her heart.

"Tell Mike that I send my love," she said.

WHEN MY SISTER Robin was three years old, Mother noticed that she didn't have much energy. Mother would ask what she wanted to do, and Robin would say that she wanted to sit on the bed or lie on the grass. That didn't sound normal for a three-year-old, so she took Robin to our family doctor in Midland, Dorothy Wyvell.

Dr. Wyvell ran some tests. Mother worried that the results were bad when the doctor called and told her to come back to the office with Dad. Every parent can imagine the agony of the conversation that transpired. Dr. Wyvell told them that Robin's blood test had revealed that she was suffering from leukemia. Not only did she have the disease, but her white blood cell count was off the charts—the highest that Dr. Wyvell had ever seen.

My parents had expected that something was wrong, but they had not imagined this. Finally my father asked, "What's the next step? How do we treat her?"

As she began to answer, Dr. Wyvell's eyes filled with tears. She was not only my parents' doctor; in close-knit Midland, she was also a friend. "There's nothing you can do," she said. "She probably has only a few weeks left. You should take her home and make her as comfortable as you can."

My father could not accept that there was no hope to save his little girl. He went home and called his mother's brother Dr. John Walker at Memorial Sloan Kettering, the best cancer hospital in New York. His uncle told him about some recent advances in treatment that might help Robin. He also confirmed what Dr. Wyvell had told them: Childhood leukemia had no cure.

My parents took Robin to New York. They knew the odds were long, but they refused to give up on their daughter. As Dr. Walker told my father, "You'll never be able to live with yourself if you don't try to treat her."

My parents never really told me what was going on. They just said that Robin was sick and that she and Mother were going to New York to see Uncle John so that she could get better. My father shuttled back and forth between New York and Midland. Sometimes Robin's cancer would go into remission, and she would come home for a few weeks. Then she would suffer a setback, and they would fly back to New York. When my parents were gone, they left me and my brother Jeb, who had been born a few months earlier, with Midland friends and neighbors. They became our surrogate parents without a second thought.

My parents approached Robin's illness differently. My father was a whirlwind of activity. When he was in New York, he was meeting with doctors, checking test results, and asking about new treatments. In Texas, he raced out of the house early in the morning, stopped at church to pray for Robin, and then threw himself into his work. Looking back on it, I can see that the frantic activity was his way of coping with the helplessness he felt. George Bush, the Navy pilot who swam to the life raft and paddled away from death, must have found it unbearable not to be able to do anything to help the girl he loved.

In contrast to my father's constant motion, Mother spent almost every waking hour at Robin's bedside, playing with her, reading to her, and trying to keep her spirits high. She stayed with the Walkers in New York, and family members would drop by the hospital to offer support. My great-grandfather, gruff old G.H. Walker—who at age seventy-eight was in the final year of his own life—spent hours teaching Robin how to play gin rummy. She called the game "Gin Poppy," the nickname the family used for my dad.

Robin's treatment was painful. The chemotherapy and blood transfusions drained her strength. Mother imposed a rule: No crying in front of Robin. My father had a hard time abiding. Mother sat stoically by her side, comforting her daughter as she suffered and slipped away. As the biographer Richard Ben Cramer described my mother's character in those days, "It was beyond strength—it was heroic, an act of will and love."

One day when Robin was resting, Mother went to visit Dad's parents in Greenwich, Connecticut. My grandfather Prescott Bush, who had just been elected to the U.S. Senate, took her for a long walk through Greenwich's Putnam Cemetery. There he showed her the burial plot that he and my grandmother had selected as their final resting place. There was room for an extra headstone. That was his gentle way of telling my mother that they would take care of Robin when the time came, and that he wanted his granddaughter to be at his side. (Decades later, my parents moved Robin's grave to the plot where their graves will be at Dad's presidential library in College Station, Texas.)

The end arrived on October 11, 1953. Robin died peacefully after battling for seven months. In one of her final moments with my father,

Robin looked up at him with her beautiful blue eyes and said, "I love you more than tongue can tell." Dad would repeat those words for the rest of his life.

I HAVE A vivid memory of the day my parents told me that Robin had died. One of my teachers at Sam Houston Elementary School had asked me and one of my classmates to carry a record player to another wing of the school. As we walked outside, I saw my parents pull up in their pea-green Oldsmobile. I had no idea why they had shown up at school in the middle of the day. As I sprinted over to the car, I thought that I saw Robin's blond curls in the backseat. I was so excited that she had come home. But when I got to the car, she wasn't there. Mother hugged me tight and told me that she was gone. On the drive home, I saw my parents cry for the first time.

After Robin's death, my parents switched roles. My father became the strong one, dealing with the funeral planning and logistics. One of their first decisions was to donate Robin's body to Memorial Sloan Kettering. The doctors told them that they could learn from studying her disease, and my parents hoped that Robin's death might lead to some benefit for other suffering children. Childhood cancer research became a lifelong cause for them. Today the childhood cancer clinic at Houston's MD Anderson Cancer Center bears Robin's name.

After seven months of staying strong, Mother cratered. She suffered bouts of depression that would plague her periodically. At twenty-eight years old, her dark brown hair started to turn white.

While I was too young to fully understand Robin's death, I sensed that Mother was hurting. She later told me that I stopped playing with my friends so that I could stay inside and try to cheer her up with jokes. My father found ways to lift her spirits, too. He planned visits with friends and gently helped my mother to move forward with life. Instead of focusing on Robin's loss, they gave thanks for the years they were able to spend with her.

Robin's death did not drive my parents apart, unlike many couples who find their relationships broken after losing a child. In their case, the shared pain brought them together, and their marriage emerged stronger. When they needed each other most, they were both willing to go three-quarters of the way.

MY FATHER NEVER talked much about losing Robin. Back in that era, people didn't really discuss topics like that. A few years after Robin died, Dad wrote his mother a touching letter about how lonely he felt. "We need some soft blond hair to offset those crew cuts. We need a doll house to stand firm against our forts and rackets and thousand baseball cards," he wrote. "We need a girl." His prayer was answered when my sister Dorothy was born in 1959. When he first saw her in the hospital, he pressed his face against the nursery glass and sobbed.

During the 1980 presidential campaign, a journalist asked my father whether he had ever faced any "personal difficulty." The subtext of the question was whether someone with a life as comfortable as George Bush's could relate to ordinary people.

My father could have mentioned that he'd been shot down by enemy fire in World War II, or that he had almost died of a staph infection in high school. Instead he stared at the reporter and asked, "Have you ever sat and watched your child die?"

The journalist said no.

"I did, for six months," Dad said.

That ended the interview. Anyone who had ever lost a child knew exactly what he meant.

My father never stopped thinking about his daughter. For as long as I can remember, he has kept a three-by-five framed photo of her on the desk in his office. Late in his life, as he contemplated his own mortality, Dad asked his minister whether he would meet Robin and his mother in heaven. It was telling that those were the two people who he wanted to see. He asked whether Robin would still look like a child, or whether she would have "grown up" over the sixty years since her death. That's part of the great mystery. But I think Dad knows in his heart that he will see his daughter again.

HAT IN THE RING

B Y THE AGE OF TWENTY-FIVE, George Bush had passed up the safety of college to serve his country as a naval aviator during World War II. He had passed up the financial security of Wall Street to learn the oil business in West Texas. His spirit of adventure and zeal for new challenges made it impossible for him to stand still. Over the next two decades, he pushed himself from one frontier to the next. In his business career, he went from an employee to an entrepreneur, from a small city to a big city, and from onshore oil to the new horizon of offshore drilling. His financial success made it possible for him to push himself again, from private business into public service, and from local politics to the national stage. Not every risk my father took in those years paid off. That taught him another lesson: If you refuse to give up, opportunity can arise not only from victory, but also from defeat.

AS AN EMPLOYEE of Dresser Industries, George Bush saw the oil business up close, and he had learned a lot. One thing that he learned was that he wanted to enter the business on his own. Soon he set a new goal: to become an independent oilman.

Before my father could strike out on his own, he had to inform Neil Mallon that he planned to leave Dresser. As Dad would later tell the story, he was nervous about his meeting with Neil. He didn't want to abandon the man who had given him his first shot in the business. When Dad broke the news that he was leaving, Neil was silent. Then he grabbed a yellow legal pad and spent thirty minutes telling my father how he ought to set up the business. Neil's handling of the situation set a good example for Dad and later for me. Rather than harbor resentments or stand in the way of a talented employee, he chose to encourage and mentor. My father remained grateful for the rest of his life. Just ask my younger brother Neil Mallon Bush.

My father approached a friend and neighbor on Easter Egg Row, John Overbey, with the idea of starting a new partnership. Overbey was a University of Texas graduate who was savvy in the world of oil leases and royalties and had a good nose for finding information from old-time ranchers, scouts at oil companies, and fellow independents. My father brought a different set of skills. He had good relationships with prospective investors, especially on the East Coast.

By the spring of 1951, Bush-Overbey was up and running. Dad frequently traveled to the East Coast to look for money. Several of the company's first major backers were family members or friends, including his father and his uncle George Herbert Walker, Jr., who was eager to take a bet on his favorite nephew. He also raised money from people like Eugene Meyer, then the President of the **Washington Post** newspaper corporation. Unfortunately, the paper wasn't always so keen to support anyone named George Bush in later years.

My father was aggressive in raising money but cautious in spending it. Bush-Overbey took small stakes in a variety of projects, which offset risk but limited the chance of a big payout. On most mornings, Dad would get into the office early, fire up his typewriter, and write letters. He wrote to people he had met around town or on his trips, potential lessors, and investors. Over the years, he would apply his assiduous letter writing to politics and diplomacy. Today there are thousands of people around the world who can reach into a desk drawer and produce a thank-you note from George Bush.

NOT FAR FROM the one-room Bush-Overbey office in downtown Midland was the law firm of Liedtke and Liedtke. Bill and Hugh Liedtke were brothers from Tulsa, Oklahoma, where their father was a lawyer for Gulf Oil. The Liedtkes had plans to build a large independent oil company, and they needed an ambitious partner to help. George Bush was the perfect fit, and Dad was eager to join forces. John Overbey wasn't interested in the corporate life, so after a two-year partnership with Dad, he went his own way on good terms and became a successful independent oilman.

Dad agreed to raise half of the money to capitalize the new company. The Liedtkes would raise the other half. Once again, my father turned to his uncle Herbie and his Wall Street friends. They had seen decent returns from Bush-Overbey, and Dad convinced them that he could deliver even more. He lined up a half million dollars in capital. The Liedtkes did too.

Before they started making deals, they had to choose a name for the new company. The partners decided that their name should start with either an A or a Z, so that they wouldn't get lost in the middle of the phone book listings. By chance, the movie **Viva Zapata!**, starring Marlon Brando, was playing at Midland's downtown theater. The bold Mexican revolutionary general captured their independent, risk-taking spirit. Plus his name started with the right letter. In 1953, Zapata Petroleum was born.

It didn't take long for the firm to live up to its daring name. Hugh Liedtke proposed that Zapata take $850,000 and invest it in one place, the Jameson field in Coke County. Some early exploration by another operator had proved that

the field contained oil, although nobody knew
how much. Betting the company on one investment was the opposite of the strategy of Bush-
Overbey. But the prospect of hitting a big find
was what made my father love the oil business.

The gamble paid off. By the end of 1954, Zapata had drilled 71 holes, and all 71 produced
oil. Eventually, they went 127 for 127. Dad and
the Liedtkes delivered a healthy return to their
investors and walked away from the project
with a lucrative payout. George Bush was too
modest—and too smart—to spend wildly. He
had a growing family to support, and he knew
how unpredictable the oil business could be.
We did move to a new, three-thousand-square-
foot house on Sentinel Drive on the outskirts
of Midland. The house had a swimming pool
and backed up to Cowden Park, where I played
my Little League games. For a little guy, that
was about as good as it could get. Before long
George Bush had another business idea, and
soon we were on the move again.

THE OCEAN HAS always fascinated my father. His favorite place in the world is Walker's

Point in Maine. As a boy, he spent his summers swimming, sailing, and fishing in the Atlantic. His grandfather Bert Walker introduced him to speedboats, which became a lifelong passion. Well into his eighties, he loved to take his powerboat, the **Fidelity**, on the water and crank her up as fast as she would go. In the 1950s, the future of offshore oil exploration was bright. So as a young oilman, George Bush was intrigued by underwater drilling.

The first oil exploration in the shallow waters off the Gulf of Mexico began in the late 1930s. Geologists believed that deeper waters could contain bigger deposits. Accessing those deposits required an offshore drilling platform that was big enough to reach the ocean floor, stable enough to withstand the waves and winds, and mobile enough to explore multiple locations. That kind of equipment required significant up-front capital expenditures. In 1954, Zapata Petroleum decided to create a new venture, Zapata Offshore, to build rigs and lease them out to oil operators. The new subsidiary was led by George Bush.

My father's first big move was to bet on a brilliant but unconventional engineer, R.G.

LeTourneau. LeTourneau—whose formal education ended in seventh grade and who was known to sketch his mechanical designs on legal pads rather than draw up blueprints—had an idea for an offshore drilling platform. Unlike other models in use at the time, it would include three legs and multiple motors, which would provide greater stability and speed. Dad and the Liedtkes were intrigued, but the cost was steep: three million dollars.

LeTourneau had enough confidence in his design that he offered to build the drilling platform if Zapata would advance him four hundred thousand dollars and promise a stake in the company if the rig worked. The venture was risky, but Zapata decided to bet on the eccentric engineer.

In 1956, LeTourneau's revolutionary rig, nicknamed "the Scorpion" or "the three-legged monster," made its debut in the gulf. Mother and I flew out on a small prop plane with three of Dad's fellow oilmen to witness the christening. I was amazed by the size of the rig. The platform measured 185 feet by 150 feet, each leg extended 140 feet, and the contraption weighed nine million pounds. Many years later in Midland, I was reminded of Dad's entry into the offshore oil business when I ran into one of the other fellows aboard the prop plane that day. He informed me that I owed him a new hat. "Why's that?" I asked. "Because you vomited in my old one on the flight over," he said.

Over time, George Bush and the Liedtkes decided to split Zapata into two separate companies. My father would take the offshore assets; Bill and Hugh Liedtke would keep the onshore assets. The Liedtkes went on to phenomenal success, merging with South Penn Oil and creating one of the world's great energy companies, Pennzoil. Dad made a lot less money in the offshore business, but he was thrilled that his friends had done so well. He loved the work that he had chosen. And he never judged his worth by the size of his wallet.

IN 1959, SHORTLY after the division of Zapata, my father moved our family five hundred miles east across the state to Houston, where most offshore drilling companies were based. I'm sure it was tough on my parents to leave Midland, where they had made so many friends. But they were confident about their ability to adjust to a new home. And we did, thanks in large part to Mother. Despite the fact that she was raising four children (me; Jeb, born in 1953; Neil, born in 1955; and Marvin, born in 1956) and pregnant with a fifth (Dorothy, born later in 1959), she coordinated all the moving logistics and oversaw the construction of a new house on Briar Drive. Mother made sure the house quickly became a home.

Houston was a bustling big city that opened up new horizons—for Dad's business career and for me. I remember the first time we were hit by one of Houston's famous torrential rainstorms. It felt like living in a tropical jungle compared to our time in Midland. I started at a new school, Kinkaid, that offered more options than my schools back in West Texas. And unlike Midland, Houston had professional sports. I remember watching the Houston Oilers play the Dallas Texans in one of the first AFL championship games. In 1962, the city attracted a major league baseball team, the Colt .45s. They would soon be renamed the Astros and play in the Astrodome, known at the time as the eighth wonder of the world. For a sports-minded kid, Houston was heaven.

The offshore business involved serious financial risk. Without drilling contracts, Zapata's rigs and workers would be idle. Dad traveled the world to drum up new business. His experience working with foreign businessmen and government officials laid an important foundation for his later diplomatic positions. Running the company also taught him key management principles. He learned the importance of hiring knowledgeable people and listening to their advice, of delegating responsibility and holding people accountable, and of making tough decisions and accepting the consequences. When things went right, he shared the credit. When things went wrong, he took the heat. This experience helped him develop the leadership style that he would employ for decades to come.

Although the oil business was filled with uncertainty, my father rarely showed stress. Any problems he had were kept inside. His vigorous exercise regimen helped. There were times when my father's tireless pace caught up with him. On a business trip in England in 1960, he collapsed on the floor of his hotel room. Fortunately, he managed to push the help button on the way down. The British doctor told him that he had food poisoning, but when he got back to Texas his doctor diagnosed him with a bleeding ulcer. The cause may have been stress, or it may have been exhaustion. Either way, the doctor told my father that he was lucky to be alive.

IN HIS EARLY YEARS, George H.W. Bush did not appear to be a very political person. He followed the news and voted when he was of age, but he didn't belong to any political organizations. Aside from his race for senior class President at Andover, he had never been involved in a campaign.

That began to change in 1950, when my grandfather decided to run for the U.S. Senate from Connecticut. My father was twenty-six and launching his career in the oil business, so he couldn't do much to help his dad. Nevertheless, he followed the race closely, and his father's decision to run got him thinking about whether he might like to do the same in the future.

Prescott Bush was not a typical politician. At fifty-five years old, the only public office he had held was moderator of the Greenwich town meeting. He considered himself a Republican based largely on his pro-business beliefs, and he had been an active fund-raiser for the party in Connecticut. Party officials had approached him about running for Congress in 1946, and my grandfather was interested. But his partners at Brown Brothers Harriman discouraged him. They considered their investment house more important than the House of Representatives.

Another opportunity arose four years later when Connecticut's junior U.S. Senator, Raymond Baldwin, resigned to accept a seat on the state supreme court. In November 1950, the state held a special election to choose a Senator to serve out the final two years of Baldwin's term. Connecticut Republicans convinced my grandfather to run. This time his Wall Street partners supported the decision.

As a formal man who had spent most of his life in the boardroom, my grandfather had to adjust to life on the campaign trail. He worked hard, traveled throughout the state, and enlisted the singing talents of the Yale Whiffenpoofs to lighten up his campaign events. He ran television ads, a relatively new technique at the time that he had learned about while serving on the board of directors of CBS.

A few days before the election, the syndicated columnist Drew Pearson broadcast a false report that my grandfather was President of the Birth Control League. The charge hurt with the state's heavily Catholic population, which opposed birth control so strongly that it was illegal to sell contraceptives in Connecticut. My grandfather lost the election by just over a thousand votes, less than one-tenth of one percentage point. It wouldn't be the last time that suspicious election-eve maneuvering affected a candidate named Bush.

I'm sure my grandfather was disappointed to lose, but he had run a strong campaign and grown more comfortable on the stump. He ran again for the same Senate seat in 1952. This time he lost in a close primary. After the defeat, Prescott Bush resolved that he was done with politics. He had given it his best shot, and a career in the Senate was not to be.

Then fate intervened. Less than two months later, Connecticut's other U.S. Senator died unexpectedly. State Republicans again urged my grandfather to run, and he agreed to do it. His perseverance paid off, and he won the special election by a healthy margin. Prescott Bush, whose political career had seemed doomed a few months before, was sworn in as a U.S. Senator from Connecticut. George Bush learned an important lesson: Do not allow defeat to extinguish your dreams. If you keep working and remain optimistic, opportunities can come your way.

THANKS TO HIS character and his contacts, Prescott Bush became a highly respected Senator. He had served on the Yale Board of Trustees with the Senate Majority Leader, Republican Senator Robert Taft of Ohio. He also made friends with Senators on the other side of the aisle, including Lyndon Baines Johnson of Texas, who became Majority Leader in 1955, and a fellow member of the New England delegation, John F. Kennedy of Massachusetts. Back in the 1950s, the Senate was a lot more collegial than it is today.

My grandfather's most influential friend in

the capital was President Dwight Eisenhower. One key to developing the friendship was my grandfather's golf game. Ike loved to play golf, and there was no better golfer in the Senate than Prescott Bush. Ike especially liked that the Senator, unlike most politicians, refused to let the President win. Years later, my brother Marvin invited me to play a round at the Burning Tree Club in Maryland, one of the places where my grandfather and President Eisenhower used to play. Marv introduced me to our caddie, who told me he had carried the bag for my grandfather decades earlier. After watching me play about five holes, he delivered his assessment. "Your grandfather was a hell of a lot better than you are," he said. "He could shape it left, shape it right, make it move. When you hit it good, you're just lucky." The fellow wasn't afraid to speak the truth.

One of Prescott Bush's fellow Senators was Joseph McCarthy of Wisconsin. At the time, McCarthy was very popular with a certain segment of the country for his fervent anticommunism, which included making (often baseless) allegations that communists had infiltrated the top levels of the government. During his 1952

Senate campaign, my grandfather appeared at a campaign event with McCarthy. The other Republican candidates at the event lauded McCarthy, earning big cheers from the crowd. My grandfather considered McCarthy a demagogue and a bully. Prescott Bush was last to speak. "While we admire his objectives in the fight against communism," he said, "we have very considerable reservations concerning the methods which he sometimes employs."

The crowd booed lustily, but my grandfather was not intimidated. He later rejected a campaign contribution from McCarthy. Years later, when I learned about my grandfather's stance, I admired his willingness to stand up to extremism. Boston Mayor James Michael Curley once summarized the philosophy of many politicians as, "There go the people. I must follow them, for I am their leader." Prescott Bush had the courage and integrity to reject that view.

In 1956, my grandfather ran for reelection. He had established a strong record as a Senator, sponsoring important legislation like the Federal Highway Act and the bill creating the Peace Corps. He also earned a reputation for working tirelessly to serve his constituents. He spent Saturday mornings in the office answering every piece of mail that he had received that week. My father learned a valuable lesson: In politics, there is no substitute for staying in touch with the people you serve. Later, Dad followed his father's practice of devoting Saturday morning to answering his mail.

My grandfather's opponent in 1956 was Thomas J. Dodd, a Democratic Congressman and lawyer. Dodd took a populist line of attack against my grandfather. "I notice Senator Bush seems to have a lot of time to play golf," he said. "I can't afford to play golf."

Then someone asked Dodd what his favorite hobby was. He said it was horseback riding. Without missing a beat, my grandfather said, "Well, I congratulate my opponent. I've never been able to afford a horse."

My grandfather went on to win reelection by more than ten percentage points. (Years later, I had the chance to work with the affable Chris Dodd, the son of my grandfather's opponent and a Senator from Connecticut for thirty years.)

In 1962, Prescott Bush was sixty-seven years old, suffering from arthritis, and exhausted from his demanding travel schedule. "You would be a fool to run again," his doctor advised him, and he complied. I think he had second thoughts, especially after his health started to improve. He lived ten more years, and who knows what he might have accomplished in the political arena during that decade. His experience showed the importance of timing in politics. For Prescott Bush, the timing wasn't right to continue. For his son, the time was right to begin.

IT MIGHT SEEM hard to believe now, but for almost an entire century—from Reconstruction until 1961—not a single Republican won a statewide election in Texas. Between 1896 and 1959, the state never sent more than one Republican at a time to the U.S. Congress or the state senate. No more than two Republicans served together in the state legislature. In the 1950 and 1954 gubernatorial races, the Democratic candidate, Allan Shivers, won nearly 90 percent of the vote against his Republican opponents.

Despite the party's minority status, I don't think that Dad ever doubted that he was a Republican. His father's politics had influenced him, and he agreed with the fundamental goals of the Republican Party: a vibrant free-enterprise system, a smaller and more accountable federal government, and greater decision-making at the state level. In Texas, Republicans and many Democrats weren't all that far apart on those issues. Yet the Democrats were the party of power, and most Texans saw no reason to switch their allegiance.

As a Republican in Midland, Texas, Dad used to joke that he could hold party meetings in his living room and still have chairs left over. He strongly believed that Texas would benefit from a two-party system in which voters had an alternative to the Democratic political machine. So he got involved with the local Republican organization. He served as the Republican precinct chair in Midland and as a delegate at county conventions. He was a local leader in the Eisenhower presidential campaigns in 1952 and 1956. Those elections marked minor triumphs for Texas Republicans. For only the second and third times in history, the Republican presidential candidate won Texas's electoral college votes.

My father's first significant jump into politics came after we moved to Houston. He became involved with the Republican Party of Harris County, the largest county in the state. Dad worked hard to help elect Republican candidates, including John Tower, who won the 1961 special election to fill the U.S. Senate seat vacated by Vice President Lyndon Johnson. Tower was Texas's first elected Republican U.S. Senator since Reconstruction, and his election gave the party a sense of optimism.

In 1962, a handful of Houston friends asked Dad to run for Chairman of the Harris County Republican Party. He agreed and campaigned hard for the job, visiting every one of the more than two hundred precincts in the city, including some of the African-American areas that had probably never seen a Republican. Eventually, his only rival for the position withdrew, and the party elected my father unanimously. In retrospect, I am surprised that he agreed to take the job. Serving as a local party Chairman requires long hours of recruiting precinct Chairmen, building voter lists, and performing other thankless tasks at the grassroots level. As he had shown in the oil business, George Bush was not afraid to start at the bottom.

Dad's job was complicated by an active fringe element in the party, the John Birch Society. The Birchers were extremists who peddled a variety of conspiracy theories. They claimed that Eastern elites like the Rockefellers wanted America to surrender its sovereignty to some kind of world super-government. As a result, the Birchers wanted to pull the United States out of the United Nations. They also wanted to impeach Supreme Court Chief Justice Earl Warren and to repeal the Sixteenth Amendment, which authorizes the federal income tax, without replacing it with any reasonable alternative. George Bush understood that the more the Republican Party became identified with the Birchers, the less likely that Republicans would ever emerge as a viable alternative to Democrats in Texas.

Diplomacy was my father's first instinct, and he tried hard to bring the Birchers into the fold. He instructed the party leadership to stop referring to Birchers as "nuts," and he appointed Birch Society members to chair several important precincts. The move didn't work. The Birchers railed against his leadership and refused to work with the so-called Republican establishment. So Dad purged the Birchers from their leadership posts and moved on without them.

Running the county party turned out to be a valuable experience. He learned how to recruit and motivate volunteers. He gained experience managing a political organization. He formed friendships with other Republican county Chairmen and Republican leaders throughout the state. And he learned that there are some people on the extremes of the American political spectrum who would rather hurl invectives than work for the common good.

ON SEPTEMBER 11, 1963, George Bush held a press conference in Austin to announce his candidacy for the United States Senate. I had just started my senior year at Andover. I was no expert on politics, but I knew enough to recognize that this race was a long shot. My father was a thirty-nine-year-old businessman and county party leader who had never held public office. He had little name recognition outside

Houston and Midland. And he was a Republican in a state that almost uniformly elected Democrats.

My father never asked my opinion about his decision to run, and I didn't expect him to. Of course, he talked to Mother. She later told me that her only reservation about Dad's running for office was that he would win and they would run out of money. After all, there were no East Coast trust funds to support them. Mother did not want money to buy lavish things; as she put it, "I just wanted to make sure we could afford to send your brothers and sister to college." My father convinced her that they were financially secure, and from then on she was all in. Working hard to help George Bush's campaign succeed was another time that she went three-quarters of the way for the man she loved.

George Bush was in the race for the right reasons. He felt the same duty to serve others that led Prescott Bush to serve as the Greenwich town moderator and to give up his Wall Street career to serve in the Senate. He also knew from watching Prescott Bush that it was possible to enter public service and remain a good father and a good man. That was a lesson that I learned from them both. Needless to say, Prescott Bush fully supported his son's decision to run, even if he knew it was a long shot.

The first stage of the contest was the Republican primary, a four-way race that pitted my father against Jack Cox, Robert Morris, and Milton Davis. Cox was the front-runner. Like Dad, he came from the oil business in Houston. He had served in the Texas state legislature for six years before joining the first wave of Democrats to switch parties. In 1962, Cox had won more than 45 percent of the vote in his run for Governor against Democrat John Connally.

My father dashed back and forth across the huge state. There was no coffee gathering or chamber of commerce banquet too small for him to attend. He laid out his case for "responsible conservatism" and his vision for a two-party state. After each campaign event, he sent handwritten notes to the people he had met. He must have written thousands of them that spring. Republicans responded to his warm personality, his energy, and his impressive biography. One person at a time, George Bush was building a political following.

Dad's hard work paid off in the primary. He

won 44 percent of the vote, compared with 32 percent for Cox. Texas election law requires a nominee to get 50 percent of the vote, so he and Cox squared off again in a runoff. He had to skip my high school graduation because of the election, but I didn't mind. I wanted him to win. And he did. He prevailed in the runoff with about 62 percent of the vote.

THE 1964 SENATE RACE in Texas may have included involvement from more future and former Presidents than any other Senate campaign in history. Dad was one of them, of course. I campaigned for him during the summer after I graduated from high school. So did Richard Nixon, whom my grandfather had gotten to know in the Senate. Dwight Eisenhower, still a close friend of Prescott Bush's, supported Dad. The sitting President, Lyndon Johnson, campaigned for the Democratic incumbent, Ralph Yarborough, who also had the support of President Kennedy before he was assassinated.

Senator Ralph Yarborough was a liberal populist who subscribed fully to the big-spending plans of the Great Society. He supported the

Civil Rights Act of 1964, which many Texans opposed as an overreach by the federal government into an issue that they felt should be decided by the states. Yarborough attacked my father's ties to the oil industry and tried to portray him as a wealthy Northeastern carpetbagger. One critic printed a flyer claiming that my mother was an heiress who spent all her time on Cape Cod. Shortly thereafter, my dad received a letter from Marvin Pierce. Mr. Pierce delivered the bad news that Mother was not an heiress. Nor had she ever been to Cape Cod.

In his opening speech of the general election, Dad called Yarborough "a man who has fostered, finagled for, and flourished on a diet of spend, spend, spend the taxpayers' money." Dad's platform called for a tax cut and a balanced budget, smaller government that encouraged free enterprise, and a "courageous" foreign policy "designed to extend freedom."

Given that Texas Democrats far outnumbered Republicans, Dad had no choice but to appeal to the conservative wing of the Democratic Party and try to outhustle his opponent. He chartered a bus nicknamed the "Bandwagon for Bush." I traveled with him on a bus trip to West

Texas, where we stopped in Democratic strong-
holds such as Abilene and Quanah. Those trips
were like the ultimate father-son camping experience. We would pull into a town square, and a
country band called the Black Mountain Boys
would start playing in hopes of drawing some
kind of a crowd. The Bush Belles, an enthu-
siastic and brightly clad group of housewives,
would pass out campaign pamphlets. My job
was to run back and forth to the bus to make
sure that the Belles and other campaign volunteers had all the materials that they needed.
Then Dad would mount the podium and give
a speech. Some in the audience applauded and
cheered. Others just looked startled at the sight
of a real-life Republican.

Campaigning with my dad was a thrilling
experience. I was amazed by my father's energy and his drive. I learned about the elements
of a campaign, including the "stump speech."
At first I was surprised that Dad delivered the
same speech at every campaign stop. For those
traveling with him, hearing the same lines over
and over again could be tiresome. (Perhaps that
was the reason Mother started needlepointing purses for key volunteers during campaign

trips.) For the crowd in each city, however, the speech was brand-new. And even if the entourage was bored, Dad was not. He was a sincere and emotional speaker who recognized that every minute is precious in a campaign. I grew to love the daily rhythms of the campaign—the crowds and the competition. It might have been that summer of 1964 when I caught the political bug myself.

Dad's campaign gained some momentum throughout the summer and fall, but it received a devastating blow on the day the President entered the race. While Ralph Yarborough may have been beatable in Texas in 1964, President Lyndon Baines Johnson was not. Even though Yarborough had taken positions to LBJ's left—and even though LBJ liked and respected Prescott Bush—the President couldn't afford to lose a Democratic seat in the Senate. Johnson praised Yarborough as a fellow Democrat and deftly tied Dad to Republican presidential candidate Barry Goldwater, who had lost traction after LBJ's "daisy ad" portraying him as eager to engage in a nuclear war.

In the final weeks of the campaign, it was obvious that LBJ was surging in his home state.

Dad convinced several major Texas newspapers to endorse both him and LBJ. Ticket splitting offered the only path to victory for George Bush, who remained upbeat to the end. On Election Day, my grandparents and I flew down to Houston from Connecticut, where I had started my freshman year at Yale. I remember driving to the Hotel America for the "victory" party right after the polls closed. We were listening to a radio broadcast that was interrupted by the news that Ralph Yarborough had won reelection.

As an eighteen-year-old kid who loved his dad, I took the loss hard. I felt like getting out of the hotel ballroom as quickly as I could. My father showed me a different way to deal with defeat. He gave a gracious concession speech and spent the night shaking hands and thanking supporters and campaign staff.

When the final vote tally came in, George Bush had something to be proud of. While LBJ had beaten Goldwater by 700,000 votes in Texas, Dad lost to Yarborough by only about 300,000 votes. More than 1.1 million Texans voted for my father—the highest statewide total

Even as a young man at Phillips Academy, George Bush displayed a natural leadership ability. People have always gravitated toward him and wanted to follow him. *George Bush Presidential Library and Museum (GBPLM)*

George Bush enlisted on his eighteenth birthday and became the youngest pilot in the Navy. His plane was shot down over the Pacific on September 2, 1944. *GBPLM*

Lieutenant George Bush married Barbara Pierce on January 6, 1945, while on leave from the Navy. Dad says the engagement ring is a star sapphire; Mother still suspects it might be blue glass. *GBPLM*

I was born on July 6, 1946, while Dad was a student at Yale. It's hard to imagine how he did it all—top student, star athlete, loyal friend, and devoted husband and father. As Mother put it with characteristic bluntness, "He worked hard." *GBPLM*

As Captain of the Yale baseball team, Dad met Babe Ruth during his senior year. The photo became iconic: one great man near the end of his life, another embarking on his. *GBPLM*

With Dad at the christening of "the Scorpion," his company's revolutionary offshore oil rig, in 1956. His experience running Zapata Offshore helped him to develop the leadership style that he would enjoy for years to come. *GBPLM*

Campaigning with Dad was a thrilling experience. But after hearing the stump speech over and over, Mother started needlepointing purses for volunteers. *GBPLM*

The lesson of George Bush's first political campaign, for the United States Senate in 1964, was that there are some races that you just can't win. The loss stung, but it didn't dampen his enthusiasm for politics or his desire to serve. *GBPLM*

In 1966, George Bush was elected to the United States House of Representatives. Mother moved to the capital with him and took to Washington quickly. *GBPLM*

Out of both respect and sympathy, George Bush went to Andrews Air Force Base to see off outgoing President Lyndon Johnson. Dad was the only Republican Congressman there.
LBJ Presidential Library/ Frank Wolfe

After Dad's unsuccessful Senate campaign in 1970, President Richard Nixon made him Ambassador to the United Nations. After Watergate, when George Bush was Chairman of the Republican National Committee, he wrote in a private letter to President Nixon, "I now firmly feel that resignation is best for this country, best for this President." *GBPLM*

Hosting a gathering for Cameroon National Day at the Ambassador's Residence at the Waldorf Astoria. As UN Ambassador, Dad mastered the art of personal diplomacy. *GBPLM*

that any Republican had ever received, including Dwight Eisenhower in his two presidential campaigns.

The LBJ landslide was unstoppable across Texas. After the 1964 election, there were no Republicans in the state senate and only one Republican in the 150-member state house, Frank Cahoon of Midland. In hindsight, it's hard to see what more Dad could have done. The lesson of 1964 was there are some races that you just can't win. Two years later, however, he found one that he could.

BETWEEN 1950 AND 1960, Texas's population expanded from 7.7 million to 9.6 million. Houston grew from under 600,000 to almost a million. In 1965, Houston's one congressional district split into three. My parents lived in the newly created Seventh District. As a former Chairman of the county party and a strong candidate in 1964, Dad would have a good shot at that new seat. The loss in the Senate race stung, but (like Prescott Bush's losses in 1952) it didn't dampen my father's enthusiasm for politics or his desire to serve. He announced his candidacy for Congress in January 1966 and ran unopposed for the Republican nomination.

The Democrat in the general election was Frank Briscoe, the District Attorney for Harris County. Unlike Ralph Yarborough, Briscoe was a conservative. Since he and Dad agreed on most policy issues, the race turned on personality. Dad ran billboard ads that showed him carrying his suit jacket casually over his shoulder, a youthful and energetic image. His campaign's official slogan was "Elect George Bush to Congress and Watch the Action." He gave more than one hundred speeches in the fall campaign. Former Vice President Nixon and House Minority Leader Gerald Ford both came to Houston to campaign for him.

Briscoe took a personal approach too—he personally attacked George Bush. Like Ralph Yarborough, he called him a carpetbagger. But Dad turned the provincialism into an advantage. He repeated the mantra he had adopted in 1964, "Texan by choice, not by chance." That attitude appealed broadly, since a majority of the voters in the district were new Texans. Dad's memorable phrase, along with his billboards, provided my introduction to messaging in politics. Then, as now, a catchy and accurate slogan can help a candidate grab the attention of busy voters, especially those who are open-minded enough to consider crossing party lines. I like to think that I picked up a few supporters by describing myself as a "compassionate conservative" in the 2000 campaign.

As a college student on the East Coast, I didn't have the chance to give Dad much help on the 1966 campaign. I did fly down from Connecticut for the election-night party in Houston. This time the victory party lived up to its name. Dad won 57 percent of the vote. George Bush was headed to Congress as the representative of Texas's Seventh District—a district that has remained Republican ever since.

MAN OF THE HOUSE

UNLIKE SOME MEMBERS of Congress, Dad decided to move his family with him to Washington when he was elected. He was a family man first, and he wanted to be around as much as possible while my younger brothers Neil and Marvin and my sister Dorothy grew up. (Jeb and I did not live with our parents in Washington; I was finishing college, and he was in high school at Andover.) My parents sold their house in Houston, bought a town house there for Dad's trips back to his district, and moved into a home in Washington's Spring Valley neighborhood. They purchased the house sight unseen from Senator Milward Simpson of Wyoming, whose son Alan later followed his father into the Senate and became a lifelong friend of my parents'.

I didn't see my parents all that often in the late 1960s. I was in college and then figuring out what I wanted to do with my life—a transitional period that I once described by saying, "When I was young and irresponsible, I was young and irresponsible." One thing I'm sure of is that I tested my father's patience during those years. After a hard-fought tennis match in Washington, Dad's friend Jimmy Allison and I became quite inebriated. I later drove my tennis partner, my brother Marvin, back to my parents' house. Everything went fine until I struck our neighbor's garbage can, which had been placed on the curb. I then zoomed into the driveway. Mother had watched the scene unfold. She was furious.

"Your behavior is disgraceful," she said. I stared at her blankly. "Go upstairs and see your father," she said.

I defiantly charged upstairs and put my hands on my hips. "I understand you want to see me."

Dad was reading a book. He lowered his book, calmly slid off his reading glasses, and stared right at me. Then he put his reading glasses back on and lifted up the book.

I felt like a fool. I slunk out of the room, chastened by the knowledge that I had disappointed my father so deeply that he would not speak to me.

That was as close as we got to an argument. Dad was not the kind of man who engaged in verbal fisticuffs. He would let my siblings and me know when we were out of line, and he expected us to correct the problem. Eventually, we did.

George Bush's great gift to his children was unconditional love. No matter how we expressed our individuality, no matter how badly we misbehaved, he always loved us. Over time, that love itself became a powerful source of independence. There was no point in competing with our father—no point in rebelling against him—because he would love us no matter what. I took that lesson to heart when I became a parent. When Barbara and Jenna were teenagers, they had independent streaks that reminded me a lot of times past. I used to tell them, "I love you. There's nothing you can do to make me stop loving you. So stop trying."

* * *

DAD ENJOYED serving in Congress. In the Capitol, he earned a reputation as a hardworking Congressman. He frequently flew back to Houston, where he stayed in close touch with his friends and constituents in the district. Like his father, he worked six days a week and spent most Saturday mornings signing letters and writing personal notes. Sundays were reserved for church in the morning and hamburger lunches in my parents' backyard in the afternoons. The lunches, which became somewhat legendary, featured an eclectic blend of invitees: family members, staffers, fellow Members of Congress, neighborhood friends, visiting constituents, and Washington insiders like the journalist Charlie Bartlett. Dad also included friends that he had met in earlier phases of his life. One of my father's most impressive qualities was his ability to make new friends while keeping old ones. No matter how high he rose in business or politics, George Bush never discarded old friends. The hamburger lunches were a great illustration of Dad's range of friends. The diverse group of guests would mingle on the lawn, chatting and drinking beer, while Congressman Bush flipped the burgers.

Mother was a willing hostess. She took to Washington quickly, setting up the new house and helping my younger siblings settle into their new schools. She easily made a circle of close friends, and she loved to organize tours of the Capitol and other Washington landmarks for visiting family and guests. Whenever my younger siblings had free time, she made sure they took advantage of the opportunity to experience the history and culture of the nation's capital.

One of my favorite memories of visiting Washington during Dad's congressional years came when he brought me with him to the House gym. He knew the name of every worker and towel attendant in the facility. Dad loved to play paddleball, a fast-moving game that requires good hand-eye coordination. One of his favorite playing partners was Congressman Sonny Montgomery, a Democrat from Mississippi. They played to win, but all the while they whooped and hollered and needled each other, having a lot of laughs. It was a good reminder that Congressmen from opposite parties could put their differences aside and enjoy each other's company.

Like every new Member, Congressman Bush was assigned to several legislative committees. My father hoped for a position on either Ways and Means or Appropriations. Those powerful committees are usually off-limits to freshmen, but Dad had developed a relationship with Minority Leader Gerald Ford during his campaign, and his father pitched in by calling his old friend Wilbur Mills of Arkansas, the Ways and Means Committee Chairman. The House Republican leadership showed its confidence in Dad by making him the first freshman in sixty-three years to receive a seat on Ways and Means.

While my father benefited from his father's connections, he also benefited from his mother's lessons. He worked tirelessly, kept his promises, and was willing to stay out of the limelight in order to share credit with others. Those qualities were often in short supply in Congress, and that made people gravitate to George Bush. He became especially close with other young Members of Congress, including Bill Steiger of Wisconsin, Jerry Pettis of California, John Paul Hammerschmidt of Arkansas, and Bob Price of Texas. In a preview of things to come, his fellow Republicans elected him president of the freshman class.

In the late 1960s, two issues dominated life in Washington: the Vietnam War and civil rights. My father had supported the American effort in Vietnam from the beginning. He believed that allowing communists in North Vietnam to overrun the South would deny the people of South Vietnam the opportunity to live in freedom. He also worried about the spread of communism throughout Southeast Asia. The United States had made a commitment to defend the South Vietnamese, and he believed strongly that America had to keep its word.

The day after Christmas 1967, Congressman George Bush embarked on a sixteen-day trip through Vietnam, Laos, and Thailand. He met with senior American officials. He also spent time with junior officers and enlisted men, including bomber pilots based on a carrier in the Tonkin Gulf, and asked for their unvarnished opinions on the war. Most told him that they were doing a lot better than the newspapers suggested.

My father came away impressed by the troops and convinced that America was making what he called "remarkable military progress." He also saw the resilience of the Vietcong guerillas. In a letter to his constituents, he described the intricate tunnels that the Vietcong dug through the jungles as evidence of their persistence. "I am now convinced that our objective is realistic," he told a reporter. "We can succeed if we have the will and the patience."

Back at home, the war grew more divisive. Dad recognized the right of antiwar activists to express their views, but he was troubled by vitriolic and violent protests that demoralized the troops. He defended LBJ against the ugly personal attacks lobbed by activists. As the months went by, the Johnson administration failed to offer a clear rationale for America's escalating involvement in the war. Thousands of young men were being drafted to fight a war that fewer and fewer people understood. For George H.W. Bush, the enduring lesson of Vietnam was that any commitment of the American military must include a clearly defined mission that the people can understand. Decades later, when he sent American troops to remove Saddam Hussein from Kuwait, that's exactly what he provided.

* * *

MY FATHER'S TRIP to Vietnam also influenced his outlook toward the other explosive question facing the country: civil rights. Leaders like Martin Luther King, Jr., and Thurgood Marshall were forcing the issue to the center of American politics. Throughout the South, civil rights activists opposed segregationist policies through sit-ins, freedom rides, and marches. The nation's television screens were filled with scenes of horrible violence, including the brutal crackdown on protesters by sheriff Bull Connor and the church bombings in Birmingham, Alabama, that killed four young African-American girls. I later learned that one of them was a friend of my Secretary of State Condoleezza Rice's. In 1963, President Kennedy proposed legislation prohibiting racial discrimination in public accommodations such as hotels, buses, and restaurants. In one of the most impressive acts of presidential leadership, President Johnson steered the Civil Rights Act through Congress in 1964.

My father had always been a strong believer in equal treatment of all people. Like his father,

he had raised money for the United Negro College Fund. As party Chairman and a Congressman, he had reached out to African-Americans
in Houston. In the 1964 Senate campaign, Dad
had opposed the Civil Rights Act on federalism
grounds. He believed that states, not the federal government, should control the regulation
of public places.

Vietnam changed his views. During his trip
to the front lines of the war, my father saw
black and white men risking their lives side by
side. In April 1968, the House of Representatives took up the Fair Housing Act, which outlawed racial discrimination in selling, renting,
or advertising residential property. My father
understood the argument that the federal government should not be able to dictate the conditions for the use of private property. But in
his heart, George Bush is a fair man. He could
not imagine telling an African-American veteran that he wasn't allowed to buy a house for
his family just because he was black.

Dad's congressional district was nearly 90
percent white and heavily opposed to the open-
housing bill. He estimated that the letters to
his office ran thirty to one against the legis-

lation. But on April 10, 1968, Congressman Bush voted in favor of the Fair Housing Act. He was one of only nine Texans to vote for the bill. (The other fourteen members of the Texas House delegation, thirteen Democrats and one Republican, opposed it.) President Johnson signed the bill into law the next day.

The reaction was swift and nasty. Dad's office received one angry phone call after the next, and at least one person threatened his life. The congressional postal office later reported that he received more mail than any other Member of Congress that year, much of it ranting against his vote on the open-housing bill.

When he went home to Houston the weekend after the vote, Dad confronted the issue head-on. He held a town hall meeting that was packed with hundreds of constituents. Many of them greeted their Congressman with catcalls and boos, much like the reaction when Prescott Bush had denounced McCarthy.

What this bill did, he said, was "try to offer a promise or a hope—a realization of the American Dream." He recounted his conversations with African-American soldiers in Vietnam, some of whom had told him about their desire to come home, get married, and buy a home. "Somehow it seems fundamental," he said, "that a man—if he has the money and the good character—should not have a door slammed in his face if he is a Negro or speaks with a Latin American accent." (**Negro** was an accepted word at the time.)

He acknowledged the differences of opinion. "I voted from conviction," he said. "I knew it would be unpopular—I knew it would be emotional—but I did what I thought was right; what more can I tell you!"

To his amazement, the crowd gave him a standing ovation. Most of them probably didn't change their minds about the open-housing bill, but they did change their minds about their Congressman. They recognized that he had courage and that he was honest. In the fall of 1968, seven months after the open-housing vote, George Bush ran for reelection unopposed.

I followed the open-housing debate, and I was very proud of my father. I admired the way that he took a principled position, defended his decision, and stood up to the political mob— all while maintaining his dignity. The lesson of his vote on the open-housing bill is that although citizens might not agree with the decision you make, they appreciate a leader who is willing to make a tough decision. George Bush did that throughout his career. I kept his example in mind when I faced tough decisions of my own, such as ordering the troop surge in Iraq or approving major government intervention in the marketplace to prevent a meltdown during the financial crisis.

IN THE PRESIDENTIAL race of 1968, Richard Nixon defeated Vice President Hubert Humphrey, who had stepped forward to run when LBJ shocked the country by declining to seek reelection. Nixon carried thirty-two states and more than three hundred electoral votes. He took his oath of office on January 20, 1969. An hour later, LBJ departed the nation's capital, where he had been a fixture since his election to Congress in 1937. He left with few friends.

Out of both respect and sympathy, Dad decided to go to Andrews Air Force Base to see off the former President. Amid the large crowd, a few other Congressmen showed up, including LBJ's longtime friend Jake Pickle, but Dad was

the only Republican. When Lady Bird Johnson's press secretary, Liz Carpenter, noticed
Dad standing in the crowd, she pointed him
out to the outgoing President. LBJ walked over,
shook his hand, and said, "George, I'm grateful
that you're here. Come visit me and Lady Bird
at the ranch sometime."

A few months later, Dad accepted the offer.
LBJ drove him around the sprawling grounds
of his ranch in Johnson City, Texas. At lunch,
Dad asked him a question: Should he leave his
safe seat in the House to run for the Senate
against Ralph Yarborough in 1970? The former
President, who had served in both the Senate
and the House, replied in classic LBJ style.

"George," he drawled, "the difference between the Senate and the House is the difference between chicken salad and chicken shit."

While he didn't put it quite so colorfully,
President Nixon agreed that Dad should run.
He promised to help with the campaign and
assured Dad a soft landing if he didn't win the
race.

Not everyone thought that Dad should run.
Many in his district urged him to keep his coveted seat on the House Ways and Means Com-

mittee. Once again, however, George Bush decided to take a risk. In January 1970, he announced that he would leave his safe seat in the House to run for the Senate. While many factors played a role in Dad's decision, I've always suspected that part of the reason was that he wanted to serve in the same body in which his father, Senator Prescott Bush, had served.

By the time Dad launched his 1970 Senate campaign, I had finished my pilot training and was flying planes with the Texas Air National Guard in Houston. I had time between training sessions to help out with the campaign. I traveled across the state with him on his kickoff tour. This time I was very optimistic, and so was Dad. The state's demographics were changing, Dad had built a good reputation, and Senator Yarborough was increasingly out of step with most Texans.

On the day my father cruised to victory in the Republican primary, the dynamics of the race changed dramatically. I remember riding with Mother, Dad, and some of his campaign aides when a radio broadcaster announced that Lloyd Bentsen had defeated Ralph Yarborough in the Democratic primary. That was not good news. Bentsen was a decorated World War II pilot, a former House member from South Texas, and a successful business executive in Houston. Like my father, Bentsen was a young, charismatic candidate who had run hard to the right of Yarborough. The philosophical distinctions in the race had just been erased, and Bentsen would benefit from a huge advantage in voter registration. Dad suddenly faced an uphill battle. The car fell silent for a few seconds. Then my father tried to reassure us. "It's okay," he said. "We can still win this thing."

Two factors ultimately doomed Dad in the race. First, Bentsen was able to appeal to Texans' longtime political heritage with his effective slogan "Texas needs a Democratic Senator." (The other Senator at the time was John Tower, a Republican.) Second, the Texas legislature had placed a constitutional amendment on the ballot that would allow each county to vote on whether to approve the sale of liquor by the drink. The measure drew heavy opposition from rural Texans in dry counties, who derided the amendment as an "open saloon" law. As a result, rural turnout was high—and in those days rural Texans voted overwhelmingly Democratic. I remember going to rural Kaufman County in 1970 to shake a few hands on Dad's behalf. When I arrived at the county courthouse, the building was nearly vacant. I asked where everybody had gone. One of the few people left said, "They heard a Republican was coming." (In a sign of the changes in Texas politics, I received a warm greeting when I returned to the Kaufman County courthouse as a Republican candidate for Governor in 1994. On Election Day, I carried the county.)

Thanks to Bentsen's strength as a candidate and the rural Democratic turnout, he defeated Dad 53 percent to 47 percent. This loss hurt a lot more than 1964. That one could be explained away by the Johnson landslide. This one seemed like the death knell for George Bush's political career.

Dad was gracious in defeat. He thanked everybody that he could find. He returned to Washington for the conclusion of his congressional term—likely the final months of his career in elected office. He was not bitter. He held no grudges. He accepted the voters' decision and prepared to move on with his life. Then one day he got a phone call from the President. Richard Nixon wanted to see him at the White House. From the despair of a second defeat, a career-changing opportunity arose.

DIPLOMACY

AS A CONGRESSMAN FROM HOUSTON, home of the Johnson Space Center, George Bush took a keen interest in the space program. When **Apollo 8** became the first spacecraft to fly around the moon in December 1968, my father wanted to honor the commander of the mission, his friend Frank Borman. Some Congressmen might have issued a press release or introduced a congressional resolution. That was not George Bush's style. To celebrate Frank Borman's accomplishment, he hosted a dinner in his honor at the Alibi Club in Washington, DC. The guest list was classic George Bush: some Members of Congress, some Washington friends, and some pals from Houston, like C. Fred and Marion Chambers. Generously, Dad included me on the list.

"How would you like to fly up to Washington for a dinner with an astronaut?" he asked in a phone call.

I was at Moody Air Force Base in Valdosta, Georgia, for pilot training with the Texas Air National Guard. "That sounds interesting, Dad," I said.

Then he revealed an ulterior motive. "I also invited Tricia Nixon. I thought it might be fun for you to take her to the party."

I was briefly speechless. "I'm going to have to get back to you on that," I said.

I wasn't sure how I felt about flying to Washington for a blind date with the President's oldest daughter. I mentioned the invite to several of my flight school buddies. They didn't believe me. Only a fifty-dollar wager would quiet their needling. I called Dad back.

"Count me in," I said.

On the appointed evening, I pulled up to the White House gate in my parents' purple Gremlin, which was outfitted with Levi's jean seat covers. A White House usher met me at the Diplomatic Reception Entrance and took me upstairs. I asked if the President was there. The usher said that he and Mrs. Nixon were traveling.

I awkwardly sat on the couches overlooking the Rose Garden and awaited my date's arrival. Eventually Tricia emerged, and I introduced myself. We went downstairs and climbed into a white Lincoln Town Car. As we hit the seats, one of the Secret Service agents in the front swiveled his head and said, "Good evening, Miss Nixon."

Off we went to the Alibi Club, where we were seated at a round oak table. Being a swashbuckling pilot, I had taken to drink. During dinner, I reached for some butter, knocked over a glass, and watched in horror as the stain of red wine crept across the table. Then I fired up a cigarette, prompting a polite suggestion from Tricia that I not smoke. The date came to an end when she asked me to take her back to the White House immediately after dinner. When I returned to the party, my father was standing around chatting with a few friends.

"How'd it go, son?" he asked.

Before I could answer, one of his friends leaned in and whispered, "Get any?"

I smiled. "Not even close."

More than forty years later, when I drove through the White House gates as President, I thought back to that first visit and had a good chuckle.

MY FIRST TIME meeting Richard Nixon came when my father brought me with him to an ecumenical church service that the President held in the East Room. I admired the beauty of the room—the tall ceilings, elegant chandeliers, and full-length Gilbert Stuart portrait of George Washington that Dolley Madison rescued before the British burned the White House in 1814. The idea of a church service in the White House struck me as unusual. So did the President. When I shook hands with him, he seemed somewhat stiff and formal. I had voted for Richard Nixon, but I didn't feel very warm about him.

Part of the problem was that Nixon's style of leadership did not seem to fit the times. In the late 1960s and early 1970s, Americans were grappling with race riots in major cities, the assassinations of Martin Luther King, Jr., and Bobby Kennedy, an unpopular war in Vietnam, and a changing culture in which drug use was becoming prevalent and women were demanding their rightful place in society. A country looks to its leaders to set a mood, and the rattled nation needed a President to project optimism, unity, and calm. Instead, Richard Nixon came across as dark and divisive. His White House, led by senior aides H.R. Haldeman and John Ehrlichman, seemed cold and conspiratorial. And that was before the news broke about secret tapes and enemies lists.

On the other hand, I have always appreciated President Nixon because of the opportunities he created for my father. In December 1970, Dad was serving out the final month of his term in the House of Representatives. He had given up his seat to run for the Senate and wasn't sure what he was going to do next. With two Senate losses in the past six years, his political future did not look bright. But President Nixon—who had been told that his own political career was finished after losing the 1962 California Governor's race and declaring, "You won't have Nixon to kick around anymore"— found a place for George Bush.

About a month after the 1970 election, Dad met with the President at the White House. Mother called to tell me that Dad had been nominated to serve as United States Ambassador to the United Nations. I was surprised. I thought back to his campaign speeches blasting the UN as an ineffective institution that should have little influence on American foreign policy. At the time, the Texas crowds had responded with loud cheers. I wondered what they'd say when they heard about UN Ambassador Bush.

Looking back on it, I see why the UN position appealed to my father. His travels abroad and experience negotiating offshore drilling contracts with foreign companies and governments had sparked an interest in international issues. The new position got him out of Washington and gave him a life after defeat. Plus the job came with a seat in the Cabinet, which would allow Dad to see the workings of the White House up close.

My father's first mission was to get confirmed. Previous UN Ambassadors included heavyweights like Adlai Stevenson, a former Governor of Illinois and two-time Democratic presidential nominee, and Arthur Goldberg, who left his lifetime appointment on the Supreme Court to take the job. The **New York Times** editorialized, "Nothing in [George Bush's] record qualifies him for this important position." Thankfully, most Senators disagreed—and were willing to overlook Dad's skepticism about the UN during the 1964 campaign. The Senate confirmed him handily, and he took his oath as Ambassador in February 1971. Once again, he and Mother were on the move. This time they did not have to find a place to live. One of the perks of the UN job was that it came with housing: a penthouse apartment on the forty-second floor of the Waldorf Astoria.

OVER THE YEARS, George Bush became an expert at starting new jobs. As soon as he was appointed to the position at the UN, he reached out to a wide variety of people for advice, including former President Lyndon Johnson. When he made his first visit to the U.S. mission at the UN headquarters in New York, he ate lunch with some of the top administrative staff. He took a tour of UN agencies in Europe and received detailed briefings on each agency's operations. While he admired the service of many American diplomats, he recognized quickly that the UN was inefficient and that its management structure provided no account-ability. When I became President thirty years later, little had changed. I grew increasingly frustrated with the UN's inability to achieve results as well as with its propensity to send mixed signals, such as giving Cuba and Libya seats on the Human Rights Council or failing to stop the genocides in Rwanda and Darfur. Nevertheless, I learned that many of my fellow world leaders, especially in Europe, needed the UN imprimatur to convince their parliaments to fund operations in Afghanistan and Iraq.

As UN Ambassador, Dad devoted his energy to building trust with his fellow Ambassadors. He chatted his way through the required din-ners and cocktail parties. He also created other opportunities to get to know his colleagues. He and Mother took Ambassadors and their fami-lies to Broadway shows, a John Denver concert at Carnegie Hall, and baseball games at Shea Stadium. He invited the Italian and French Ambassadors and their families to Walker's Point, asked his mother to host a luncheon for the Chinese delegation in Greenwich, escorted a group of Ambassadors to NASA headquarters in Houston, and organized a private screening of **The Godfather**. He recognized that the key to effective diplomacy was developing personal relationships—an approach that can be called "personal diplomacy." The brand of diplomacy that my father developed at the UN became a hallmark of his foreign policy for years to come, especially during the presidency.

One of my parents' favorite places to entertain was the spectacular apartment at the Waldorf. The nine-room suite had once belonged to Douglas MacArthur, and it measured up to his luxurious taste. The first time I visited my parents at the Waldorf, I found Dad in the living room, which was forty-eight feet long with elegant flooring and woodwork.

"Is this big enough for you, Dad?" I asked.

"It's adequate," he deadpanned.

Mother and Dad had a very happy life at the Waldorf, and so did my little sister Doro. As I told John Negroponte when I appointed him UN Ambassador years later, "I don't think you'll have any problem adjusting to the accommodations."

The most controversial policy issue facing the UN during Dad's tenure was the question of which delegation should represent China. The country held a coveted seat on the Security Council that two rival factions—the Nationalists, based in Taiwan, and Mao Zedong's Communists, based on the mainland—were vying to fill. The United States had always supported the Nationalists as China's representative at the UN. But as Mao Zedong and the Communists grew in power, they claimed that they were the only legitimate Chinese government and pushed to exclude Taiwan from the UN.

In the fall of 1971, the UN General Assembly held a vote on who would represent China. The Nixon administration supported "dual representation," meaning that both mainland China and Taiwan would have seats. My father, tapping into the personal relationships he had developed, reached out to almost a hundred UN delegates, explaining his concerns about emboldening the Communists and urging them not to turn their backs on the Taiwanese. Dad's position was undercut, however, when President Nixon dispatched National Security Adviser Henry Kissinger to Beijing to set up a historic visit to the People's Republic of China. Kissinger's trip weakened Dad's hand by reinforcing Mao's claim that he was leading the true Chinese government.

Dad did his best, but the dual-representation strategy failed and Taiwan lost its UN seat by a few votes, fifty-nine to fifty-five. Several delegates who had promised to support Taiwan either switched their position or abstained from the vote. In a show of sympathy, Ambassador Bush rose from his seat on the floor of the General Assembly and accompanied Taiwan's disgraced Ambassador, Liu Chieh, out of the UN. They were heckled and jeered on the walk down the aisle. Mother, who had come with Dad to watch the historic vote, remembers delegates spitting at her. The UN, created as an idealistic forum to pursue peace, had become a venue of ugly anti-Americanism.

In September 1972, a Palestinian terrorist group known as Black September kidnapped and killed eleven Israeli athletes at the Summer Olympics in Munich. Israel responded by launching attacks against Syria and Lebanon. A majority of the UN Security Council supported a resolution that condemned the Israeli military response but was silent about the terrorist attack against the athletes. Because the

United States holds one of the five permanent seats on the Security Council, it has the power to veto any Security Council resolution. The administration chose to exercise America's veto power for only the second time to block the anti-Israel resolution. Over the next few decades, U.S. Ambassadors to the UN repeatedly used the veto power to defend our ally Israel from unfair condemnation.

In all his government positions, George Bush took his duties seriously. But he never took himself too seriously. During his time as Ambassador, **New York** magazine published an article by sportswriter Dick Schaap identifying the "10 most overrated men in New York City." Dad made the list, as did other local luminaries including New York Senator Jacob Javits, Cardinal Terence Cooke, and **New York Times** publisher Arthur Sulzberger. Some on the list had an ego delicate enough to take offense. Not Dad. He decided to hold a party for everyone on the list. As he wrote on the invitation, "I'd like the chance to look you over to see why you are so 'overrated.'" Almost all of them (plus Dick Schaap) showed up for a lighthearted evening at the Waldorf.

* * *

THE ASSIGNMENT in New York gave Dad a
chance to see his parents more often. In September 1972, his father, Prescott, went to see
his doctor for a persistent cough. After a few
tests, he was admitted to Memorial Sloan Kettering, the hospital where Robin had died in
1953. Unfortunately, his prognosis was bleak.
He had advanced lung cancer. He passed away
a month later at age seventy-seven.

My grandmother wanted the funeral to be an
uplifting celebration of Prescott Bush's life. She
wrote all the eulogies and had the church choir
sing "Gampy's" favorite hymns. She asked my
brothers, male cousins, and me to serve as pall-
bearers. After the service, Dad, his brothers, and
his sister stood on the steps of the church, shaking hands and thanking every guest for coming
to pay their respects. It was hard for Dad to
say good-bye to the man who had served as his
mentor and example. He would carry the lessons of Prescott Bush with him for the rest of
his life.

Before long, Dad found a silver lining in his
father's death. Prescott Bush, who always in-

sisted on integrity in government, did not have to witness what happened in the nation's capital over the next two years.

AS AMBASSADOR to the UN, my father played no role in the 1972 presidential campaign, in which President Nixon won reelection over the Democratic candidate, Senator George McGovern. The campaign effectively ended before it began when it was revealed that McGovern's first selection as a running mate, Senator Tom Eagleton, had undergone electric shock therapy for mental health problems. Nixon went on to a landslide victory, but his reelection came with short coattails. While the President carried every state except Massachusetts (he also lost the District of Columbia), Republicans lost two seats in the Senate and gained only twelve in the House.

A couple of weeks after the election, the President asked my father to meet him at Camp David, the rustic presidential retreat in the Catoctin Mountains of Maryland named for President Eisenhower's grandson, who was also President Nixon's son-in-law (he married President Nixon's younger daughter, Julie). The President told Dad that he wanted him to leave the UN and replace Senator Bob Dole of Kansas as Chairman of the Republican National Committee. From Nixon's perspective, the choice made a lot of sense. Dad had experience running a party organization in Texas, and he was a fresh face with the energy and credibility to promote the Nixon agenda and strengthen the party. From Dad's perspective, the job was at best a step sideways. He worried that some might think he had failed as a diplomat. He had also been around the Nixon White House enough to know that he didn't like some of their tactics. He had no interest in smearing decent people on the other side of the political aisle.

Nevertheless, if leading the Republican Party was how he could best serve the country, he felt obliged to say yes.

A few days later, Bob Dole came to see him in New York. He told Dad that he was there to feel out his interest in succeeding him at the RNC. Dad felt bad for Dole; no one had told him that he had already been replaced. My father gently broke the news to the embarrassed Senator. The situation revealed that the White

House was either overly secretive or dysfunctional.

In early 1973, Mother and Dad cleared out of Apartment 42A at the Waldorf Towers and headed back to the nation's capital. Dad figured that the job would be relatively routine. He assumed that he would spend most of his time fund-raising, recruiting candidates, and meeting with party officials, many of whom he already knew. He did not expect that nineteen months later, he would be sitting in the East Room of the White House, listening to Richard Nixon become the first and only President in American history to resign.

IN THE SUMMER of 1972, five men were caught breaking into the headquarters of the Democratic National Committee at the Watergate apartment complex in Washington, DC. The burglars were affiliated with the Committee to Re-Elect the President—known as CREEP. The White House denied any connection to the burglary, and the allegations had little impact on the 1972 election. By early 1973, shortly after Dad took over as RNC Chairman, there were indications that some people close to President Nixon had played a role in a cover-up.

President Nixon assured the country that he knew nothing about Watergate. For more than a year, Dad defended the President. George Bush, who always believed the best of people, trusted the President when he gave his word. As details about Watergate continued to drip out, Dad grew increasingly concerned. The Senate opened an investigation. Senior White House aides resigned. A special prosecutor was appointed. Then it came out that the President had secretly taped his conversations in the Oval Office. He refused to turn over the tapes, as the special prosecutor had demanded. When the Attorney General and Deputy Attorney General refused to execute Nixon's order to fire the special prosecutor, the President dismissed the special prosecutor and accepted the resignations of the Attorney General and Deputy Attorney General—a move that became known as the Saturday Night Massacre. Eventually, the White House released a limited number of transcripts of the Oval Office conversations. But there were key gaps, including an infamous eighteen and a half minutes that had been "accidentally erased."

I watched the scandal unfold from Cambridge, Massachusetts, where I was attending Harvard Business School. The campus environment was hostile to Republicans, especially Richard Nixon. I kept my head down, studied hard, and generally did not discuss politics. One exception came when I visited Dad's only sister, my energetic and spirited aunt Nancy, in Lincoln, Massachusetts. We would play nine holes at her favorite golf course and commiserate about the putrid swamp that George Bush had waded into.

The more I learned about Watergate, the more disgusted I became. I was shocked that the President had surrounded himself with people who had acted like the law didn't apply to them. And I was angry about the dilemma they had created for my father. On one hand, he was trying to defend a President to whom he felt loyal. On the other hand, he had to protect the party against Democratic efforts to anchor every Republican to the sinking ship that was the Nixon White House.

In late July 1974, as the Watergate scandal was reaching its crescendo, Dad wrote a long letter to my brothers and me. To that point, he had not shared his thoughts about how agonizing the experience had been. Always an optimist, he opened the letter by reflecting on all the things he had to be thankful for, including our close family and the opportunity to serve the country he loved. He praised President Nixon's positive features. Then he reflected on Nixon's flaws: his insecurity, his poor judgment, his disrespect for Congress, and, above all, the harsh and amoral way in which he spoke about his supposed friends on the White House tapes.

One of those supposed friends was George Bush. Nixon had called Dad a "worrywart" and complained that he hadn't used the RNC aggressively enough to defend him. The President's suggestion that Dad was weak hurt him. For many excruciating months, he had spoken up for Richard Nixon. "It stings but it doesn't bleed," he wrote in his letter to us. He closed with the lessons he hoped we would learn from the Watergate debacle:

Listen to your conscience. Don't be afraid not to join the mob—if you feel inside it's wrong. Don't confuse being "soft" with seeing the other guy's point of view. . . . Avoid self-righteously turning on a friend, but have your friendship mean enough that you would be willing to share with your friend your judgment. Don't assign away your judgment to achieve power.

He couldn't have realized it at the time, but his words set a standard that both Jeb and I would strive to follow when we held public office.

The final straw came on August 5, 1974. The Supreme Court had ruled that the White House must turn over all the tapes to Leon Jaworski, the new Watergate special prosecutor and a friend of Dad's from Houston. The tapes revealed that Nixon had spoken to one of his aides about thwarting the FBI's investigation into the Watergate break-in. That was proof that he knew about the cover-up and that he had lied to the country. The revelation shattered Dad's trust in Nixon.

The day after the smoking-gun tape became

public, Nixon held a meeting with his Cabinet and key political advisers. Dad attended the meeting and witnessed a surreal scene in which the President spent the meeting talking about the economy and other policy issues rather than confronting the only question that really mattered. Later that day, Dad gave Nixon's Chief of Staff, Alexander Haig, a candid assessment. After speaking to some of his old friends in Congress, he had learned that the President would not have the votes to survive an impeachment proceeding.

Despite his deep disappointment, my father refused to condemn Nixon publicly. While he might have benefited in the short run, Dad saw little point in "piling on," as he put it. He voiced his opinion privately in a letter to the President on August 7. As far as I know, he is the only party Chairman in American history who has ever written such a letter. "I now firmly feel that resignation is best for this country, best for this President," he wrote. "I believe this view is held by most Republican leaders across the country." Writing with his characteristic sympathy, Dad continued, "This letter is made much more difficult because of the gratitude I will always have for you. If you do leave office, history will properly record your achievements with a lasting respect." The next day, President Nixon announced that he would resign.

Mother and Dad were relieved by the President's decision. They went to the White House for his farewell address. As Dad described it, the White House was filled with "an aura of sadness, like someone had died." In the East Room, where I had first met Nixon at the ecumenical church service a few years earlier, he concluded his speech by saying, "Always remember, others may hate you, but those who hate you don't win unless you hate them, and then you destroy yourself."

IT WOULD HAVE been hard to imagine at the time, but serving as party Chairman during Watergate proved to be a valuable experience. Dad met hundreds of party leaders and grassroots Republican activists—a network that would prove vital in his later campaigns. Although he saw how people in honorable positions could do dishonorable things, he didn't let the experience jade his view of public service.

The Watergate experience confirmed a key lesson: A leader must surround himself with people of good character and set high standards. Watergate also reinforced the importance of personal relationships. Nixon seemed to have few real friends. He seemed introverted, mysterious, and suspicious. A cost of his isolation was that he had no one to keep him grounded or talk him out of his worst instincts. By contrast, my father was extroverted, optimistic, and determined to see the best in people. As a result, he managed to maintain his friendships in Washington throughout Watergate— and he struck up some new ones. One unlikely friend was Bob Strauss, Dad's counterpart at the Democratic National Committee. They bonded over their experiences and shared many laughs. They came to respect each other so much that Dad later named Strauss Ambassador to the Soviet Union. The contrast was striking. Richard Nixon kept a list of his political enemies; George Bush turned his political opponents into friends.

Unfortunately, the hangover from Watergate would affect every President who followed Richard Nixon. A generation of reporters saw the **Washington Post** win a Pulitzer for exposing the scandal, and many dreamed of being the next Woodward or Bernstein. A strong and skeptical press corps is good for democracy. Often the media's first instinct is to portray every story as a scandal, however, which presents a distorted picture of government and leaves the public cynical.

As for George Bush, his character and good judgment allowed him to survive Watergate with his reputation and integrity intact—a feat that seems more impressive with time.

AFTER WATCHING Richard Nixon board the helicopter on the South Lawn for his departure from the White House on August 9, 1974, Mother and Dad returned to the East Room to see the new President, Gerald Ford, take the oath of office. Ford remains the only President who was never elected; Richard Nixon appointed him after his first Vice President, Spiro Agnew, resigned to avoid jail time for tax fraud.

Ford offered an immediate contrast with Nixon. He was a big, sturdy Midwesterner with an optimistic demeanor, exactly the kind of healer the nation needed. When President Ford uttered his famous line "My fellow Americans, our long national nightmare is over," it seemed to me that he was referring to more than Watergate. My hope was that a long era of tension and pain—the race riots, Vietnam, Nixon's enemies list—was coming to a close.

Ford immediately had to make a major decision. Former President Nixon could have faced criminal charges for his involvement in Watergate. President Ford understood that a trial of the former President would have forced the American people to relive the traumas of Watergate for years to come. He removed that possibility by granting Nixon a full and unconditional pardon. His decision was deeply unpopular, and many think it cost him the 1976 election. George Bush respected the President's decision. Not only was it necessary, but it also showed political courage.

I spent the summer of 1974 in Fairbanks, Alaska, where I was working a job for Alaska International Air. I had gone there between my first and second years of Harvard Business School both to satisfy my sense of adventure and to assess the business opportunities. I was startled by the beauty of Alaska and enjoyed the hiking, the fishing, and the long summer days. I was also surprised, however, by how dependent the state and its businesses were on the federal government. That did not appeal to me, and by the end of the summer I concluded that business opportunities were better in Texas.

One morning I picked up the local newspaper in Fairbanks and read that George Bush was on the short list of people who Gerald Ford was considering to fill the vacant vice presidency. It had never occurred to me that Dad would be a candidate for the job. I called Dad, who confirmed that the report was true.

"Well, there are some people who think I could do a good job," he said, "but I wouldn't make much out of it."

He was on the list partly because an RNC poll of party leaders showed that Dad had more support than anyone else. Some of his friends on Capitol Hill were lobbying the new President on his behalf. If Dad wanted to be VP, I was rooting for him hard. Deep down I wondered whether Ford could pick someone with such a recent connection to Nixon.

Sure enough, I heard on the radio a few days

later that Ford had selected Nelson Rockefeller, the Governor of New York, to be the new Vice President. I could only imagine what Prescott Bush would have thought of that choice.

Two days later, President Ford called my father to the Oval Office to discuss his future. Dad told him that he had enjoyed his time at the UN and that he would like to expand his diplomatic experience. The President told him he could take his pick of ambassadorships—including Great Britain and France, two coveted posts once held by John Adams and Thomas Jefferson.

A Ford aide had tipped Dad off about the subject of the meeting, so he was prepared. He told the President that he would like to go to China. Dad was aware that the American representative to China did not have the rank of Ambassador, because the United States did not have full diplomatic relations with the People's Republic of China. But he wasn't hung up on titles. He had spent time thinking about China, and he was convinced that America's relationship with China would be pivotal in the future—an insight that few had at the time.

In the fall of 1974, President Ford named him head of the United States Liaison Office in Beijing (then known as Peking).

Looking back on it, Dad's decision to take the top diplomatic post in China was probably the most surprising career move he had made since he and Mother set out for West Texas in 1948. Just as he didn't want to pursue the conventional path of an investment banker on Wall Street, he did not want to be stuck attending diplomatic dinners in London or Paris. Like West Texas, China represented the frontier—an exciting place to live, with a distinctive culture and great promise for the future. For someone worn out by the Washington scene, China was a perfect place to escape to.

LIAISON BUSH ARRIVED in China in October 1974. Before leaving Washington, he had done a lot of homework on his new post. He had met with China experts throughout the U.S. government. On the flight over, he stopped in Japan and consulted with the U.S. Ambassador in Tokyo. He and Mother took Chinese lessons. They certainly didn't master the language. But they did know how to say **hello** and **thank you**—a good start for any diplomat.

Upon arrival, Dad asked for detailed briefings from his deputy, the experienced foreign-service officer John Holdridge, and he befriended everyone in the office from the junior officers to his driver and Chinese interpreter. He peppered his new colleagues with questions about China, their children, their interests, and their backgrounds. He and Mother worked hard to make the Liaison Office and their personal residence less formal and more welcoming. They invited staff members over for dinners, bought a Ping-Pong table, and added other personal touches. George Bush was a team player, and he was building Team China.

Another priority was to develop personal relationships with his fellow diplomats. He attended dozens of receptions at other embassies and frequently entertained his counterparts at the Liaison Office. Some people might have considered those events drudgery. Not George Bush. At every cocktail party and in every receiving line, he saw an opportunity to meet a new person and build a new relationship. In his view, no country was too small to merit his attention. Nothing galled him more than what he liked to call bigshot-itis. His first visitor at the Liaison Office was the head of the delegation from Kuwait, a small Middle Eastern kingdom that would play a major role in his presidency decades later.

Just as he had at the United Nations, George Bush blended his personal life and his diplomacy. He loved to play tennis, so he organized regular matches with his fellow diplomats at the International Club. Dad loved the competition and the exercise. He also recognized that his colleagues were a lot more likely to return his call if they had also returned his serve.

He devoted a lot of attention to Chinese officials. He already knew the foreign minister, Chiao Kuan Hua, who had been the first Ambassador from the People's Republic to the UN. Even though Dad had opposed the People's Republic on the Taiwan vote, they had become friends. The foreign minister fondly remembered the lunch that Dad's mother had hosted for the Chinese delegation in Greenwich, and he was eager to reciprocate the hospitality.

Despite his role as America's senior diplomat

in China, Dad's policy influence was limited. The major decisions on China came from President Ford and Henry Kissinger. Dad might have been frustrated by the lack of collaboration, but he understood the President's desire to manage the relationship from the White House. During his time as President, he often dealt directly with foreign leaders like John Major of Great Britain or Brian Mulroney of Canada. I did the same with some of my closest counterparts, such as Tony Blair of Great Britain.

The biggest headline of Dad's tenure in China came when President Ford made a state visit in 1975, the first since President Nixon's historic trip three years earlier. Dad accompanied the President to his meeting with Mao Zedong, the revolutionary leader of the Chinese Communist Party. It was fascinating for him to meet Mao, who had grown reclusive as his health failed. In hindsight, it was even more important that Dad got to know the small, smiling Vice Premier who sat at Mao's side. His name was Deng Xiaoping. Thirteen years later, he and my father would meet again—this time as leaders of their nations.

The new post in China left my parents with

more free time than they'd had in years. They explored Beijing on their bikes and walked around the city with C. Fred, their cocker spaniel named for their Houston friend. C. Fred always drew interested looks from the locals, because the Communists had banned dogs. Mother and Dad continued to take Chinese lessons, and on Sundays they worshipped in a local church—one of the few sanctioned by the Chinese government—where services were conducted in Chinese.

Mother and Dad encouraged family and friends to visit them in China. One of the first to accept the invitation was my grandmother, who came for Christmas 1974. In typical Dorothy Walker Bush style, she arrived on an exhausting flight from New York and shortly thereafter joined Dad for a bicycle ride to the Forbidden City. It's safe to say she was the only seventy-three-year-old Western woman pedaling through the December chill that day.

Texas friends made the trek to China as well. Jake Hamon, one of Dad's buddies from the oil business, visited with his wife, Nancy, in March 1975. Nancy came clad in a sable coat and hat. The outfit had at least one admirer in the house.

As my parents chatted with the Hamons, Mother looked over with horror to see C. Fred chewing on a furry object. Years later, when Laura and I invited Nancy to a Valentine's Day party at the White House, she was still chuckling about her mangled hat.

I visited Mother and Dad in China shortly after I graduated from Harvard Business School in 1975. The Liaison Office was comfortable, but I was taken aback by the primitive conditions elsewhere. Most people traveled by bicycle or horse cart. The summer was hot and dry, and the city was covered with dust blown in from the desert. It reminded me of Midland, Texas. Unlike in Midland, however, there were no signs of capitalism. Everyone wore the same dull gray clothes, rationed out by the Chinese government. Dad had a vision that China would emerge as a world power in the future, and he turned out to be right. In 1975, however, the country had a long way to go.

As part of the trip, I experienced Dad's personal diplomacy up close. On the Fourth of July, he held a big celebration at the Liaison Office, complete with hamburgers, hot dogs, and American beer. No American official had ever hosted anything like that before, so the event drew a big turnout from the diplomatic corps. I vividly remember a Scandinavian Ambassador exiting the party, somewhat wobbly, with a giant mustard smear on his bright white shirt.

ON NOVEMBER 2, 1975, Mother and Dad got up early and went for a bike ride through Beijing. They were enjoying a crisp fall morning when Dad spotted a messenger from his office pedaling toward them. He had a telegram from the White House marked: "George Bush. Eyes Only." Dad was shocked by what he read. President Ford wanted him to leave China and return to the United States to serve as Director of the Central Intelligence Agency.

As my parents knew from their meager access to American news, the CIA was facing withering criticism from the public, the media, and Congress. In December 1974, the **New York Times** had published a front-page article revealing that the CIA, under multiple Presidents, had engaged in illegal activities, including monitoring domestic antiwar activists and other dissident groups. Congress formed the

Church and Pike Committees to investigate. Angry legislators demanded transparency and a massive overhaul of the agency. As my father read the message to Mother, she broke down in tears. The President had just asked the man she loved to reenter the swamp.

Mother wasn't the only one who had misgivings about the offer. Dad was reluctant too. Democrats had made huge gains in the 1974 congressional elections that followed Watergate, and my father knew that dealing with the most liberal Congress in recent memory would be very unpleasant. He also wanted to keep the door open to pursue further political ambitions. He had been considered for VP in 1974, and Republicans in Texas were talking to him about running for Governor in 1978. Those plans would be threatened if he took the CIA job. As he put it in a letter to his brothers and sister, the CIA was a "graveyard for politics."

Yet again, Dad's sense of duty prevailed. He had dealt with the CIA during his time at the UN and in China, and he knew the importance of their work. A few hours after he received the telegram, Dad cabled back to Washington to accept the job. As he explained to the President and Kissinger, "My Dad inculcated into his sons a set of values that have served me well in my own short public life. One of these values quite simply is that one should serve his country and his President. And so if this is what the President wants me to do the answer is a firm 'YES.' "

The CIA position required confirmation by the Senate. The nomination became controversial when some Senators loudly claimed that George Bush was too political for the job. Dad pointed out that he had held nonpolitical posts at the UN and in China, and he assured the Senators that partisanship would play no role in the assignment. Still, they demanded more. In a historically unusual letter, President Ford provided a written guarantee that he would not consider George Bush for Vice President when he ran for reelection in 1976. The President was willing to do what was necessary to get his nominee confirmed, and Dad's commitment to serve his country was strong enough that he gave up his constitutional right to run for office. The Senate confirmed him by a vote of sixty-four to twenty-seven.

* * *

DIRECTOR BUSH BEGAN the new job by developing a strong and trusting relationship with his new colleagues. That task was especially important at the CIA, where agency morale was sagging because of the beating the CIA had been taking in Congress and the press. The agency's image had been tarnished badly.

From the beginning, Dad made it clear that he believed in the agency's mission and would stand up for its people. In his appearances before Congress and the media, he stressed the importance of a robust intelligence capacity. While acknowledging past abuses, he explained the measures the agency had taken to correct them. Most important, he called the intelligence officers "patriots," a term that few people were willing to use in public when the daily headlines blared about the CIA's past transgressions.

He showed his support for the agency in other ways. President Ford had offered him an office in the Old Executive Office Building, right next to the White House. Accepting the office would have signaled his importance in Washington, where proximity to the President is a proxy for power. He turned the President's offer down. He felt that his office should be at agency headquarters in Langley, Virginia. There he took the employee elevator, not the one reserved for the Director. Around Christmas 1976, he arranged for the great jazz artist Lionel Hampton to perform a concert for the employees in "the Bubble," the CIA's large auditorium. (Unlike the Christmas party back in West Texas, Dad didn't tend bar.)

Director Bush traveled to CIA stations abroad to thank analysts and case officers. Some in the clandestine service had never met a CIA Director. He also made some difficult personnel decisions that were necessary to improve the agency—another reason why it was so important for him to develop trust early on. He gently eased out older agency leaders, which gave him a way to promote junior officers and address the recruitment problem. And he spoke out forcefully against leakers, including former CIA agent Philip Agee, who had just released a tell-all book. My father could forgive a lot of mistakes, but he believed that it was disgraceful for a man to violate his oath and reveal state secrets, especially when it could lead to the loss of innocent American life.

It didn't take long for word to get around Langley that George Bush cared deeply about the CIA's mission and people. He found the work fascinating; his inquisitive nature was sated by the agency's cadre of brilliant analysts. Remarkably, in just one year, he developed a strong bond with the people of the CIA— dedicated public servants who did not often receive the public appreciation that they deserved. One historian called him the most popular director since Allen Dulles in the 1950s.

Dad's affection for the CIA lasted long past his year at Langley. As President, he asked for in-person CIA briefings almost every day. When I was elected President, he advised me to do the same. I took his advice and found the briefings by the smart, capable CIA analysts one of the most interesting aspects of my job. Like Dad, I gained great respect for the fearless officers of the clandestine service.

TRUE TO HIS WORD, Dad stayed out of politics throughout his time at the CIA. President Ford's poll numbers had suffered after his pardon of Nixon, and the economy was struggling. In November 1976, he lost a close election to Jimmy Carter. Dad had met Carter during the campaign when the Georgia Governor requested intelligence briefings so that he could be up to speed if he won the election. After Carter's victory, Dad offered to stay on. He had been at the agency for only a year, and he felt that he could provide stability while the President filled the rest of his national security team.

Jimmy Carter decided to let Dad go, a move that I thought was a mistake. When he became President twelve years later, Dad retained CIA Director William Webster, who had been appointed by Ronald Reagan. When I took office, I retained Director George Tenet, who had been appointed by Bill Clinton. I thought my decision would send a signal of continuity and nonpartisanship in an important national security post. I was disappointed that President Obama chose not to keep Michael Hayden, a lifelong public servant whom I had appointed to lead the CIA in 2007. Nobody knew the intelligence business better than Mike, a career professional in the field, and his knowledge would have been very valuable to the President.

Ultimately, a Democratic President did recognize Dad's contributions to the CIA. In 1998, Bill Clinton signed legislation sponsored by Congressman Rob Portman of Ohio that renamed the agency's headquarters. When I made my first visit to Langley, Director George Tenet said, "Mr. President, welcome to the George Bush Center for Intelligence."

IN THE SPACE of one decade, George Bush had served as Ambassador to the United Nations, Republican Party Chairman, Liaison Officer in China, and Director of the CIA. He had seen a President fall and a new world power begin to rise. He had dealt successfully with diplomats, communists, and spies. He had led organizations through crises and emerged with his reputation enhanced. Yet when George Bush boarded a commercial flight to Houston after Jimmy Carter's inauguration, most observers believed his political career was over. According to conventional wisdom, none of the jobs he had held in the 1970s were viewed as a springboard to political success.

Of course, George Bush never put too much stock in conventional wisdom. He believed that his diplomatic jobs had prepared him well for further public service. And he turned out to be right. Not only is my father the only President to have held all four of those jobs, he is the only President to have held **any** of those four jobs. In hindsight, the experience and judgment he gained along the way equipped him to become one of the best-prepared Presidents of the modern era.

RUNNER-UP

OVER HIS CAREER IN BUSINESS and government, George Bush had navigated his way through many unfamiliar situations. In the spring of 1977, shortly after he left the CIA at the end of the Ford administration, my parents encountered a new challenge: They were home alone.

Mother and Dad had returned to Houston shortly after Jimmy Carter's inauguration. They bought a house, their twenty-fifth different address in thirty-two years of marriage. All their children had grown and were living on their own. My parents used their newfound time to reconnect with their many Texas friends and dote on their first grandchild, George Prescott Bush, son of my brother Jeb and his wife, Columba. They enjoyed the respite from the

In 1974, President Ford named George Bush as America's representative to China. Dad recognized that China, like West Texas, represented an exciting frontier. Mother and Dad got around Beijing on bicycles. *GBPLM*

A few hours after receiving a telegram from the White House asking Dad to return from China to run the CIA, he cabled back, " . . . if this is what the President wants me to do the answer is a firm YES." President Ford offered him an office next to the West Wing, but Director Bush felt his office should be at Agency headquarters in Langley, Virginia. *GBPLM*

Planning Dad's first Presidential run in 1979 with his close friend and adviser James A. Baker III. Jimmy is a brilliant strategist, a skillful negotiator, and one of the best joke-tellers I have ever heard. I count him among the greatest political figures of the twentieth century. *Bush Family Photo*

Franklin Roosevelt's Vice President complained that his job was "not worth a warm bucket of spit." Fortunately, Ronald Reagan's Vice President had a more positive experience. Dad and the President had lunch together every week, a tradition I continued with Vice President Dick Cheney.
GBPLM/Cynthia Johnson

One of my favorite memories of Dad's 1988 Presidential campaign was when he invited our family to join him on a trip through the Midwest around Halloween. I still smile at the image of Barbara and Jenna walking down the aisles of Air Force Two trick-or-treating the national press corps. *GBPLM*

When the 60-year-old Vice President went to the Old Timers baseball game at Mile High Stadium, he donned the Denver Bears uniform and slapped a single into right field. *GBPLM/David Valdez*

On the sunny morning of January 20, 1989, George H.W. Bush was sworn in as the forty-first President of the United States. As I watched him raise his right hand and repeat the oath, I felt a wave of immeasurable pride.

GBPLM/Carol Powers

Playing horseshoes with Soviet President Mikhail Gorbachev at Camp David in 1990. Dad's strategy was to develop their friendship while encouraging Gorbachev to allow the Soviet Union to unwind peacefully. On Christmas Day 1991, Gorbachev signed paperwork disbanding the Communist regime. *GBPLM/David Valdez*

Dad was a prolific writer of personal letters. Today there are thousands of people around the world who can reach into a desk drawer and produce a thank-you note from George Bush. *GBPLM/David Valdez*

I once asked my mother how she and my father have managed to stay happily married for almost seventy years. "Both of us have always been willing to go three-quarters of the way," she said. *GBPLM*

President George H.W. Bush's record includes a number of major domestic accomplishments. One of his proudest is the Americans with Disabilities Act. *GBPLM/Joyce Naltchayan*

Waiting with Laura for the First Lady to throw out the first pitch at a Texas Rangers game. Dad never had to worry about whether Mother could handle the pressure of the presidency while holding our family together. I was blessed that Laura gave me the same peace of mind. *GBPLM/Carol Powers*

Meeting with General Colin Powell, Defense Secretary Dick Cheney, Chief of Staff John Sununu, and National Security Adviser Brent Scowcroft after Saddam Hussein invaded Kuwait. "This will not stand," Dad told the press, "this aggression against Kuwait." Those were not hollow words.
GBPLM/Susan Biddle

As a combat veteran, Dad understood the agony of war firsthand and felt a special connection to the troops as Commander-in-Chief. In 1990, Mother and Dad spent Thanksgiving Day with service men and women deployed to Saudi Arabia. *GBPLM/Susan Biddle*

political arena. Mother called it "a second honeymoon." But Dad could not take it easy for long. He missed the action. And he believed he had more to contribute. As he wrote to his friend Gerry Bemiss, "I don't want to slip into that 3 or 4 martini late late dinner rich social thing. There is still too much to learn."

My father wasn't the only one in the family with a drive to contribute. In our old hometown of Midland, I was preparing to enter the political arena that he had just left—and that he was about to reenter, in a big way.

A DECADE on a government salary, combined with the expenses of educating five children, had taken its toll on my parents' finances. In 1977, my father's uncle Herbie—a founding owner of the New York Mets who helped inspire my dream to own a baseball team—died at age seventy-two. His wife, Mary, decided to put Walker's Point up for sale. The big house had been damaged by a storm the previous winter, and she didn't want the expense of maintaining it. She had received a generous offer from a buyer outside the family. Fortunately, she gave my father the option to match the price. He had loved Walker's Point his whole life, and he hated the thought of losing the family's traditional gathering place—his "anchor to windward." At the time, he didn't have the cash to buy the property. He asked his aunt if she would give him a little more time to get the money together. She agreed, and he purchased the property in 1981.

My father didn't like the idea of cashing in on his government service, but he had always been interested in the business world. Joining a few corporate boards of directors gave him a way to stay engaged and make some money. He accepted seats on the boards of Eli Lilly, Texasgulf Oil, and First International Bancshares in Dallas. He also received an offer to get back into the oil business from H. Ross Perot, a Dallas businessman who had founded a successful technology company. Dad thanked Ross but declined the offer. He explained that he didn't want to take on any long-term business commitments. That was not the last George Bush would hear from Ross Perot.

While Dad enjoyed his corporate roles, politics and public service remained his passions.

Some of his Texas friends urged him to run for Governor in 1978. But his interests were elsewhere. He had served in the Cabinets of two Presidents, and he knew how to handle the pressures of politics and policy. As much as Mother loved their quiet life together, she knew that their second honeymoon would be brief. Dad wanted to serve, and he wanted to serve on the big stage. Soon they began to travel the country, sounding out the prospects of a presidential campaign.

AFTER GRADUATING from Harvard Business School in 1975, I returned to Midland, Texas. Like my dad a generation earlier, I was attracted to Midland by the entrepreneurial climate and the excitement of an oil boom. My debut in the oil business came as a land man. My duties were to hustle around checking court records and trading minerals and royalties. Occasionally I took a small interest in a deal. I had some marginal success, and my cost of living was low.

On July 6, 1977, my thirty-first birthday, Midland's longtime Congressman, George Mahon, announced that he would retire after forty-four years in the U.S. House of Representatives. The prospect of running for Mr. Mahon's seat intrigued me. I liked politics, and I'd gained valuable experience working on Dad's campaigns in 1964 and 1970, as well as on Senate races in Florida (for Edward Gurney, who won) and Alabama (for Red Blount, who lost). I felt strongly about the issues. I believed that the country was headed in the wrong direction under Jimmy Carter, especially on energy regulation and tax policy. The political bug was biting hard.

Dad was surprised when I told him that I was considering running for Congress. He suggested I visit his friend former Governor Allan Shivers to ask his advice on the race. Shivers was a political icon. For decades, he held the record for the longest continuous service as Governor of Texas (until my successor, Governor Rick Perry, surpassed him). When I told Governor Shivers that I was considering running in the Nineteenth Congressional District, he looked me straight in the eye and told me that I couldn't win. The seat had been held by a conservative rural Democrat for the past forty-four years, and the district was drawn perfectly for a conservative rural Democratic state senator, Kent Hance.

I thanked the Governor for seeing me and left somewhat perplexed. Had Dad known what Shivers would say? If so, why had he sent me? It was not Dad's style to try to dictate the course of my life. On a decision of this magnitude, he wanted me to make up my own mind. In hindsight, I suspect that the Shivers referral was his way of warning me that the race would be difficult and that I should prepare for disappointment.

I entered the race anyway. I was independent-minded enough—or, some might say, stubborn enough—to give it a shot. As expected, once I told him that I had decided to run, my father was behind me 100 percent.

My congressional campaign was a small operation. Most of those involved were friends, family, or volunteers. My brother Neil was the campaign manager. My treasurer was Joe O'Neill, a childhood friend who had graduated from Notre Dame and the University of Michigan's business school, served in the Army Special Forces, and returned to Midland to work in the oil business. One night in the summer of 1977, Joe and his wife, Jan, invited me to a barbecue in their backyard. They told me there was someone that they wanted me to meet: Jan's good friend from Midland, Laura Welch.

I was struck by Laura's beauty. She had gorgeous blue eyes and a bright smile, which she flashed frequently in response to my jokes. As we chatted, we learned how much we had in common. She had grown up in Midland at the same time that I had, and we had overlapped for one year at San Jacinto Junior High. It turned out that we had even lived in the same apartment complex in Houston after college (she graduated from Southern Methodist University in Dallas and then earned a master's in library science from the University of Texas). She was smart and dignified and had a calm, natural manner. It wasn't exactly the same as when George Bush met Barbara Pierce at that Christmas dance back in 1941. Nobody danced a waltz in Joe and Jan's backyard; our second date was at a putt-putt golf course. Like my parents, however, we fell in love quickly. We were both over thirty and ready to settle down. We got married a few months later.

Laura knew she was marrying into a political family. She was less interested in the politics and more interested in the family. As an only child, she was thrilled to gain three brothers-in-law and a sister-in-law. She quickly developed a comfortable relationship with my parents, who welcomed her as a daughter of their own. Among other things, Laura bonded with Mother over their responsibilities as spouses of candidates. Laura was supportive of my race, but she had no interest in a starring role. I liked that about her; I was not looking for the stereotypical "political wife." She even vowed that she would never give a political speech. Fortunately, she broke that vow. She became a very effective advocate in my 1978 congressional campaign—and in many other campaigns that followed.

The front-runner in the 1978 Republican primary was Jim Reese, a former mayor of Odessa who had run a strong race against Mahon in 1976. Reese had lined up some impressive endorsements, including that of former California Governor Ronald Reagan. I had met the Governor at a rally in Jacksonville, Florida, during my time working on a Senate campaign. Reagan made a powerful impression. He was

tall and handsome and carried himself like the
Hollywood star that he once was. He gave a
fantastic speech that electrified the crowd. I
was not surprised that he had almost defeated
President Gerald Ford in the 1976 primaries or
that he was considered a strong candidate for
the Republican nomination in 1980.

Naturally I was disappointed that Governor
Reagan had endorsed my opponent. When I
mentioned the situation to Dad, he said immediately, "Reagan will call you if you win your
primary." Sure enough, when I upset Jim Reese
for the Republican nomination, the phone rang
the next day. "George, this is Ron Reagan," he
said. "Congratulations on proving me wrong.
I just want to let you know that I'll do anything I can to help you win the seat." I thanked
him for the call and hung up impressed by his
generosity. I did not ask for his help. I naively
thought that voters would appreciate that I was
willing to run without inviting him or my dad
to campaign in the district.

I campaigned hard through the summer and
fall of 1978. After the primary, Laura and I left
our home in Midland and rented a house in
Lubbock, the largest city in the congressional

district. It was asking a lot of my new bride to make her leave her home so soon after we got married. But she embraced the challenge. While we had taken a short trip to Mexico after the wedding, she thought of the campaign as our real honeymoon. We spent long hours together on the road, driving across the sprawling district for campaign stops in small towns like Levelland, Plainview, and Brownfield. On the Fourth of July, we rode in a white pickup truck in a parade in the heavily Democratic northern part of the district. Nobody waved to us—at least not using all five fingers. It's safe to say that Laura had not envisioned doing anything like this when she planned her career as a public school librarian. For me, she was going three-quarters of the way.

On election night, I came up short. I won my home county of Midland and some of the southern part of the district. But as Governor Shivers had predicted, the district was drawn perfectly to suit Kent Hance. He stressed his Texas roots and painted me as an Ivy League–educated outsider, which played well in the mostly rural district. He won 53 percent to 47 percent.

Even though I lost the race, I learned a lot—

about campaigning, and about the partner at my side. And thanks to my father's example, I knew that life would go on after defeat. In some ways, losing the election might have been for the best. To this day, my friend Kent Hance reminds people that he is the only politician ever to beat me. "I'm responsible for George W. Bush being President," he says. "If it wasn't for me, he'd still be stuck in Congress."

I DON'T REMEMBER the exact moment when Dad told me he had decided to run for President. It was obvious that he was leaning strongly in that direction in 1977 when he created the Fund for Limited Government, a political action committee that allowed him to raise money as he explored his options.

It did not require much exploration to recognize that George Bush faced an uphill climb for the Republican nomination. Unlike other prospective candidates, he was not an elected official. He had no natural constituency. His national name recognition was so low that in many early presidential polls he didn't register enough support to be included in the results.

He was listed under the asterisk as one of "others receiving votes." His early campaign aides formed the "asterisk club." George Bush had overcome long odds before, and he intended to do it again.

The competition for the 1980 Republican nomination promised to be intense. In addition to Governor Reagan, the field included Senator Bob Dole of Kansas, a former RNC Chairman and Gerald Ford's running mate in 1976. Another presidential hopeful was John Connally, a former Democratic Governor of Texas whom Richard Nixon had recruited into the Republican Party by appointing him Treasury Secretary. Connally, who had been in the car with John F. Kennedy on the day that he was assassinated in Dallas, was charismatic and had a strong following in the boardrooms of corporate America. Rounding out the field were Howard Baker, a respected Senator from Tennessee, and two Congressmen from Illinois, John Anderson and Phil Crane.

The Chairman of the Fund for Limited Government was my father's close friend and confidant from Houston, James A. Baker III. Dad first met Jimmy Baker shortly after he and

Mother moved to Houston in 1959. While Dad was building his offshore oil business, Jimmy was making his name as a lawyer. A graduate of Princeton and the University of Texas School of Law, Jimmy was a brilliant strategist, a skillful negotiator, and a man who could always make Dad laugh. He was one of the best joke-tellers that I have ever heard (most of his best jokes cannot be repeated). He and Dad struck up a friendship as tennis partners at the Houston Country Club. Before long, they were club champions in men's doubles.

Jimmy had grown even closer to Mother and Dad when his wife, Mary, died of breast cancer in 1970. My parents reached out to help comfort their grieving friend. Dad explained how he had dealt with Robin's death by plunging into his work, and he asked Jimmy if he wanted to spend more time on his 1970 Senate campaign. He accepted the offer. For the rest of Dad's career, James Baker was his most trusted and valuable political adviser—including in the 1980 presidential campaign.

Another Houston friend taking a leading role in the 1980 effort was Bob Mosbacher, who volunteered to head up Dad's fund-raising effort.

His job was to raise enough money for Dad to travel the country and set up political organizations in a few key states. One of the first staffers hired was Karl Rove, a twenty-eight-year-old political whiz who had led the College Republicans while Dad was at the RNC. Karl played an important role in Dad's campaign and later became one of my closest advisers and a dear friend.

No account of George Bush's team would be complete without mention of Don Rhodes. My father first met Don in 1964, when he volunteered on Dad's Senate campaign. Don would stop by the office on the way home from his job as a convenience store clerk. He worked grueling hours stuffing envelopes and checking mailing lists. At first, few people took Don seriously. He was different. He hardly spoke. And when he did, it was in a loud, slurred way. Many around the campaign pitied Don. Few thought he was capable of more than menial tasks.

Don never talked about his background, except for one aspect: He loved his Texas A&M. Over time, some of his life story emerged. His slurred speech was a result of bad hearing. His social awkwardness was a result of his troubled home environment. A childhood friend of Don's later told us that his mother was a prostitute who died when Don was young, leaving him an orphan in Houston.

Over the years, Don Rhodes became one of my father's most loyal and trusted aides. Dad saw something in the former convenience store clerk that others did not: a man who needed a friend, and a man he could trust completely. My parents' trust in Don was so deep that they allowed him to handle their day-to-day finances. It was not uncommon for my siblings in college to get a call from Don reminding them to pay a bill or check the balance in their bank account.

One of my favorite memories of Don came after the strike that ended the major league baseball season in 1994. Don was so angry that he vowed not to attend a ball game for ten years. When the Houston Astros opened their beautiful new ballpark in 2000, Dad asked Don if he would like to join him for opening day. Of course, he had great seats. Don looked Dad straight in the eye and said, "I told you I wasn't going to a game for ten years, and it hasn't been ten years yet."

When Don died in 2011, my father called Don "the most unselfish, most caring friend" he ever had. That was high praise from George Bush. After Don's funeral, his ashes were scattered in my parents' future gravesite at the George Bush Presidential Library. That was a fitting tribute to Don Rhodes. He was not just a staffer; he was a member of the family.

ON MAY 1, 1979, my father officially announced his campaign for the presidency. Dad's limited national following and skeletal staff dictated his strategy for the primaries. In 1976, Jimmy Carter had devoted all his resources to the early states of Iowa and New Hampshire. His victories there had provided the momentum that propelled him all the way to the nomination. Dad adopted a similar approach.

As in his earlier political races, George Bush resolved to outwork his opponents. He visited every one of Iowa's ninety-nine counties, many of them multiple times. He would show up for pancake breakfasts, county fairs, chamber of commerce dinners, and coffees at people's

homes. He followed up with hundreds of handwritten letters. In the month before the caucus,
he held dozens of campaign events. He talked
about the struggling economy, rising inflation,
and declining American power abroad. His
message was that Jimmy Carter had to go—
and that he had the energy and experience to
replace him.

Dad was not the only one working hard. My
brother Jeb came back from Venezuela, where
he had been working for the international office
of a Texas bank, to work full-time on the campaign. Neil worked on the campaign in New
Hampshire, and Marvin spent almost a full
year in Iowa. Doro enrolled in a typing class
and volunteered on the campaign in Massachusetts. Dad's brothers and sister all pitched in as
well. And Mother maintained a full campaign
schedule, speaking in living rooms and meeting halls across Iowa about why George Bush
would be a great President. Our love for him
was so powerful that it was easy for the family
to go all in.

I made it to Iowa for the final weeks before
the caucuses. I traveled the northeastern corner of the state with Congressman Tom Tauke.

We met with groups of caucusgoers and tried to persuade them to turn out for George Bush. I loved every minute of the retail politics.

Ronald Reagan was clearly the front-runner going into the caucuses, but Dad had lined up support from respected Iowans like former RNC Chair Mary Louise Smith and Congressman Tauke. More important, he had spent a lot more time in the state than Reagan. That was crucial. Iowans appreciate candidates who give them personal attention. On caucus night, Dad's hard work paid off. He was first to the finish line with just over 30 percent of the vote. The candidate who had once been an asterisk in the polls had just won the first major contest of the presidential race.

THE UPSET VICTORY triggered a wave of national publicity. George Bush's name was in the headlines; his picture was on the magazine covers. Amid the euphoria of the Iowa triumph, however, he was uncharacteristically boastful. Looking ahead to New Hampshire, he said, "We'll do even better there." He continued, "There'll be absolutely no stopping me." In one of his most memorable lines, he announced that he had "Big Mo" (momentum) on his side. That was true, but not for long.

In retrospect, the Big Mo quote represented a missed opportunity. With the spotlight on him after his Iowa win, Dad had a chance to emphasize his vision for the country. Instead, he became entangled in the world of political process, and ultimately he allowed his candidacy to get defined by others. I learned a valuable lesson: Every time you have the microphone in a political campaign, you should use the opportunity to talk about your vision for the future. (Of course, I didn't always heed those words. In 2000, I won in Iowa and lost in New Hampshire to John McCain, in part because I let him define me.)

Compared to Iowa, New Hampshire seemed like familiar territory. Dad had been born in neighboring Massachusetts, grown up in nearby Connecticut, and spent summers across the border in Maine. He had a strong network of supporters in the state led by former Governor Hugh Gregg. (Years later his son, my close friend Judd Gregg, would serve as a Governor, a Senator, and Chairman of my New Hampshire campaigns.)

Despite the home-field advantage, the atmosphere in New Hampshire was different from Iowa. New Hampshire voters are an independent lot, and they have a history of derailing front-runners. Dad's front-runner status also led to intensified press scrutiny. In an interview with Mother, Jane Pauley asked, "Mrs. Bush, people say your husband is a man of the eighties and you are a woman of the forties. What do you say to that?" Mother defused the insult with a quip. "Oh, you mean people think I look forty?" Life as the presidential front-runner would not be easy.

The key moment in New Hampshire came at the debate two nights before the primary. In an attempt to dramatize the event, the debate organizers decided to invite only the two front-runners, Ronald Reagan and George Bush. The Reagan campaign supported the format and picked up the cost of the room rental. Dad hadn't suggested the idea, but he relished the chance to go head-to-head with Reagan.

Naturally, the other candidates were incensed

that they hadn't been invited. They decided to protest their exclusion by showing up at the debate and demanding to be heard. It later became clear that the Reagan campaign had coordinated their appearance, creating a political setup: They wanted to put George Bush on the defensive at the debate—and they did.

After the moderator, Jon Breen of the **Nashua Telegraph,** introduced Dad and Reagan to the audience, the other candidates popped out from behind the curtain and stood angrily on the stage. Reagan argued that they should be allowed to join the debate, but the moderator insisted on adhering to the agreement. Dad sat awkwardly in his chair as the spectacle unfolded around him. His instincts had kicked in. Rules were rules, and Dad had been raised to follow them. Plus he did not want to embarrass Mr. Breen in front of the national audience.

Reagan, on the other hand, had no problem showing up his host. When Breen threatened to cut off his microphone, Reagan thundered, "I am paying for this microphone, Mr. Green." The crowd roared with approval. (They didn't care that his name was Breen, not Green.) The remark echoed a line from Spencer Tracy in the movie **State of the Union,** and the former actor had won over his audience big-time. Dad's silence made him look weak and further infuriated the other candidates. The debate ended up as a one-on-one affair, but the only story anyone remembered was the controversy about the microphone. One press account said that Dad had shown "the backbone of a jellyfish." Bob Dole said that George Bush "wants to be King" and compared his actions to the those of the Gestapo. Other candidates piled on.

It was agonizing for me to listen to the jilted candidates hammer Dad. Looking back on it, the New Hampshire debate was the first time I experienced the unique brand of pain that the child of a public figure feels. I was used to hearing my father get criticized in his Texas campaigns and in his Washington jobs. This was different. The stage was bigger, the stakes were higher, and the barbs were more personal. How could anyone accuse George Bush of being selfish and uncaring? Didn't they know anything about his life? It made me furious.

Over the years, I would have that feeling again. When I was President, people often asked how I could handle all the criticism. The answer was that putting up with criticism of me was nothing compared to listening to attacks on a man I admire and love. There was one thing that lessened the pain: Dad never seemed to be bothered by the attacks. No matter how nasty or untrue the allegations might have been, he never complained or vented his frustration in front of his family. Looking back on it now, I can see that he was trying to send us a message: The critics were not getting to him, so we shouldn't let them get to us either. I adopted the same approach when my daughters got upset about the criticism that I received when I was in office.

As expected, the New Hampshire primary did not go well for George Bush. Ronald Reagan won in a landslide, claiming 50 percent of the vote. Dad finished second with 23 percent. Bob Dole dropped out of the race shortly thereafter. John Connally, who had pinned his hopes on South Carolina, dropped out when he finished a distant second to Reagan there. By mid-March, the 1980 Republican nomination was essentially a two-man race.

*   *   *

THE LOSSES in New Hampshire and South Carolina returned Dad to his underdog status. Reagan had more money and greater name recognition, and now he was the candidate with Big Mo. Dad's competitive instincts were strong. He fought hard and held his own. He won primaries in Massachusetts, Connecticut, and Pennsylvania. To have any chance of winning the nomination, Dad had to draw some contrasts with Reagan. But negative campaigning never came naturally to him, especially against a fellow Republican. His campaign slogan was "A President We Won't Have to Train"—a reminder that Governor Reagan had limited experience outside California. He jogged regularly to highlight his relative youth and energy (and to burn off some of the late-night campaign junk food). He occasionally discussed their differences on policy issues, most famously by labeling Reagan's plan to cut taxes and balance the budget "voodoo economics."

The toughest blow for Dad in the 1980 primaries came in Texas in early May. For the third time in his career, Dad campaigned across his home state. But Ronald Reagan was strong in Texas. He had won all one hundred of Texas's delegates against Gerald Ford in 1976, and in 1980 key elected officials like Republican Governor Bill Clements decided to stay on the sidelines. Like his Senate races, the Texas primary left Dad disappointed. Reagan won 53 percent to 46 percent.

Dad continued to battle. He won an impressive victory in Michigan in late May. However, Reagan was on the verge of picking up a massive number of delegates in his home state of California, which would essentially clinch the nomination. George Bush was not a quitter. His instinct was to finish the race. Jimmy Baker had a different perspective. He strongly suggested that Dad get out before he did irreparable damage to his political future.

Dad finally accepted his friend's advice. After spending Memorial Day weekend at home in Houston, he announced that he was ending his campaign and endorsing Ronald Reagan. He had a lot to be proud of. A year or two earlier, few would have imagined that he would be the runner-up for the nomination. Even in defeat, he showed his characteristic sense of humor. On the campaign plane's final flight, he played the Kenny Rogers song "The Gambler": "You've got to know when to hold 'em, know when to fold 'em." George Bush was folding his hand, but he wasn't out of the game.

ABOUT SEVEN WEEKS after the primaries ended, my parents attended the Republican National Convention in Detroit. The big question was whom Governor Reagan would pick as his running mate. The rumor swirling around the convention was that he was considering creating a "co-presidency" by selecting former President Gerald Ford. That idea made no sense to me. No former President had ever returned as Vice President, and I did not see how the sitting President could agree to share power with a predecessor.

Laura and I did not attend the convention. Instead we went to New York, where I had meetings with investors to discuss the oil and gas exploration company that I had started in 1979. One of our friends in New York invited us to dinner at the '21' Club. Near the end of the meal, the maître d' approached and said excitedly, "Mr. Bush, there's something on the news that I think you'll want to see." He wheeled out a portable television, and Laura and I watched in shock as Lesley Stahl of CBS News announced to the nation that Ronald Reagan had picked George Bush as his running mate. We hurried back to the hotel, where I called my surprised but thrilled dad to congratulate him and booked a flight to Detroit.

The vice presidential selection is the first big decision that a presidential nominee makes. Not surprisingly, I thought Ronald Reagan's choice sent all the right signals. The pick gave him a running mate with a foreign policy background, experience in Washington, and a reputation for loyalty. Once again, a political career that seemed lifeless had been reborn.

The 1980 race proved to be a transformative election. The country was suffering from crippling unemployment, inflation, and interest rates. The Soviet Union had invaded Afghanistan and Iranian radicals had seized dozens of hostages from the American embassy. Jimmy Carter had few answers beyond lamenting the national malaise. The American people were ready for a change, and Ronald Reagan provided it. With his sunny optimism and confidence in the country, he gave Americans hope for a better future.

On Election Day, Ronald Reagan took 44 states and 489 electoral votes, the most that any nonincumbent has ever received. Mother and Dad headed back to Washington, where George Bush would soon become the forty-third Vice President of the United States.

WITHIN A HEARTBEAT

IN JANUARY 1981, Laura and I flew to Washington for the Reagan-Bush inauguration. Dad had invited the full flock of children, siblings, aunts, uncles, cousins, and, of course, his mother. The day before the ceremony, some of us attended a luncheon generously hosted by Ronald Reagan's "Kitchen Cabinet"—longtime friends and confidants, like Holmes Tuttle and Justin Dart. There I met Tuttle's and Dart's sons, Robert Tuttle and Steve Dart, along with Tuttle's grandnephew Jim Click. All three of those men remain good friends of mine, and Robert Tuttle later became my Ambassador to Great Britain.

Of course, the highlight of the lunch was greeting the President-elect. Ronald Reagan had an ease about him that made you feel comfortable. In some ways, he was like Dad: charming, friendly, and warm. Even in our brief meeting, I sensed that the new President and Vice President would enjoy a good working relationship.

The next morning we took our seats on the inaugural platform. For the first time, the inauguration was held on the West Front of the Capitol Building. The day was sunny and warm—the fifty-five-degree temperature far exceeded that of most Washington winter days—and the view over the National Mall was spectacular. I looked out with awe at the huge crowd stretching back toward the Washington Monument, the Lincoln Memorial, and Arlington National Cemetery.

I had no idea that the 1981 inauguration would be the first of six that I attended. (The others came in 1985, 1989, 2001, 2005, and 2009.)

At the time, my overwhelming emotion was happiness for Dad. I watched with joy as Mother held the Bible while Dad took his oath of office from Justice Potter Stewart, their longtime friend and former neighbor on Palisade Lane in Northwest Washington, DC. When President Reagan began his inaugural address,

I was inspired by his optimism and determination to move the country forward. As he said in his speech, "Americans have the capacity now, as we've had in the past, to do whatever needs to be done to preserve this last and greatest bastion of freedom."

Following the ceremony, Dad and the new President attended a luncheon at the Capitol. President Reagan surprised the guests with a dramatic announcement: After 444 days in captivity, the American hostages in Iran had been released. I've always wondered whether the Iranians chose the timing because they feared Ronald Reagan or wanted to insult Jimmy Carter. Either way, the Reagan presidency was off to a great start. When the hostages touched down at Andrews Air Force Base a week later, Vice President Bush was there to welcome them home.

After watching the inaugural parade and attending the inaugural balls, my siblings and I spent the night at the Vice President's Residence at the Naval Observatory. Situated on a grass lot spanning approximately seventy-two acres, the spacious house was perfect for Mother and Dad. It had plenty of spare bedrooms for family gatherings, and the grounds included a tennis court and a jogging track, which enabled my parents to exercise frequently. The house was open to our family for the next eight years. As Mother later pointed out, that was the longest period that she and Dad had stayed in any house during their married life.

WHILE SERVING AS Franklin Roosevelt's Vice President, John Nance Garner (the first Texan to serve as VP) complained that his job was "not worth a warm bucket of spit" and "the worst damn fool mistake [he] ever made." Fortunately, Vice President Bush had a more positive experience.

My father's office was on the first floor of the West Wing, down the hall from the Oval Office and right next to the President's Chief of Staff: James A. Baker. As President Reagan had wisely recognized, Baker was a perfect fit for the job. As a skillful lawyer, campaign veteran, and former official in Gerald Ford's Commerce Department, he brought expertise on policy, politics, and personnel. Just as important, he had the even temperament and sound judgment to help guide the White House through any crisis. Of course, it was helpful for Dad to have his close friend as one of the President's top advisers. And it said a lot about Ronald Reagan that he had enough confidence to hire his primary opponent's campaign manager as his White House Chief of Staff.

Continuing a tradition started by Jimmy Carter and Walter Mondale, Vice President Bush and President Reagan had lunch together once a week in the private dining room next to the Oval Office. Their favorite menu item was Mexican food. The lunches provided an opportunity for Dad to give the President his candid advice on a wide range of subjects. Dad pledged to the President that their conversations would remain confidential. To this day, I have no idea what they discussed or whether they had any differences of opinion.

What I do know is that George Bush was loyal to Ronald Reagan and to his agenda. Dad recognized that it was the President who set policy for the administration; the Vice President's job was to support the President's decisions. In Dad's view, the highest form of disloyalty was for a Vice President to leak disagreements or try to create separation from the President. He impressed upon his staff that the President should never have to worry about being undermined by his Vice President (or any member of his staff, for that matter). I am sure the President's staff noticed and appreciated Dad's approach to the job. Before long, he showed his loyalty in a way that no one could have anticipated.

ON MARCH 30, 1981, George H.W. Bush flew from Washington to Fort Worth, where he attended a routine event at the Hotel Texas—a local landmark because President John F. Kennedy spent his final night there in 1963. Dad then drove to Carswell Air Force Base and boarded Air Force Two for a flight to Austin, where he had been invited to address a joint session of the state legislature.

Back in Washington, a deranged man named John Hinckley shot President Reagan as he was walking out the side door of the Washington Hilton. The shooting wounded Press Secretary James Brady, Secret Service agent Timothy McCarthy, and D.C. police officer Thomas Delahanty. The President was rushed to George

Washington University Hospital, where doctors discovered that he had suffered heavy internal bleeding because a bullet had lodged in his lung. They inserted a tube in his chest and wheeled him into the operating room to begin surgery. (From behind an oxygen mask, the President joked, "I hope you're all Republicans.")

Dad first heard about the shooting shortly after Air Force Two lifted off in Fort Worth. His lead Secret Service agent, Ed Pollard, initially informed him that the President had not been harmed. A few minutes later, the agent burst back into the cabin. The President **had** been shot. His condition was unknown, and Dad had to get back to Washington immediately. Around the same time, the secure phone on the plane rang. Secretary of State Alexander Haig was asking for the Vice President. Dad tried to talk to him, but all he could hear was static. The faulty communications added to the uncertainty about the President's condition. Twenty years later, on September 11, 2001, I would experience similar frustrations with the communications equipment on Air Force One.

Dad took a moment to process what he had learned. He jotted his reactions on one of the flight cards aboard Air Force Two. (The card is now an artifact at the George Bush Presidential Library at Texas A&M.) He thought first about the President as his friend—"decent, warm, kind," he wrote. Then he turned to his responsibilities. He scribbled a reminder to avoid panic. He wrote the word **uncertainty**, which he knew the country would be feeling. He knew how important it would be to project stability and help calm the nerves of the rattled nation.

When Air Force Two landed at Andrews Air Force Base, the Secret Service wanted Dad to take a helicopter directly to the South Lawn—where the President lands in Marine One. Dad refused. He did not want to send the signal that the President had lost command. He instructed the chopper to take him to the familiar landing zone at the Naval Observatory, and he took a car from there to the White House.

"Only the President lands on the South Lawn," he said.

By the time Dad arrived in the Situation Room, the President had come through the surgery and had a good prognosis for recovery. Dad went to the Press Briefing Room to make a concise, upbeat statement on the President's condition—a stark contrast to the haphazard briefings that senior officials had delivered earlier in the day. The next day, Dad visited the President in the hospital and presided over a Cabinet meeting. Journalists noted that Vice President Bush sat in his usual position, rather than in President Reagan's chair. I'm confident that my father never even considered taking the President's seat. He understood that his job was to support the President, not supplant him. Within two weeks, the President was back at the White House. Within a month, he was addressing a joint session of Congress.

Crisis has a way of revealing character. The President—and the country—had just seen that Vice President George Bush was a man they could trust.

AS THE PRESIDENT'S confidence in his VP grew, so did Dad's role in the administration. President Reagan asked him to spearhead a number of important policy initiatives. He headed up the administration's task force on federal deregulation. As a former businessman, he understood the burdens inflicted by red tape, and his group made recommendations to cut or revise hundreds of needless or wasteful regulations. Dad also led a task force aimed at reducing drug trafficking in South Florida, which was a major problem in the early 1980s. The administration pursued a strategy to interdict drug supplies coming from South America up the East Coast.

Another of Dad's responsibilities was representing the President and the country abroad. In all, he visited more than sixty countries in eight years. Those diplomatic missions came naturally given his experience in China and at the United Nations. He built trust with leaders in crucial parts of the world like the Middle East and Asia. He developed a good relationship with Prime Minister Margaret Thatcher of Great Britain. He traveled to Central America, where his presence helped demonstrate America's commitment to democratic governments facing threats from communism. He went to Africa to help oversee the delivery of food and medicine to drought victims and refugees. And he spent time behind the Iron Curtain in Europe, where he met with key figures like Lech Wałesa, the leader of the Solidarity movement in Poland.

One of his most difficult trips was to Lebanon in 1983. Dad flew to Beirut three days after Hezbollah terrorists bombed the U.S. Marine barracks and killed 241 Americans. He did his best to console the families who had lost loved ones in the attack. As a safety precaution against further attacks by Hezbollah or other terrorists, President Reagan decided to pull American troops out of Lebanon. Unfortunately, al Qaeda interpreted America's withdrawal as a sign of weakness. Osama bin Laden later cited the U.S. pullout from Lebanon as evidence that America was a "paper tiger" that "after a few blows ran in defeat."

Dad comforted Americans after tragedy several more times. In 1985, Hezbollah terrorists hijacked TWA Flight 847 en route from Athens to Rome. They diverted the plane to Lebanon, where they murdered an American Navy diver on board and held the other passengers— including several Americans—hostage. When the hostages were released, President Reagan dispatched Dad to meet them in Germany before they returned home. In 1986, after the space shuttle **Challenger** exploded, President Reagan sent Dad to Florida to console the family members of the astronauts on board. To this day, he stays in touch with June Scobee Rodgers, the widow of **Challenger** commander Dick Scobee. Dad's kindness, decency, and ability to connect with people made him an ideal choice.

In retrospect, Dad's most important trips as Vice President were the ones he took to the Soviet Union. In the span of three years, three Soviet leaders died: Leonid Brezhnev, Yuri Andropov, and Konstantin Chernenko. President Reagan asked Dad to attend each of their funerals, leading Jim Baker to describe Dad's vice presidential role as "You die, I fly."

The trips gave Dad insight into the Soviet system. He was impressed by the power on display at the funerals: the precise military marches, the casket drawn by a Soviet tank. To most of the world, the Soviet Union looked like an unstoppable empire. But underneath the facade of strength, Dad sensed that the foundation of the Soviet Union was crumbling. The aging and dying leaders symbolized the declining appeal of the communist system. As he told his congregation at St. Martin's Episcopal Church after his trip to Brezhnev's funeral in 1982, "Something was missing. There was no mention of God. There was no hope, no joy, no life ever after. . . . So discouraging in a sense, so hopeless, so lonely in a way."

My father's most significant trip to Moscow came for Chernenko's funeral in 1985. After the now-familiar solemn ceremony in Red Square, Dad met the new Soviet leader, Mikhail Gorbachev. It didn't take him long to recognize that Gorbachev was different. A generation younger than his predecessors, Gorbachev had a warm, charismatic personality and spoke without notes. Instead of repeating the usual platitudes, he seemed genuinely interested in improving his country's relationship with the United States.

George Bush has always been a good listener and a good reader of people. When he heard Gorbachev say that he wanted to "start anew," he believed that there was a real opportunity for U.S.–Soviet relations to enter a new phase. Dad reported back that he felt the President could forge a unique working relationship with Gorbachev. Reagan and Gorbachev met later that year at a summit in Geneva. The following year, they held a historic summit in Reykjavik, Iceland. Those meetings were the beginning of one of the most important diplomatic relationships of the twentieth century—one that both Ronald Reagan and Dad would nurture skillfully until the peaceful end of the Cold War.

MY FATHER ENJOYED his time as Vice President. Unlike some of his vice presidential predecessors, Dad never felt excluded or, as they say in Washington, out of the loop. Dad admired the difficult decisions that President Reagan made. Over time, Dad and President Reagan developed more than just a solid working relationship; they became good friends.

One reason that my father and President Reagan got along so well was that they shared a sense of humor. In a memo to the President recapping a trip to Finland, Dad described a visit to a Finnish sauna. "I felt a little self-conscious at first sitting around stark naked with four Finnish guys I'd never laid eyes on before," he wrote. "We all did the whole treatment including jumping in the ice cold ocean.

We saw less of each other after the jumping in that ice cold water." President Reagan loved to share stories and jokes in return. When Dad asked the President how his meeting had gone with Bishop Desmond Tutu, the President responded, "So-so."

When White House doctors diagnosed President Reagan with intestinal polyps in 1985, he checked into Bethesda Naval Hospital for surgery. Before he went under, he delegated presidential power to the Vice President, becoming the first President to invoke the Twenty-Fifth Amendment. (I later did the same thing when I had minor procedures during my presidency.) Dad served as Acting President for almost eight hours. He was in Maine at the time and deliberately kept a low profile. He did play a game of tennis. According to one of his friends with him that day, he stumbled while trying to run down a lob shot, hit his head on the tennis court, and briefly blacked out. Fortunately, he regained his faculties quickly, and nobody had to notify Tip O'Neill, the Speaker of the House and the next in the line of presidential succession.

After the President returned to the White House residence, Dad went to visit and wish him a speedy recovery. He found President Reagan lying on a couch in a red robe with a flower in his mouth, as if he had been prepared for a funeral. As Dad tried to process the scene, the President jumped up off the couch, and they both roared with laughter.

Mother enjoyed the vice presidential years too. She used her platform as Second Lady to promote important causes, especially literacy and volunteerism. Unfortunately, she did not have as close a relationship with Nancy Reagan as Dad did with the President. Mrs. Reagan was cordial, but she did not go out of her way to make Mother feel welcome. I was surprised when Mother told me shortly after Dad was elected President that in her eight years as the wife of the Vice President she had never toured the White House residence. When I became President, Laura and I made it a point to invite Dick Cheney, Lynne Cheney, and their family to the residence and to include them in White House events.

THROUGH ALL THE travel and politics of the vice presidential years, family remained central to my father's life. He visited Walker's Point for family gatherings every summer. He loved to entertain there. When the National Governors Association held its 1983 meeting in Portland, Maine, Dad invited all the Governors and their families to a clambake. For one night at least, there was no partisanship on display. The guests included members of both parties, including two Governors that George Bush would see a lot of in the future: Michael Dukakis and Bill Clinton.

As Bill Clinton tells the story, he and Hillary brought their three-year-old daughter, Chelsea, to the gathering. As they waited in the receiving line, they schooled her on how to greet the Vice President. When the big moment arrived, she blurted out, "Where's the bathroom?" To Governor Clinton's astonishment, the Vice President left the receiving line, walked Chelsea to the house, and introduced her to his mother, who showed her to the bathroom. The gesture of kindness made an impression for years to come.

Throughout his years as Vice President, Dad maintained a close bond with his mother. She visited Washington frequently, and even when she wasn't in town, she kept an eye on her son. After one of President Reagan's State of the Union addresses, she called to inform Dad that she had caught him looking down during the speech. "When the President is speaking, you should be listening," she admonished him. He protested that he had been reading a printed copy of the speech. She was not persuaded. He might have been Vice President of the United States, but he was still Dorothy Walker Bush's son.

No matter what was going on in the world, Dad was never too busy to talk on the phone or send a letter to check in with my siblings and me. In a typical note to us in 1983, he wrote, "I'm getting a little older. I'm not sure what the future holds. I don't worry about that. Win or lose, older or younger, we have our family."

Dad didn't just express his commitment to his family. He lived it. When my brother Marvin checked into the hospital suffering from a severe form of colitis, Dad visited every day. On the days when Marvin was in the most pain, my father rescheduled meetings and practically moved his office to the hospital so that he could sit at his son's bedside. Marvin lost forty-five pounds, and at one point his vital signs failed. I know my parents were thinking of Robin and praying that they would not lose another child.

Fortunately, Marvin rallied and regained his health. To help lift his spirits after a difficult surgery, Dad reached out to a friend in the front office of the New York Mets, Arthur Richman. Before long, ballplayers were calling Marvin to cheer him up. He made a full recovery and soon had a reason to celebrate when he and his wife, Margaret, adopted their first child, their daughter, Marshall, from the Gladney Home in Fort Worth, Texas. They later adopted a son, Walker, from the same wonderful place. Dad remained grateful to the Mets for their generosity—until they beat the Houston Astros in the 1986 National League Championship series. For his part, Marvin remembered how much it helped to have people call to cheer him up. When Speaker Tip O'Neill underwent surgery for a similar condition, Marvin called to lift his spirits. The Speaker later told my father, "Anybody who raised a person as fine as Marvin ought to be all right."

Marshall and Walker were not the only additions to the family during those years. My siblings and I produced eight grandchildren in eight years—including Laura's and my twin daughters, Barbara and Jenna, who entered the world on November 25, 1981. Dad summed up his feelings about family in a letter to Jeb and Colu after their third child, John Ellis Bush Jr., was born in 1983: "Last night's phone call brought us true happiness," he wrote. "Nothing else matters. The birth of JB Jr. put everything that is important into perspective."

Twenty-eight years later, in August 2011, Jeb Jr. and his wife, Sandra, were on the receiving end of another note from George Bush. In a sign of the times, it arrived not through the postal service but via e-mail. "I haven't seen you yet and I love you already," Dad wrote. "You are one very lucky little girl." The message was signed "Gampy" and addressed to his first great-grandchild, Georgia Helena Walker Bush.

LIKE MOST MODERN Vice Presidents, George Bush spent a good amount of time tending to the political grassroots. That came naturally to Dad given his love of people and his experience as a party Chairman. As the 1984 election approached, Dad traveled to all fifty states to tout the President's record and fire up campaign volunteers. He attended a steady stream of fundraisers and rubber-chicken dinners. I think his favorite event was an Old Timers baseball game at Mile High Stadium. He had been campaigning in Colorado and sent word that he'd like to drop by the game. The organizers of the exhibition game surprised him by inviting him to take the field at his old position: first base.

For a sixty-year-old politician, that was a risky proposition. The game offered plenty of potential for national embarrassment. But the former captain of the Yale baseball team still had a lot of young man in him. He put on the uniform of the Denver Bears, a team in the American Association league. When he came to bat against former Baltimore Orioles and Chicago Cubs pitcher Milt Pappas, a three-time All-Star who had pitched a no-hitter, he slapped a single into right field. It certainly didn't hurt that Milt had served up a fat fastball for the Vice President to hit. Pappas and Dad stayed in touch for years after the game.

Dad held his own in the field as well. Orlando Cepeda, a Hall of Fame slugger who played most of his years for the San Francisco Giants, hit a rocket down the first-base line. Dad made a slick play, stabbing the hot shot and tossing the ball to the pitcher to beat Cepeda to the bag. I still remember his look of joy as he jogged back to the dugout.

Dad's political travels intensified once the Democrats selected their presidential nominee for 1984: Walter Mondale, who had served as Vice President under Jimmy Carter. Mondale had won a tough primary over Senator Gary Hart of Colorado. Typical of the sound-bite era in American politics, the race was defined by a single phrase. In one of the Democratic debates, Mondale criticized Hart's lack of substance by demanding, "Where's the beef?" a line he borrowed from a commercial for Wendy's hamburgers. Like Ronald Reagan's devastating question at his 1980 debate with Jimmy Carter—"Are you better off than you were four years ago?"—Mondale's sound bite effectively encapsulated his criticism of Hart.

President Reagan held a comfortable lead in polls for most of the summer, but shortly before the Democratic convention, Mondale shook up the race by naming Congresswoman Geraldine

Ferraro as his running mate. The first woman ever to appear on a presidential ticket, Ferraro was a savvy politician and former prosecutor from Queens, New York. She had little experience on the national stage, but her selection generated excitement and big crowds across the country. Dad sent a letter to the Congresswoman the day of her nomination. "Dear Geraldine, It **is** a good job," he wrote. "Congratulations on your selection. Good luck—up to a point."

A month before the election, Dad had the unenviable task of debating Ferraro in what remains one of the most anticipated vice presidential debates in American history. His knowledge and experience dwarfed hers, but he was wary of appearing condescending. He knew the press was ready to pounce on him for even a hint of sexism. He prepared for the debate by sparring with Congresswoman Lynn Martin of Illinois (he was impressed enough that he later named her to his Cabinet). All things considered, the big night in Philadelphia went well for Dad. He treated his opponent respectfully, but he did not hesitate to point out their differences or call out her mistakes, such as when she mischaracterized the administration's position on the START treaty and missiles in Europe. Years later, when I debated Ann Richards in the race for Governor of Texas, I remembered Dad's example as a lesson in how to be firm without being insulting.

The biggest headline of the debate came the next morning. As Dad met with some lively longshoremen in New Jersey, a relieved and energized George Bush offered a review of his performance in language fit for the docks. "We tried to kick a little ass last night," he said. Unbeknownst to him, a TV microphone picked up their interaction. The press had a field day, blowing the comment out of proportion and accusing Dad of sexism. Fortunately, campaigns move fast, and for most voters the incident was quickly forgotten.

That incident was just one example of the tense relations between Dad and the media during the 1984 campaign. When I joined Dad for the final days of the campaign, I could tell that relations with the traveling press had grown hostile. They hammered Dad with repetitive questions about his position on abortion and his privileged upbringing. My impression was that many members of the press corps, particularly the women, were actively rooting for Geraldine Ferraro.

Mother was infuriated by the negative coverage, and eventually she snapped. After a reporter repeated the latest of many allegations that Dad was a rich elitist, she pointed out that Congresswoman Ferraro and her husband actually had a higher net worth.

"That four-million-dollar—I can't say it, but it rhymes with **rich**—could buy George Bush any day," she said. It was a classic Barbara Bush blurt, and she regretted it the moment it left her lips. Mother called and apologized to Geraldine Ferraro, who immediately forgave her. My siblings and I weren't quite so generous. We took great delight in calling Mother the "poet laureate" of the family.

Years later, Dad went on to develop a genuine friendship with Geraldine Ferraro. Near the end of her life, Dad sent an e-mail to her: "I often think of our strange but wonderful relationship," he wrote, "and I hope you know that I consider you a real friend. In fact, I hope it's okay if I say I love you."

In hindsight, the incidents with the press in

1984 were a good learning experience. A presidential campaign is grueling and stressful. Even the most seasoned campaigner can be tempted to vent frustrations, and you never know what a stray microphone might pick up. I was reminded of that reality in 2000, when an unexpectedly live microphone in Naperville, Illinois, captured me delivering an unflattering review of a **New York Times** reporter to Dick Cheney. The lesson was to stay disciplined, keep your composure, and stay on message. And if your wife happens to put her foot in her mouth, go three-quarters of the way to forgive her.

FOR ALL THE drama of the campaign, the election turned out to be one of the most lopsided in history. President Reagan won every state except Minnesota (plus the District of Columbia). Early in their second term, the President generously let Dad use Camp David for a weekend. He invited a group of his siblings and children to meet the campaign team that he had begun to assemble for the 1988 presidential race. One of the strategists that we met that day was Lee Atwater, a brilliant South Carolinian who had been one of President Reagan's key advisers. Jeb and I pressed Lee on whether he would be loyal to Dad first and foremost. As Jeb put it, "If someone throws a grenade at our dad, we expect you to jump on it." Lee assured us that he would be fully devoted to George Bush.

Then he laid out an interesting idea. "If you're so worried about my loyalty," he said, "why don't you come up to Washington to work on the campaign and keep an eye on me?"

THE ROAD TO THE WHITE HOUSE

WHEN LEE ATWATER SUGGESTED that I move to Washington to help in Dad's campaign, I was intrigued. The timing seemed right. I had just merged my oil business into a larger company. I was interested in exploring other opportunities. And there was no better cause: George Bush would make a great President.

I also knew that Dad would need all the help that he could get. My father and I both love history, and the history of Vice Presidents seeking the presidency did not provide much hope. Dad was up against the Van Buren factor: Not since Martin Van Buren defeated William Henry Harrison in 1836 had any Vice President been elected to follow the man who had selected him.

When I arrived at the campaign in the fall of 1986, Lee Atwater asked what title I wanted. I consulted with Dad, who told me that I didn't need a title. After all, I already had the title of son. His point was that proximity to power is power. He was right. Everyone involved in the campaign knew that I could talk to the candidate at any time, and that was more valuable than a title. Proximity to power was also a reason that Mother and Laura were so effective throughout our careers. Everyone knew that my father and I spoke frequently to them and trusted their judgment. So when Mother or Laura had a request or a piece of advice, our aides were usually wise enough to comply.

I had no specific portfolio at the campaign. My duties included raising money, delivering surrogate speeches, encouraging volunteers, dealing with reporters (occasionally), fielding suggestions and complaints, and discussing strategy with Dad's senior aides. I also took it upon myself to be a loyalty enforcer, ensuring that campaign staffers were there to serve George Bush and not their own interests. One memorable example involved Lee Atwater.

Early in the campaign, **Esquire** magazine ran a profile of Lee in which he conducted part of the interview while using the restroom. The theme was that Lee was the bad boy of Republican politics—that he was so important to George Bush that he could get away with anything. I was furious. I told Lee that his job was to make George Bush look good, not make himself look good.

"By the way, if you think I'm mad," I said, "you ought to hear what Mother says."

Lee immediately apologized to Mother and toned down his public behavior.

IN THE FALL of 1986, it seemed that being Ronald Reagan's Vice President would be a strong asset in the 1988 race. The President had been reelected in a nationwide landslide. But there's a reality about every two-term presidency: Toward its end, Americans grow weary of the President. (Tell me about it!) The first signs of President Reagan's slipping popularity came in the midterm elections of 1986. Republicans lost five seats in the House and eight in the Senate. For the first time in the Reagan presidency, Democrats had control of both houses of Congress.

In November 1986, several media outlets reported that the Reagan administration had secretly sold weapons to Iran in return for co-operation in releasing American hostages who had been captured by Hezbollah in Lebanon. Though the desire to free the hostages was understandable, the revelation was startling. The administration had previously professed that it would never pay ransom for hostages. Plus Congress had outlawed arms sales to state sponsors of terrorism, one of which was Iran.

As bad as the story looked, it soon got worse. In late November, Attorney General Ed Meese revealed that more than half of the money that the Iranians had paid for the weapons had been diverted to support the Contras, an anticommunist rebel movement in Nicaragua. That was a problem because two years earlier, President Reagan had signed a bill that prohibited government aid to the Contras.

The press, on high alert for a scandal similar to Watergate, demanded to know what the President knew and when he knew it. The administration initially denied that President Reagan had approved an arms-for-hostages deal but later backtracked and acknowledged that he had. The President insisted that he had not known that members of the National Security Council staff had diverted funds to the Contras. Ultimately, President Reagan accepted responsibility for the actions of his administration and appointed an independent counsel to bring charges against anyone who had broken the law. National Security Adviser John Poindexter and Lieutenant Colonel Oliver North were found guilty (their convictions were reversed on appeal).

The scandal, which became known as Iran-Contra, put Dad in a difficult position. While he was aware of the arms sales to Iran, he knew nothing about the diversion of funds to the Contras. Regardless, he knew the press and his political opponents would try hard to wrap him into the scandal. Although none of the commissions that studied the scandal concluded that he had done anything wrong, the specter of Iran-Contra haunted him. President Reagan's approval rating plummeted below 50 percent in the weeks following the revelations.

Even worse, a poll showed that 39 percent of voters favored a Democrat in 1988, while only 27 percent favored another Republican.

The big question facing George Bush was whether to distance himself from the President. Some advisers and friends told him it was his only hope to win the nomination. Reporters pressured him to explain where he disagreed with the President. George Will of the **Washington Post** mocked him as Reagan's "lapdog." Dad refused to take the bait. He was a loyal man in good times and bad. He understood the political risks, but he was not the kind of person to turn his back on his friend.

AS THE 1988 primaries approached, the campaign strategy began to take shape. Unlike Dad's 1980 campaign, which focused primarily on Iowa and New Hampshire, the campaign built a national infrastructure. The campaign paid particular attention to the seventeen states that scheduled their primaries for the same date in early March, Super Tuesday. Those primaries represented a firewall—if George Bush crashed and burned in the early states, victories on Super Tuesday would keep the damage from spreading.

While Dad's place as the front-runner had its advantages, it also created challenges. He spent all of 1987 with a target on his back, and the press and his political rivals in both parties let plenty of arrows fly. One of the most outrageous charges was that he had engaged in an extramarital affair. The whisper campaign started in June 1987. Tellingly, the gossip peddlers could not agree on who the "other woman" was. Around the same time, Senator Gary Hart withdrew from the Democratic presidential race amid allegations of adultery.

As I watched the Washington circus unfold, I grew incensed. The rumors were not only false; they were hurtful to Mother and Dad. Lee Atwater and I agreed that we should not let the gossip go unanswered. He set up an interview for me with a **Newsweek** reporter.

"The answer to the Big A question is N-O," I said.

When Mother heard about my interview, she was furious.

"How dare you disgrace your father by bringing this up?" she demanded.

Although Mother was the one who expressed her displeasure, I was certain that she was reflecting Dad's concern too. They feared that my denial would give credence to the gossip and spark a new round of coverage. My quip did make national news. Thankfully, the story died shortly thereafter.

In retrospect, I don't know whether my response helped. It's possible that the story was so ridiculous that it would have died on its own. Mother was correct that sometimes the best way to handle a false allegation is just to ignore it. That was generally my approach when people leveled false charges at me during my candidacies. But when the lie impugned the character of a man I loved and respected, I couldn't hold back.

It turns out I wasn't the only one in our family who felt that way. When I was running for reelection as President in 2004, my daughter Jenna wrote me a letter offering to work on my 2004 campaign. "I hate hearing lies about you. I hate when people criticize you. I hate that everybody can't see the person I love and respect, the person that I hope I someday will be like. . . . I may be a little rough around the edges, but with the proper training I could get people to see the Dad I love."

ON OCTOBER 12, 1987, Vice President George Bush formally entered the race for President. He made the announcement in Houston. He promised to continue the policies of the Reagan administration while injecting new ideas of his own. One of those ideas was a pledge that he would repeat often in the months ahead: "I am not going to raise your taxes—period." His campaign slogan highlighted his experience: "Ready on Day One to Be a Great President." Everything went well until the balloon drop. Some of the balloons had popped overnight, and as Dad put it, "for a frightening moment it looked like a condom drop—raw rubber appearing from the ceiling."

I attended the speech, but I was fuming. On my recommendation, members of our family and campaign aides had given interviews to **Newsweek** reporter Margaret Warner for a profile about Dad. I expected the story to be objective, so I was shocked to see the cover of the magazine scheduled to hit newsstands that

week: "George Bush: Fighting the 'Wimp Factor.'" The thrust of the story was that Dad
was not tough enough to be President. I was
amazed that anyone who knew his life story—
the Navy pilot who fought in World War II,
the Congressman who endured death threats
to vote for the open-housing bill—could even
suggest that he was a wimp. (Twenty-five years
later, **Newsweek** ran a cover story headlined
"Romney: The Wimp Factor." Apparently only
Republican candidates are wimps in their eyes.)

The wimp criticism caused great concern
among Dad's friends and supporters. Many of
them had advice for the candidate—and often
I was the recipient. I knew it was important not
to burden Dad with all the suggestions being
given to me. My role was to serve as a filter. At
first my filter was not very refined. I remember
telling Dad that one of his friends had called
with the suggestion "Just be yourself." He rolled
his eyes and said, "Who the hell else would I
be?" From that point on, I was more judicious.

Over the course of the 1988 campaign, I
came to understand that most politicians have
plenty of professionals giving them advice.
What they need from their friends and loved

Dad signed this photo of us on his boat *Fidelity* in the summer of 1991. "George—My idea of Heaven! Devotedly, Dad." Mine, too. *GBPLM/Carol Powers*

George – My idea of Heaven! Devotedly, Dad *summer of 91*

The storm that gave my parents' beloved home at Walker's Point "a historic pounding" late in 1991 was a harbinger of the tumultuous year ahead for George Bush. *GBPLM/David Valdez*

Amid his own disappointment after losing the re-election, Dad invited Dana Carvey, who impersonated him on *Saturday Night Live*, to the White House to cheer up the staff. *GBPLM/Susan Biddle*

When the President-elect and Mrs. Clinton arrived at the White House on Inauguration Day, Mother and Dad received them with genuine kindness and warmth. As he wrote in a letter that he left for Bill Clinton on the Oval Office desk, Dad was rooting hard for his successor.

GBPLM/Joyce Naltchayan

On the morning of my inauguration as Governor of Texas, Mother brought me an envelope from Dad with a handwritten card and his "most treasured possession," cuff links given to him by his parents.

David Woo/The Dallas Morning News

As I took the oath of office to become Governor of Texas,
Dad wiped away a tear. It struck me that our roles had been reversed:
After years of me supporting him in public office, he was supporting me.
Fort Worth Star-Telegram/*Rodger Mallison*

Over my eight years as President, I would have many memorable
meetings in the Oval Office. None compared to standing in that majestic
room with my father on my first day.
George W. Bush Presidential Library and Museum (GWBPLM)/Eric Draper

After delivering an emotional speech at the National Cathedral three days after 9/11, Dad reached over and gently squeezed my arm. His simple, loving gesture brought me comfort, encouragement, and strength.

GWBPLM/Eric Draper

41 and I didn't talk much business during my presidency. Dad knew I had plenty of advisers; he also understood the pressure of the job. He provided love and laughter to ease my stress. (Looking on is President John Quincy Adams, President John Adams's son.) *GWBPLM/Eric Draper*

I love this picture of Mother and Dad during Laura's speech at the 2004 Republican National Convention. When I was re-elected, Dad's wound from 1992 healed a little more. *GWBPLM/Paul Morse*

I asked former rivals George H.W. Bush and Bill Clinton to team up and raise funds for disaster relief several times during my presidency. The odd couple raised hundreds of millions of dollars and developed a remarkable friendship. *GWBPLM/Eric Draper*

Our family at Camp David on Christmas 2008. *GWBPLM/Eric Draper*

For one of my final Oval Office meetings, I welcomed the living former Presidents and the incoming President, Barack Obama. The President-elect was gracious and particularly deferential to Dad, whom he later honored with the Presidential Medal of Freedom. *GWBPLM/Joyce N. Boghosian*

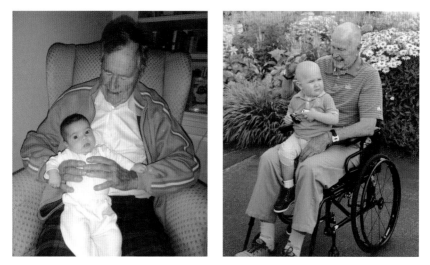

LEFT: George Herbert Walker Bush and his first great-granddaughter, Georgia Helena Walker Bush, in 2011. *Barbara Bush.* RIGHT: When Dad learned that one of his Secret Service agents had a two-year-old son with leukemia, my 89-year-old father shaved his head in solidarity with the boy.

Barbara Allison

At the dedication of the George W. Bush Presidential Center on the campus of SMU in Dallas. All my life, I've been laughing with George H.W. Bush.

George W. Bush Presidential Center/Eric Draper

Seventy years after his torpedo bomber was struck by anti-aircraft fire and Dad plummeted into the Pacific Ocean, he jumped out of a perfectly good helicopter on his ninetieth birthday. *CA Smith Photography*

ones is comfort and support. That is one reason why I was so grateful that my brother Marvin, my sister Doro, and their families lived nearby when I was President. They frequently came to the White House for family dinners, and Marv would drop by to watch sports or work out. They had no agenda. They just wanted to help me relax. I tried to provide that same kind of support for Dad.

IN THE WEEKS leading up to the Iowa caucus, CBS News ran a profile on each of the major candidates. There was some anxiety that Dan Rather would not cover the same topics that other candidates had discussed on CBS—their backgrounds, families, and experiences—but rather would exploit the opportunity to relitigate Iran-Contra. The campaign agreed to the interview, but it insisted that the interview be aired live, so that Rather's producers could not chop up Dad's quotes or take them out of context.

Shortly before the interview, Dad's top media adviser, the savvy Roger Ailes, heard rumblings from some of his friends in the TV world that

Rather was planning to focus exclusively on Iran-Contra. Sure enough, as Dad sat waiting to begin the interview, he watched as Rather played a six-minute video reviewing the allegations related to Iran-Contra. Rather's first question was why Dad continued to employ an adviser who had been involved in the scandal. Dad explained that the aide had been cleared of any wrongdoing. After several more questions on Iran-Contra, Dad told Rather that he found the topic of the discussion to be "a rehash" and a misrepresentation on the part of CBS.

The anchor pressed on with his cross-examination about Iran-Contra. Dad remained calm, but I knew he was seething. With time ticking down on the interview, Dad reminded the newsman that they had agreed to discuss other topics. When Rather followed up with yet another round of Iran-Contra questions, Dad delivered the knockout punch that he and Roger Ailes had planned.

"I don't think it's fair to judge my whole career by a rehash on Iran," he said. "How would you like it if I judged your career by those seven minutes when you walked off the set in New York?"

Rather seemed stunned by the question, which referred to his most embarrassing moment as a journalist: A few months earlier, he had gotten so angry that his broadcast was being delayed by a U.S. Open tennis match that he stormed off the set to complain to CBS executives. When coverage of the match ended sooner than expected, the anchor desk was empty, and viewers across the country were left with dead air.

Dad called me from backstage to ask how I thought the interview had gone. There was no sense of triumph or bravado in his voice. It was not in his character to humiliate someone, and I could tell he was anxious about his tough retort to Rather. I, on the other hand, was thrilled with his performance.

"You knocked it out of the park," I assured him.

Most viewers agreed. The phone lines at CBS lit up with callers objecting to Dan Rather's rudeness. The Bush campaign was flooded with calls congratulating Dad. One thing was for sure: There wasn't much talk about the wimp factor anymore.

For his part, Dan Rather's coverage of Dad's

presidency continued to be negative. When I took office, he seemed to extend the grudge to me. The low point came in 2004, when he aired allegations about my National Guard service that were based on forged documents. Once again, the public outcry was intense. This time, Dan Rather resigned from his job at CBS.

DAD'S INTERVIEW with Dan Rather brought a surge in support, but it wasn't enough to win the opening battle in the Republican primary season: the Iowa caucus. The favorite in Iowa was Senator Bob Dole of Kansas, Dad's old rival from the 1980 campaign who had since become the Majority Leader of the Senate. Dole exploited his home-field advantage in Iowa. His ads stressed his farm-state roots and assured Iowa voters that he was one of them. As expected, Dole won in Iowa, collecting 37 percent of the vote.

The shock was that George Bush finished third, behind the televangelist Pat Robertson. Robertson had no experience as an elected official and held some extreme policy positions. Yet he organized effectively in Iowa, and he correctly predicted that an "invisible army" of supporters would turn out to vote for him—25 percent of the Iowa caucusgoers, to be precise. In retrospect, the 1988 campaign provided the first glimpse of a bloc of voters whose top priority was values. Those voters later became an important part of the constituency that made me a two-term President.

Dad took 19 percent of the vote. The only major candidates who came in behind him were Jack Kemp, a dynamic Congressman from upstate New York who had first made his name as a quarterback with the Buffalo Bills, and Pete du Pont, a brainy former Congressman and former Governor of Delaware. Al Haig, the former Secretary of State and White House Chief of Staff, also picked up a few hundred votes.

Despite the defeat, Dad remained upbeat. On caucus night, he assured his supporters, "I wanted to do better, but I'm a fighter. I'm going to come back."

As the campaign shifted to New Hampshire, Dole had the momentum. The first polls after Iowa showed that he had narrowed Dad's lead in the Granite State. A few days later, Al Haig dropped out of the race and endorsed Dole.

Dole also picked up an endorsement from Don Rumsfeld, President Ford's former Chief of Staff and Secretary of Defense. Dad did not panic. As he knew better than most, Big Mo from Iowa did not always translate into success in New Hampshire.

As in his past campaigns, Dad resolved that no one would outwork him. The morning after his loss in Iowa, he showed up in New Hampshire before dawn to greet factory workers in Nashua. He embarked on an exhausting schedule of meet-and-greets organized by his effective New Hampshire campaign Chairman, Governor John Sununu. His approach reminded me of his early campaigns in Texas, where he worked hard to develop a personal connection with as many voters as he could.

Campaigning for President while serving as Vice President required a delicate balance. On one hand, traveling with the vice presidential entourage brought comfort and prestige. On the other hand, the trappings of the office could make him seem detached and aloof. Dad made it a point to combat that image. He shrunk the size of his entourage and held events at small local venues. He spent one morning at Dunkin'

Donuts, McDonald's, and a pancake house meeting with voters. (Fortunately, he also made time for jogging.) Dad drew on the network of friends and political allies that he had spent his whole career cultivating. He had been loyal to them, and now they returned the favor. One of the highlights of the campaign was a rally with Dad's friend and fishing buddy Ted Williams (to whom Dad later awarded the Presidential Medal of Freedom). In Red Sox Nation, it was hard to beat an endorsement from the Splendid Splinter.

IN A HEATED political race, the intensity of the campaign trail has a way of bringing out raw emotions. One of those emotions, it seemed to me, was Bob Dole's resentment of George Bush. Dole attacked Dad as an elitist with "rich and powerful parents" who had not "made a decision in seven years," while presenting himself as a self-made man who rose up from his hardscrabble roots in Russell, Kansas.

"Nobody ever handed me anything," Dole said.

I wondered whether their different experiences in World War II led Dole to harbor resentment toward Dad. Both had been wounded, but Dad had been able to return to his unit after being shot down, while Dole's serious injury left him confined to a hospital for the remainder of the war.

Dad hesitated to turn negative against Dole. Lee Atwater often called to express his frustration that he could not get Dad to sign off on any ads drawing a contrast with Dole. When Dad asked what I thought, I told him that I agreed with Lee. I thought it was important to put Dole on the defensive. Eventually Dad relented, and the campaign aired an ad portraying Dole as "Senator Straddle" for his shifting position on taxes. It was not a particularly harsh attack, but it succeeded in getting under Dole's skin and providing a clear contrast on an issue that mattered to New Hampshire primary voters.

As the primary approached, Dole looked bitter and irritable. He told a voter who disagreed with him, "Go back to your cave." On the night of the primary, Dad won with 38 percent of the vote. Dole finished second with 29 percent. In his victory speech, Dad compared himself to Mark Twain because reports of his death had been greatly exaggerated. When Tom Brokaw asked Dad if he had any message for his rival, he said, "Just wish him well and we'll meet him in the South."

When Brokaw asked Dole the same question, he snapped, "Yeah, stop lying about my record."

Eight days after the disaster in Iowa, the momentum had swung back to George Bush.

Fortunately, the bitterness of the 1988 primaries dissolved with time. Bob Dole and my father were both men of character, and they were able to set aside their differences and work together closely during Dad's presidency. The two old warriors grew not only to respect each other but to like each other. Shortly after Dad lost the presidential election in 1992, he attended a dinner hosted by Senate Republicans, where Minority Leader Dole gave him a warm and tearful embrace. "No President was more committed to getting the job done," Dole said. "Your place in history is secure. . . . George Bush helped change the world and that's very important to all of us." Bob Dole earned the Republican nomination for President in 1996, and Dad supported him strongly.

AFTER NEW HAMPSHIRE, the focus of the campaign shifted to South Carolina, the first primary below the Mason-Dixon Line and a bellwether for the delegate-rich South. As a native South Carolinian, Lee Atwater knew the political landscape and had assembled a powerful campaign apparatus. With its conservative electorate, South Carolina represented Pat Robertson's best chance to secure a major win. But he didn't have a strong organization, and Dad won handily with 49 percent of the vote.

Seventeen states held their primaries on Super Tuesday, March 8, 1988. The campaign's impressive fund-raising, organization, and strategy paid off with a sixteen-state sweep. For the first time in his political career, George Bush won a statewide race in Texas. By the time all the delegates were counted, George Bush was about two-thirds of the way to the nomination. Super Tuesday turned out to be not a firewall but the effective end of the campaign.

As the presumptive nominee, Dad worked hard to unify the party. He met with Members of Congress, whether they supported him or not. He called Governors across the country and invited them to Walker's Point. And in a gesture that was typical of George Bush, he and Mother hosted a dinner at the Naval Observatory for the candidates who had competed against him in the Republican primaries. Dad took the opportunity to mend any remaining wounds and enlist their support for November. He needed their help, because he was starting the general election in a deep hole.

If the presidential election had been held in the summer of 1988, Governor Michael Dukakis of Massachusetts would have won in a landslide. Dukakis had not started the Democratic primaries as a household name. He was the somewhat uncharismatic Governor of a midsized liberal state. But he ran a solid campaign and bested his rivals for the Democratic nomination—Tennessee Senator Al Gore Jr., Missouri Congressman Dick Gephardt, and civil rights leader Jesse Jackson—in a primary contest that featured repeated hammering of the Reagan-Bush administration.

In mid-July, Dukakis and the Democrats took the stage at their convention in Atlanta. Two of the featured speakers would return to play a key role in our lives. The first was Ann Richards, the feisty Texas state Treasurer and future Governor, who made headlines with her quip that Dad had been "born with a silver foot in his mouth." The other was Governor Bill Clinton of Arkansas, who gave such a long speech that his biggest applause line was "In conclusion. . . ."

One dramatic moment in the convention was the introduction of Dukakis's running mate, Senator Lloyd Bentsen of Texas. Bentsen was a respected legislator from an influential state with valuable Washington experience. And he had one other quality that Michael Dukakis was seeking: He knew how to beat George Bush. Bentsen had defeated Dad in the 1970 Senate race, and his selection by Dukakis the week before the convention was hailed as a political masterstroke. The "Boston to Austin" connection not only added a skillful campaigner to the ticket, it also echoed the JFK-LBJ presidential ticket that had delivered a victory for the Democrats over a sitting Vice President a generation earlier. The new running mates sprinted out of the convention with a big lead.

Dad spent the week of the Democratic convention on a fishing trip in the Wyoming wilderness with Jim Baker. After serving as Chief of Staff to President Reagan in the first term, Baker had become Secretary of the Treasury in the second term. He left his post, one of the most powerful in the Cabinet, to lead Dad's general election campaign.

As someone who saw the campaign up close, I can attest to the difference that Jim Baker made. Over a long presidential campaign, there is a tendency for lines of authority to blur and decision making to get sloppy. That did not happen under Jim Baker. He brought structure and clarity to the campaign. He listened carefully to advice, but there was no doubt that he was in command. He never allowed the aides on the plane to exercise outsized influence with the candidate or undermine the decisions that had been made at the headquarters (a common phenomenon on less disciplined campaigns). His closeness with Dad gave him credibility both inside and outside the organization, and it gave my father peace of mind to know that the campaign was in the hands of his trusted friend.

AFTER A GRUELING summer for George Bush, the political world descended on New Orleans for the Republican National Convention in mid-August. For over a year, Dad had walked a delicate line between his roles as Vice President and presidential candidate. He had resisted pressure to break with or criticize President Reagan—a strategy that took discipline and restraint, especially as he fell further behind in the polls. He acted out of loyalty. He was wise enough to know that weakening the President would hurt his chances in the general election. Finally, Dad had a great sense of timing. The big stage of the convention served as an opportunity to emerge from the shadow of the President and define his vision for the country.

The convention in New Orleans felt like a family reunion. We all wanted to pitch in. When Dad's name was formally placed into nomination, Jeb's wife, Columba, seconded it—first in Spanish, and then in English. George P. Bush,

Jeb and Columba's son, led the Pledge of Allegiance. My siblings and I each announced the support of the delegations from our home states: Neil from Colorado, Jeb from Florida, Marvin from Virginia, and Doro from Maine. It fell to me to announce Texas's support, which would officially put Dad over the top. I said that the Lone Star State proudly pledged its delegates "for a man we respect and a man we love . . . for her favorite son and the best father in America."

Dad opened his acceptance speech by explaining the new phase that had begun. "Many of you have asked, 'When will this campaign really begin?' I have come to this hall to tell you, and to tell America: Tonight is the night." He continued, "For seven and a half years I have helped a President conduct the most difficult job on earth. . . . But now you must see me for what I am: the Republican candidate for President of the United States."

The crowd roared, and Dad kept them cheering for the next hour. A few days earlier, Dad had asked me to read a draft of the speech. The strong argument and crisp writing impressed me, but nothing prepared me for the impact of his delivery in the Superdome that night.

"I am a man who sees life in terms of missions," he said, "missions defined and missions completed. When I was a torpedo bomber pilot they defined the mission for us. Before we took off we all understood that no matter what, you try to reach the target. There have been other missions for me—Congress, China, the CIA. But I am here tonight—and I am your candidate—because the most important work of my life is to complete the mission we started in 1980."

He delivered a forceful takedown of Dukakis's record, portraying him as a pessimist who saw America in a "long slow decline" and a "technocrat who makes sure the gears mesh but doesn't for a second understand the magic of the machine." He proceeded to lay out his vision for the country: A foreign policy based on the "knowledge that strength and clarity lead to peace," not the "weakness and ambivalence [that] lead to war." New support for charities and volunteers that would produce a "kinder, gentler nation" lit up by "a thousand points of light in a broad and peaceful sky." And an economic policy designed to create jobs without increasing taxes, culminating in his pledge "Read my lips: no new taxes."

Finally, he described his character. Dad had always been reticent to talk about himself, but in a short and self-deprecating passage, he struck just the right tone. "I may not be the most eloquent, but I learned early that eloquence won't draw oil from the ground. I may sometimes be a little awkward, but there's nothing self-conscious in my love of country. I am a quiet man—but I hear the quiet people others don't. The ones who raise the family, pay the taxes, meet the mortgage. I hear them and I am moved, and their concerns are mine."

He built to his conclusion: "I will keep America moving forward, always forward—for a better America, for an endless enduring dream and a thousand points of light. That is my mission. And I will complete it."

The crowd exploded. Laura, Barbara, Jenna, and I poured onto the stage with the rest of our family to join Mother and Dad for the balloon drop (no fear of a condom drop this time). George Bush was beaming. I can't remember another speech that so perfectly captured a moment. Dad had moved seamlessly from Ronald Reagan's Vice President to a candidate in his own right. Like many others who care deeply for George Bush, I was exuberant that night.

Years later, as I worked on my 2000 convention acceptance speech with my speechwriter Mike Gerson, I thought back to Dad's speech in 1988. One of the lessons was that a candidate must not only deliver memorable lines but also lay out a vision that the American people want to follow. That was what George Bush did in 1988. After that final night of the convention, I was convinced that many Americans could picture President George H.W. Bush.

DAD'S PERFORMANCE at the convention was flawless, with one exception: the announcement of his running mate.

Dad began the vice presidential search shortly after he secured the nomination. Unlike many presidential nominees, he was not looking for someone who could fill a hole in his résumé—the way that he had for Ronald Reagan eight years earlier and Dick Cheney, with his national security experience, did for me twelve years later. In addition to picking someone who was prepared to assume the presidency, Dad wanted to bridge a generational gap. Although he was an energetic sixty-four-year-old, he was also part of the World War II generation, which had held the presidency since John F. Kennedy's election almost three decades earlier. Dad sensed that the baby boom generation was ready for its turn on the national stage. He liked the idea of picking a running mate who could appeal to younger voters and help pave the way for a new generation of Republican leaders. There was a historical precedent that influenced Dad: In 1952, the sixty-one-year-old Dwight Eisenhower—a President whom Dad greatly admired—picked a thirty-nine-year-old Senator, Richard Nixon, to be his running mate.

Dad selected forty-one-year-old Senator Dan Quayle of Indiana to be his running mate. He had gotten to know Quayle during their years together in Washington, where Quayle had served since winning election to the House at age twenty-nine. Four years later, he had defeated three-term Democratic Senator Birch Bayh, and he had won reelection to a second

Senate term handily. He had impressed his colleagues enough to earn seats on the powerful Budget and Armed Services Committees, where he gained expertise in arms control and strongly opposed Democratic efforts to cut defense spending. Dad believed that his experience had prepared him to do the job. And he knew he would be an energetic campaigner for the ticket.

Dad kept his choice secret—from the press, from his aides, and even from Mother and me. The campaign's plan was to build drama and announce the vice presidential pick on Wednesday of convention week, the day before Dad's acceptance speech. By Tuesday morning, however, the speculation about the VP selection had reached a fever pitch. Stories about Dad's decision process overwhelmed all else at the convention. Reporters constantly hounded Bob Dole and Jack Kemp, two names on the so-called short list. Dad felt bad that he had put Dole and Kemp in an uncomfortable position. So he decided to change the plan and announce his choice of Quayle on Tuesday afternoon, a day ahead of schedule.

Dad asked me to be in the room with him

when he called Dan to make the offer. We were aboard the riverboat **Natchez,** which was about to ferry a large group of family, campaign aides, and supporters from Algiers Point across the Mississippi River to a dockside arrival rally in Spanish Plaza. Dad and Quayle spoke briefly, Quayle accepted the offer, and Dad handed the phone to Jim Baker. There was not much time for chitchat. Baker crisply told Quayle to get to the docks for the rally, where Dad would call him onto the stage for the announcement. The Senator would then get into a Secret Service limousine and be driven to meet his speech-writers, so that he could start work on an accep-tance speech that he would deliver to a national audience.

The riverboat crossed the Mississippi, and Dad was ready to make the announcement at the rally. There was one problem. Quayle was nowhere to be found. He and his wife, Mari-lyn, were still making their way to the docks. Eventually the Senator was spotted, and Dad shocked the crowd by introducing Quayle as his running mate. I thought about what must have been going through Dan Quayle's mind as he bounded up onto the platform. He was a

year younger than me, and just a few hours earlier he'd had no idea that he was about to step
onto the center of the national stage.

The spotlight quickly turned harsh. Reporters raised questions about Quayle's service in
the National Guard during Vietnam. The campaign had vetted the nominee and concluded
that there was no cause for concern. In retrospect, because Dad had kept the choice secret,
neither Quayle nor campaign staffers had time
to prepare for the barrage of detailed questions
being fired at them.

In the hothouse atmosphere of the convention, the press frenzy about Quayle's background escalated into a crisis. The coverage got
so rough that some supporters called for Dad
to dump Quayle and pick a new running mate.
George Bush didn't consider the idea. He knew
it would be a disaster to concede that his first
major decision as the party's nominee had been
a mistake. He was right. The crisis passed after
Dan Quayle's solid performance in his speech
and Dad's stellar acceptance speech on the final
night. The convention gave the Bush-Quayle
ticket one of the biggest bounces in American
political history. They came out with a small

lead. And I came away with a valuable insight. When I had to announce my own vice presidential selection, I did so in advance of the convention.

AT THE CONVENTION, George Bush had defined himself. Down the stretch, he defined Michael Dukakis. The Massachusetts Governor had left the door open by declaring in his convention speech, "This election isn't about ideology, it's about competence." It was laughable that Dukakis would claim to be more competent than George Bush, who had held more important government jobs than any presidential candidate in recent memory. On top of that, two decades in national politics had convinced Dad that voters base their decisions on values as much as any other factor. And he knew that the values of Michael Dukakis would not sit well with many Americans.

Throughout the fall, Dad labeled Dukakis a "Massachusetts liberal" and quoted his opponent's declaration that he was "a card-carrying member of the ACLU." He reminded the country that Dukakis had opposed prayer in public schools and vetoed a bill that would have required Massachusetts schools to begin each morning with the Pledge of Allegiance. "We are one nation under God," Dad would say in his stump speech, "and we ought not be inhibited from saying the Pledge of Allegiance in the schools." We knew the line of attack was working when Dukakis started saying the pledge at his campaign events.

The issue of crime produced another contrast. Governor Dukakis had supported gun control, a stance that concerned many Americans who believed that the Second Amendment protects an individual right to keep and bear arms for hunting, sports, and personal protection. He opposed the death penalty, a position that put him at odds with a majority of the population. And in the most notorious decision of his gubernatorial career, Dukakis had supported a program that granted weekend furloughs to Massachusetts prisoners, including violent offenders.

George Bush was not the first to criticize the furlough program. Senator Al Gore had attacked Dukakis on the issue during a Democratic primary debate. As Gore noted, eleven of the prisoners who had been furloughed had turned into fugitives, and two had committed murder while out on release.

One notorious Massachusetts prisoner was Willie Horton, who used his furlough to flee to Maryland and rape a woman. In late September, an independent organization called Americans for Bush highlighted the story in an ad that featured a photo of Horton. Critics charged that Dad was appealing to racist impulses, since Horton was African-American. Dad's campaign had nothing to do with that ad. As a matter of fact, it infuriated George Bush. He would never play the race card. He had run ads criticizing the furlough program, which was a legitimate policy issue, but he had never shown a photo of Horton or otherwise alluded to Horton's race. In retrospect, the Horton controversy was a harbinger of a new political phenomenon: independent groups trying to influence elections.

Dad's campaign on values—combined with his strong leadership experience and solid record—resonated with voters and helped him pull away from Dukakis. Michael Dukakis helped as well. He tried to defend his national security credentials by riding in an Army tank. His helmet was too big, and he looked more goofy than presidential.

As in most election years, the marquee events of the 1988 campaign were the presidential debates. The first debate was held in North Carolina in late September. For me, the most memorable moment happened during the preparation for the debate. Dad had invited Barbara and Jenna to spend the night at the Naval Observatory. At some point during the night, six-year-old Barbara discovered that she was missing her beloved stuffed dog, Spikey. She informed her grandfather that she could not sleep without Spikey. An intensive search of the house and yard ensued, led by Gampy himself. I don't know what Michael Dukakis was doing before the debate, but I doubt he was looking for a stuffed animal with a flashlight. Fortunately, Spikey was recovered unharmed, and most observers scored the debate as a draw.

The anticipation was great for the second and final presidential debate, which was held in Los Angeles. With just a few weeks before the election, the debate marked the last opportunity for either candidate to score points in front

of a national audience. I did not attend that debate—or any of Dad's debates. I was too nervous. To calm our nerves, my brother Marvin
and I decided to go to a Woody Allen movie. I
can't remember the name of it, but I do remember Marvin using the pay phone in the lobby to
check in with his good friend, known as PQ, to
see how the debate was going. Marvin returned
with the news that Dad was off to a good start.
Another twenty minutes passed, and Marvin
headed back to the lobby for another update.
Once again the news was positive. After a third
reassuring report from PQ, we left the theater
and made it home right after the debate ended.
A few minutes later, the phone rang.

"How'd I do, son?" Dad asked.

Without a moment of hesitation, I said,
"Dad, you hit a home run."

I was more right than I realized. Like most
debates, this one would be remembered for a
single moment. It came on the first question
of the night. The moderator, Bernard Shaw of
CNN, opened by asking Dukakis: "Governor,
if Kitty Dukakis were raped and murdered,
would you favor an irrevocable death penalty
for the killer?"

The horrifying image must have shocked most viewers, but the Governor responded as if he'd just been asked a question about the weather. "No, I don't, Bernard. And I think you know that I've opposed the death penalty during all of my life," he said. He went on to explain his policy rationale without once mentioning the prospect of his wife's rape and murder.

Dukakis's answer hurt him because it reinforced a perception among the electorate that the Governor was a cold technocrat. Dad's response was visceral. He said that he supported the death penalty for crimes that are "so heinous, so brutal, so outrageous."

Bernie Shaw did not let Dad off the hook easily. In his first question to Dad, he asked for his reaction to the possibility that he would get elected and die before the inauguration, leaving Dan Quayle to take office. The question was prompted by the most memorable line in the vice presidential debate a week earlier. When Quayle noted that he had spent as many years in Congress as John F. Kennedy had, Lloyd Bentsen snapped, "Senator, I served with Jack Kennedy. I knew Jack Kennedy. Jack Kennedy was a friend of mine. Senator, you're no Jack Kennedy." Bentsen's retort crystallized the view of some critics that Quayle was unprepared to serve as President.

Dad responded that he had confidence in his running mate's experience and ability. He also said that he had "never seen a presidential campaign where the presidential nominee runs against [the] vice presidential nominee." Dad understood a truism in American politics: People vote for President, not Vice President. Just as George Bush did not win any elections for Ronald Reagan and Geraldine Ferraro could not win an election for Walter Mondale, Lloyd Bentsen would not win the election for Michael Dukakis. When the new polls came out a few days after the final presidential debate, the Bush-Quayle ticket had a seventeen-point advantage.

ALTHOUGH HE held a solid lead, Dad refused to take anything for granted. After all, only two months earlier he had been trailing by double digits. He barnstormed across the country in the final weeks. I traveled with him on some of those trips, which brought back memories of our bus rides across Texas in 1964, when he was a first-time candidate and I was an eighteen-year-old kid. A lot had changed in the twenty-four years since then, but one thing remained the same: Dad loved spending time with his family.

One of my favorite memories of the 1988 campaign came when Dad invited Barbara, Jenna, and Laura to join him for a train trip through the Midwest around Halloween. The gesture was thoughtful; he knew they would have fun, and he enjoyed having his grandchildren around. On the flight back to Washington, Barbara and Jenna donned their Halloween costumes. I still smile at the images of our daughters, dressed as a vampire and a Juicy Fruit gum pack, walking down the aisles of Air Force Two trick-or-treating the national press corps.

Dad's 1988 campaign was the first one in which I had been involved from beginning to end. I had learned a lot along the way—about the political process, and about my father's character. Amid all the second-guessing that naturally takes place when a candidate's campaign is in peril, George Bush had remained calm and steady. He stayed focused on his long-term strategy, not the daily tracking polls. Although plenty of people doubted his chances, he remained upbeat and never wavered in his belief that he would win. Even today, I still look back with admiration at the energy, discipline, and sense of timing that he showed throughout the 1988 campaign.

ELECTION DAY finally arrived on November 8, 1988. Dad was exhausted but optimistic. Our extended family gathered to watch the returns at the Houstonian Hotel. When New Jersey and Ohio came out in Dad's column, we knew the race was over. He went on to carry forty of the fifty states, including some that no Republican has won since: California, Connecticut, New Jersey, Maryland, Michigan, and Pennsylvania. Michael Dukakis waited for the polls to close on the West Coast and then called to graciously concede.

After a brief celebration with family and campaign aides, Dad went to deliver his victory speech. Mother was at his side, and our whole family stood behind them. Forty years earlier, he, Mother, and I had moved out to a little house in West Texas, having no idea what the future would hold. The path from that day had not been easy for George Bush. He had chosen a career in politics as a Republican in a Democratic state. He had lost as many elections as he had won. He had lived under the shadows of the Van Buren factor and Iran-Contra. Through it all, he refused to give up. He kept working, kept running, kept striving to do his best. And now, after one of the great public service careers of the twentieth century, he had the job he wanted more than any other. George Herbert Walker Bush was going to be the forty-first President of the United States.

NUMBER 41

AFTER SPENDING TWO DECADES in senior government posts and watching President Reagan in the White House for eight years, George Bush understood the job of the President. And he didn't waste time getting started. The day after the election, he announced his nomination of James A. Baker to be Secretary of State. Soon after, he named John Sununu to be White House Chief of Staff. He followed up by naming his National Security Adviser: Brent Scowcroft, a savvy former Air Force general who had also served as National Security Adviser to President Ford. (Scowcroft remains the only person to hold that critical job for more than one President.)

Dad used his transition as an opportunity to continue outlining his vision for the country.

He addressed issues ranging from the economy to the Cold War with substance and command. His performance impressed journalists who had underestimated him during the vice presidency. As one TV anchor put it, it was "as if Clark Kent became Superman."

The day after the election, Mother and Dad invited our family to a church service at St. Martin's Episcopal in Houston. They asked me to lead the congregation in prayer. "Please guide us and guard us on our journeys—particularly watch over Dad and Mother," I said. "We pray that our lives be beacons to you by remembering the words of David: 'May that which I speak and that which I have in my heart be acceptable to thee, oh Lord.'" As I walked back to the pew, the exhausted and humble President-elect continued to pray.

That moment reflected my father's quiet faith. He was a religious man, but he was not comfortable espousing his faith in the public square. I was less restrained. At a Republican presidential debate in late 1999, the moderator asked the candidates which philosopher we most identified with. I said, "Christ, because he changed my heart." It was not a scripted answer; I just blurted out the truth. Dad called shortly after the debate, as he often did. "Good job, son," he said. We discussed some of the key moments. Then he said, "I don't think that answer on Jesus will hurt you too much." It was telling that his first instinct was to think that the comment would hurt me. The reaction reflected his reluctance to do anything that might be seen as imposing religion on others. In hindsight, the moment might have been Dad's way of reminding me of one of my favorite Bible verses for politicians (from the Book of Matthew): "Why do you look at the speck that is in your brother's eye, but do not notice the log that is in your own eye?"

Mother and Dad generously invited Laura, our girls, and me to fly to Washington with them later that day. To my horror, I learned that Barbara and Jenna had stopped up the toilets on Air Force Two by stuffing them full of toilet paper. To this day, Mother needles the girls about whether they did it on purpose. Fortunately, no one seemed to mind. Everyone was still riding high on Dad's victory.

Our family celebrated Christmas that year at the Vice President's residence, the last one that we spent at that wonderful house on the grounds of the Naval Observatory. Dad was just weeks away from becoming President, yet he showed no signs of stress. The only drama that I remember surrounded a horseshoe match pitting Dad and me against a Naval aide and the **Sports Illustrated** writer George Plimpton. Plimpton jumped out to an early lead, but Dad threw a ringer to complete a comeback win. "Nerts!" Plimpton exclaimed. He went on to write a fine article about the experience that captured Dad's energy, humor, and enthusiasm for life. It is one of my favorite profiles of George Bush.

ON THE SUNNY morning of January 20, 1989, our family took our places on the inaugural platform. Billy Graham delivered the invocation, and Alvy Powell of the U.S. Army Chorus sang "The Star-Spangled Banner." A few minutes after noon, Dad walked to the podium for the swearing-in. Mother held the Bible that George Washington had used to take the oath of office two hundred years earlier in 1789. Chief Justice William Rehnquist asked

Dad to raise his right hand and repeat the oath. As I watched my father, I felt a wave of immeasurable pride, along with a touch of apprehension about what might lie ahead.

Perhaps the most excited relative on the platform that day was eighty-seven-year-old Dorothy Walker Bush. My grandmother's health was so fragile that she had to fly to Washington on a plane staffed by health professionals. Nothing would stop her from witnessing this moment. Her only regret was that my grandfather, who would have been so proud of his son, could not be there to share in the joy. Dad asked her about the many inaugurations she had attended over the past fifty years. "Of course this is the best," she said, "because I'm sitting here holding the hand of my son, the President of the United States." That was about as close to bragging as Dorothy Walker Bush ever got.

The country had come a long way since Ronald Reagan stood at the inaugural platform eight years earlier. In 1981, President Reagan had begun his address by describing the "longest and one of the worst sustained inflations in our national history." Thanks in large part to the Reagan administration's policies,

Dad took office with the economy growing at 3.8 percent and unemployment at 5.3 percent. Nevertheless, the stock market had crashed in October 1987, and some industries were struggling. On the world stage, President Reagan and Gorbachev had taken steps to ease the tension of the Cold War. They had signed the INF Treaty, and the Soviet Union was withdrawing from Afghanistan. Yet the Soviets still dominated Eastern Europe, still meddled in Latin America, and still posed an existential threat because of their nuclear arsenal. And other international problems loomed, from the terrorists who had bombed Pan Am Flight 103 over Lockerbie, Scotland, a month earlier to instability in the Middle East.

As he began the biggest challenge of his career, George Bush's first action was to express gratitude. He thanked President Reagan for his service to the country. Then he led the nation in prayer: "Heavenly Father, we bow our heads and thank You for Your love." He concluded, "There is but one just use of power, and it is to serve people. Help us remember, Lord. Amen."

"I come before you and assume the Presidency at a moment rich with promise," he continued.

"We live in a peaceful, prosperous time, but we can make it better." He expressed his optimism about the future: "For a new breeze is blowing, and a world refreshed by freedom seems reborn. For in man's heart, if not in fact, the day of the dictator is over. The totalitarian era is passing, its old ideas blown away like leaves from an ancient, lifeless tree."

Then he turned to his goals at home. "My friends," he said, "we are not the sum of our possessions. They are not the measure of our lives. In our hearts we know what matters. We cannot hope only to leave our children a bigger car, a bigger bank account. We must hope to give them a sense of what it means to be a loyal friend, a loving parent, a citizen who leaves his home, his neighborhood and town better than he found it." He continued, uniting his foreign and domestic goals, "America is never wholly herself unless she is engaged in high moral principle," he said. "We as a people have such a purpose today. It is to make kinder the face of the nation and gentler the face of the world."

After the speech, Mother and Dad escorted the Reagans to their final departure aboard the presidential helicopter. Then they attended a luncheon on Capitol Hill and made their way down the parade route on Pennsylvania Avenue. That night they attended twelve inaugural balls before returning, dead tired, to the White House. Fortunately, the residence is spacious enough that they did not hear the joyous shrieks of their ten grandchildren, all of whom they had invited to spend the night. The next morning, Dad was up early, ready to get to work as the forty-first President of the United States.

GEORGE BUSH took naturally to the presidency, especially the foreign policy aspects of the job. His first major diplomatic decision was to attend the funeral of Japanese Emperor Hirohito. His choice drew fire from some of his fellow World War II veterans, who remembered the atrocities committed under Hirohito. My father understood their reaction; after all, he had fought the same enemy. But Dad believed that a nation, like a person, can change. And Japan had changed in a fundamental way. After the war, Hirohito had helped oversee Japan's transition to democracy. By 1989, Japan was one of America's closest allies, and Dad wanted to honor the relationship between the two democracies. Japan's leaders were grateful for his gesture of respect. And during my presidency a dozen years later, one of my closest friends on the world stage was Japanese Prime Minister Junichiro Koizumi.

Unfortunately for Dad, most of the media attention during his Japan trip had little to do with foreign policy. Reporters had their eyes on the United States Senate, where John Tower, the nominee for Defense Secretary, was locked in a tough confirmation battle. Tower had made some enemies on the other side of the aisle, and they came out during the hearings. The raucous debates were full of innuendo about Tower's personal life. George Bush was rightly upset that his friend was being treated so unfairly, and he tried to stand up for his nominee. In spite of Dad's strong defense of Tower, however, the Senate voted down a Cabinet nomination for the first time in thirty years. In a decision that would affect us both for years to come, the House Minority Whip, a Congressman from Wyoming, was nominated to take Tower's place. The Senate promptly confirmed Secretary of Defense Dick Cheney.

The next stop on Dad's Asia trip was China. As one of the nation's most experienced and knowledgeable China experts, he knew all the relevant players in Beijing. My parents received a warm welcome from Chairman Deng Xiaoping and Premier Li Peng, who gave them a set of bicycles—a reminder of their favorite activity during their time in the Liaison Office fifteen years earlier. On a Sunday morning, my parents attended services at the church where they used to worship and where my sister Doro had been baptized in 1975. As Dad later reflected, the church service reminded them of how much they had enjoyed their time in China—or as he called it, their "home away from home."

Not all aspects of the China visit went so smoothly. A barbecue that my parents hosted for Chinese officials produced an unexpected crisis. Ambassador Winston Lord invited a long list of guests from Chinese society, including the human rights activist Fang Lizhi. Dad later learned that Chinese security had prevented Fang from attending the event. The next day, the incident dominated the headlines. As with the Tower nomination, the news of the day overpowered the intended message of the visits.

The Fang Lizhi episode was a preview of troubles to come in China. A few months later, Chinese democratic activists decided to demonstrate for their freedom in Tiananmen Square. The protests drew worldwide attention in part because they coincided with Mikhail Gorbachev's visit to China. The Chinese government declared martial law and deployed tanks to crush the demonstrations. The world watched the drama unfold in real time. A photo of a young Chinese man standing alone in front of four oncoming tanks became the iconic image of the impending loss of innocent life.

The Tiananmen incident put the President in a delicate position. On one hand, he supported democratic reform in China. On the other hand, he saw the strategic importance of maintaining a close diplomatic and economic relationship with an emerging power. He believed, as I do, that economic progress in China will lead to political progress. And he knew from his tenure in Beijing that the Chinese government would be highly sensitive to any American action that it considered meddling in its internal affairs.

Dad struck a careful balance in response to Tiananmen. He denounced the Chinese government's use of force and imposed limited economic sanctions. At the same time, he rejected congressional calls to revoke the trade preferences that had opened up new flows of commerce and capital. The Chinese refused to respond to official diplomatic overtures. So Dad drew on his personal connections and wrote a private letter to Deng Xiaoping. "I write in a spirit of genuine friendship," he began, "this letter coming as I'm sure you know from one who believes with a passion that good relations between the United States and China are in the fundamental interests of both countries." He went on to propose sending a personal emissary to Beijing to discuss ways to lower tensions.

Within twenty-four hours, Deng had accepted Dad's offer to send an emissary. National Security Adviser Brent Scowcroft and Deputy Secretary of State Lawrence Eagleburger were dispatched to Beijing, where they met with senior Chinese officials. Dad followed up with another letter to Deng, whom he addressed as his "dear friend." He wrote, "We can both do more for world peace and for the welfare of our own people if we can get our relationship back on track. . . . If there is to be a period of darkness, so be it; but let us try to light some candles."

No one knew about Scowcroft and Eagleburger's trip until they returned to China several months later and were filmed clinking glasses with Chinese leaders. The image hurt Dad in some circles, and Bill Clinton criticized him for being soft on China during the 1992 campaign. In the long run, however, George Bush's handling of the crisis proved deft. By guiding America's relationship with China through a very challenging period, he helped pave the way for two decades of economic growth that has benefited both our nations. China's growth has lifted hundreds of millions of people out of poverty in China and created an enormous new market for American goods and services, while also increasing the prospect of political reform in China. At the 2008 Beijing Olympics, President Hu Jintao hosted a lunch in honor of a man who had been highly respected in China for more than thirty years, George H.W. Bush.

*   *   *

RELATIONS WITH CHINA posed one test during the first year of Dad's presidency. The Soviet Union posed another. From the beginning, Dad was hopeful about his counterpart in Moscow, Mikhail Gorbachev. As Vice President in 1985, Dad had been the first senior American official to meet the new Soviet leader. Dad admired Gorbachev's fresh approach, openness to the West, and commitment to reform the Soviet system—what Gorbachev called **perestroika**. When he took office, Dad had his national security team conduct a thorough review of American policy toward the Soviet Union. In a speech outlining his strategy in May 1989, he announced that the United States would move beyond "containment"—beyond the negative implications of mutually assured destruction—and toward a more cooperative relationship with a changing Soviet Union.

Gorbachev's commitment to change was tested by dramatic events in Eastern Europe. In Poland, the Solidarity movement, led by Lech Wałesa—and inspired by Pope John Paul II, the first-ever Polish pope—organized strikes in the shipyards of Gdansk. In Hungary, large protests honored a democratic leader, Imre Nagy, who had been martyred after Hungary's brief revolution in 1956. In Czechoslovakia, playwright Václav Havel organized artists and other citizens to reject communism in what would later be called the Velvet Revolution. And in East Germany, anticommunist groups held weekly prayer sessions in big-city cathedrals.

As the remarkable events of 1989 unfolded, the question was whether Gorbachev would violently suppress the freedom movements, as the Soviet Union had done in Hungary in 1956 and Prague in 1968—and as China had just done in Tiananmen Square. Dad recognized that his response to the revolutions could affect the Soviet reaction. In July 1989, he traveled to Hungary and Poland, where he spoke to massive crowds. He avoided any statements that might provoke the hard-liners in those countries or in the Soviet Union. And he immediately reached out to Gorbachev to reinforce his desire for a close relationship. "Dear Mr. Chairman," he scribbled aboard Air Force One, "I am writing this letter to you on my way back from Europe to the United States. Let me get quickly to the point of this letter," he continued. "I would like very much to sit down soon and talk to you."

Gorbachev accepted Dad's offer, and they scheduled a summit meeting in Malta for December 1989. In the meantime, the revolutions raced ahead. In November 1989, East Germany announced that it would open its border crossings to the West. Within hours, tens of thousands flocked to the Berlin Wall and began hammering it down. Dad faced enormous pressure to celebrate. Democrats in Congress urged him to go to Berlin. Journalists, eager for a dramatic story, demanded to know why he wasn't showing more emotion. "Bushism is Reaganism minus the passion for freedom," one writer complained. Dad refused to give in to the pressure. All his life, George Bush had been a humble man. He wasn't trying to score points for himself; he only cared about the results. And he knew the best way to achieve results was to think about the situation from the other person's perspective: Freedom had a better chance to succeed in Central and Eastern Europe if he did not provoke the Soviets to intervene in the budding revolutions.

"I'm not going to go dance on the wall," he said.

He pressed ahead with his outreach to Gorbachev. In December 1989, the two leaders met for a historic summit in Malta. Dad spent the night before aboard the USS **Belknap** in the Mediterranean Sea. As he prepared for the biggest meeting of his presidency, Dad thought back to his days aboard the USS **San Jacinto** in World War II. "I love the Navy," he wrote in his diary, "and I felt 31 years old walking around the decks." He even went fishing off the fantail of the ship. (Alas, all he got was a nibble.)

The next day, Dad and Gorbachev met for four hours aboard a cruise ship, the **Maxim Gorky**. They covered a wide range of subjects and agreed to continue their efforts to improve relations. The United States offered an economic aid package to help Gorbachev with his crumbling economy. At the same time, Dad made clear that he hoped the Soviets would maintain their peaceful approach to the upheaval in Central and Eastern Europe.

The strategy was controversial. Critics said he was not being tough enough. In the end, however, his approach proved to be a historic success. Unlike his predecessors in the Kremlin a generation earlier, Mikhail Gorbachev allowed the reform movements in Central and Eastern

Europe to proceed peacefully. For the first time in decades, the Berlin Wall no longer divided the East and the West. And for the first time in history, the continent came close to the vision that George Bush had defined and that would guide American policy for years to come: a Europe whole, free, and at peace.

SHORTLY AFTER the fall of the Berlin Wall, another crisis erupted. This one happened closer to home. The nation of Panama was an American ally and a country of strategic importance because of the Panama Canal. Panama's dictator, Manuel Noriega, had once cooperated with the United States to fight the spread of communism. Over time, as Noriega grew increasingly involved in the drug trade, his newfound power and wealth turned him against the United States. The Reagan administration obtained an indictment against him for drug trafficking.

Noriega's belligerence grew after Dad took office. In May 1989, he nullified the results of a democratic election. When a subsequent coup attempt failed, he executed the leaders of the uprising. A few months later, Noriega declared "a state of war" with the United States. Panamanian military forces harassed American troops stationed in the country. One Marine was shot and killed at a roadblock. Panamanian forces then assaulted another Marine and humiliated his wife.

That was the last straw. Diplomatic efforts to change Noriega's behavior were not working. Dad approved a highly classified invasion plan designed to overthrow Noriega. Operation Just Cause was set to launch early in the morning on December 20, 1989. Some twenty thousand American troops—the largest deployment since the Vietnam War—would storm the island, remove Noriega, and clear the way for the elected government to take power.

Dad slept fitfully the night before the secret mission was scheduled to launch. "I'm thinking about the kids," he wrote, "those young 19 year olds who will be dropped in tonight." He knew that some of them would not come home alive. Giving that order was the toughest decision of his young presidency.

Our family was at Camp David a few days later to celebrate Christmas. Dad was unusually reserved and somewhat grim. The pressure of his decision was weighing on him. He spent a lot of time in his small, wood-paneled office monitoring the progress of the operation. The initial reports were positive. The strike had removed the regime, and the new government had been sworn in. Yet Noriega was still at large.

On Christmas Eve, my brothers and I were playing wallyball (volleyball on a racquetball court) against several Marines stationed at Camp David. Suddenly Dad appeared on the balcony of the court with Joint Chiefs of Staff Chairman Colin Powell.

"We got him!" Dad exclaimed.

We knew exactly who he meant. The room broke out into cheers. A sweaty sergeant hugged me. Dad reported that Noriega was seeking asylum from the papal nuncio in Panama City. A few days later, he was turned over to the United States and flown to Miami, where he was eventually tried, convicted, and sent to prison.

The mission was a resounding success. Noriega was gone, and Panamanian democracy had been restored. Yet the victory came at a cost. Twenty-three Americans gave their lives, and more than three hundred were wounded.

As a combat veteran, Dad felt a special connection to the troops. He understood the agony of
war firsthand. And he believed that his job as
Commander-in-Chief was to show his personal
commitment to those who carried out his or-
ders. On New Year's Eve, Mother and Dad visited a military hospital in San Antonio, where
some of the wounded from Panama had been
sent for treatment. One Marine gave Dad a
small American flag, which he kept on his desk
in the Oval Office for the rest of his presidency.

Shortly after his visit, Dad told me about a
Navy SEAL he had visited in the hospital. It
turned out that he was a Texas Rangers fan. I
had just bought a minority stake in the Rangers and was serving as comanaging general
partner. We contacted the wounded SEAL and
told him that the Rangers would be proud to
have him throw out the first pitch on Opening Day of the 1990 season. He agreed, and
the crowd gave him a huge ovation. It was a
small gesture, but I was glad to play a part in
honoring our military. One of the lessons that
I learned was that the military must know that
their President supports them. I would not
fully understand the special relationship that a

Commander-in-Chief has with his troops for another dozen years, when I was the one who had to give the order to send our military into harm's way.

NOTHING PUT George Bush in a better mood than visiting Walker's Point. And in the summer of 1990, his spirits needed a lift. After the triumph in Panama, he had endured six months of bad news. The economy was slowing down. He was locked in a budget battle with the Democratic Congress. And my brother Neil was under investigation for his role in a failed savings and loan. In late July, Laura, Barbara, Jenna, and I visited Maine—a welcome break from the Texas heat. As usual, George Bush was nonstop activity. His idea of relaxation was playing golf or tennis in the morning, then fishing in the afternoon. A few days into our trip, Dad announced that he had to get back to Washington. On August 2, 1990, the news broke that Iraq had invaded Kuwait.

The man behind the invasion was Saddam Hussein, an oppressive and ruthless dictator who had devastated Iraq since 1979. In addition to repressing all dissent, Saddam had used chemical weapons against his own people and started a senseless war with Iran that killed hundreds of thousands of people on both sides. Then, without provocation, he had invaded the small, oil-rich nation of Kuwait—a key American ally with valuable ports on the Persian Gulf. As the Kuwaiti royal family fled, invading Iraqi troops brutalized Kuwaiti citizens and looted the country. There was talk that Saudi Arabia, another close ally of the United States, could be Saddam's next target. That would put Saddam in charge of a major share of the world's oil supply. America's vital diplomatic and economic interests in the Middle East were at stake.

Dad convened his National Security Advisers at Camp David. The usual team was joined by a new member, General Norman Schwarzkopf—the gruff, confident commander of U.S. Central Command. Dad asked for options. Some members of the team believed that tough economic sanctions could persuade Saddam to withdraw from Kuwait. Others thought an aerial bombardment would work. All agreed that a ground invasion could eventually be required. The National Security Council also discussed how to protect Saudi Arabia. Dad had spoken to King Fahd about the possibility of deploying U.S. troops to his kingdom to deter an Iraqi invasion and provide a base for the liberation of Kuwait. As the keeper of the two holiest Islamic sites, Mecca and Medina, Saudi Arabia had a zealous aversion to allowing foreign troops on its soil. The King agreed to consider the matter, and Secretary of Defense Dick Cheney was dispatched to make the case.

As Dad returned to the White House from Camp David, a huge gathering of reporters had assembled on the South Lawn. Dad told them that he was keeping his options open. Then he added, "This will not stand, this aggression against Kuwait." Those were not hollow words. George Bush understood that the President must mean what he says. Colin Powell later said that Dad's statement marked the moment when he knew that the military would have to prepare for war. The line stuck with me, at least subconsciously. A decade later, after the al Qaeda attacks on September 11, 2001, I told the country in my first public statement, "Terrorism against our nation will not stand."

Dad's strategy was to rally a coalition of nations to pressure Saddam Hussein to leave Kuwait. Thanks to years of personal diplomacy, George Bush had earned the trust of many world leaders. Now he put that trust to use. King Fahd agreed to let the United States station troops in Saudi Arabia (a decision that Osama bin Laden later cited as a reason for attacking the Saudi government). Arab leaders across the Middle East agreed to denounce the Iraqi invasion of Kuwait, a major step given that Saddam Hussein was a key figure in the Arab League. European allies like Margaret Thatcher of Great Britain and Helmut Kohl of West Germany offered their strong support. So did Japanese Prime Minister Toshiki Kaifu, who remembered Dad's early decision to attend Emperor Hirohito's funeral. A more surprising backer was François Mitterrand of France. Dad had worked hard to develop a relationship with him early in the presidency by inviting him to Walker's Point, and now the French President was offering his support.

In the most striking development, the Soviet Union joined with the United States to condemn Iraq's aggression against Kuwait. Jim Baker and Soviet Foreign Minister Eduard Shevardnadze issued a joint statement the day after the attack—a moment that Baker later said convinced him that the Cold War was over. In early September, Dad and Gorbachev met in Finland, where they resolved to work together to pressure Iraq to leave Kuwait. Their agreement marked the most significant strategic cooperation between American and Soviet leaders since FDR and Stalin. In an address to a joint session of Congress in September 1990, Dad laid out his vision for a "new world order" in which all civilized nations, including the Soviet Union, worked together to deter aggression and promote peace.

The Bush administration's diplomatic campaign also included a concerted effort at the United Nations. The Security Council had passed eleven resolutions sanctioning Iraq and demanding withdrawal from Kuwait. Saddam had ignored every one. So on November 29, 1990, the Security Council adopted Resolution 678, which offered Saddam Hussein "one final opportunity" to comply with the world's demands. The resolution set a deadline of January 15, 1991, for Iraq to leave Kuwait. If Saddam continued to defy the UN, the resolution authorized member nations to use "all necessary means" to force him to comply. The resolution passed twelve to two, with China abstaining. Dad's cultivation of François Mitterrand paid off; France's support proved critical to securing the resolution. Only Cuba and Yemen opposed the resolution. After four months of exhaustive personal diplomacy, George Bush had united the world against Saddam Hussein.

In 1990, our family spent Christmas at Camp David. It was the second year in a row that a military crisis overshadowed the holiday. Once again, Dad did his best to enjoy the family gathering. He refused to allow the burdens he carried to spoil our time together. But it was obvious that his mind was elsewhere. On New Year's Eve, he wrote a letter to my siblings and me. "I have thought long and hard about what might have to be done," he wrote. "I guess what I want you to know as a father is this: Every Human life is precious. When the question is asked 'How many lives are you willing to sacrifice'—it tears at my heart. The answer of course, is none—none at all." He continued,

"Principle must be adhered to—Saddam cannot profit in any way at all from his aggression and from his brutalizing the people of Kuwait."

With about ten days to go before the UN deadline of January 15, Dad resolved to give diplomacy one final chance to succeed. As he put it, he would go the "extra mile for peace." He wrote a personal letter to Saddam Hussein urging him to comply with the UN resolutions. He announced that he was sending Secretary of State Jim Baker to deliver the letter to Saddam. Iraqi Foreign Minister Tariq Aziz met Baker in Geneva, but he refused to take the letter. Saddam had passed up an opportunity for peace.

Before ordering the military operation, there was one more decision for Dad to make: whether to seek authorization from Congress for the use of force. Congress had not formally declared war since World War II, and several military operations—the Korean War, Grenada, and Panama—had been conducted under Article II of the Constitution, which makes the President the Commander-in-Chief of our military, without authorization from Congress. Dad and his advisers believed that Article II provided sufficient authority for him to proceed on his own, but he decided that it would be prudent to put Congress on record. The vote was close, especially in the Senate, where opponents of the war raised the specter of tens of thousands of body bags. On January 12, the Senate approved the resolution 52 to 47, and the House passed it 250 to 183.

ON JANUARY 15, 1991, the UN deadline passed without any response from Saddam Hussein. At 9:01 the next night, George Bush addressed the nation from the Oval Office. "Five months ago, Saddam Hussein started this cruel war against Kuwait," he said. "Tonight, the battle has been joined."

The first phase of the attack, Operation Desert Storm, was a massive aerial bombardment of Iraqi military targets. The objective was to degrade Saddam's capacity and convince him to withdraw his troops from Kuwait. If not, forces from twenty-eight nations were prepared to conduct a ground attack.

The hours leading up to the moment had been wrenching. Mother told me that Dad had not slept well for days. His friend the Rever-

end Billy Graham came to the White House
to conduct a special prayer service. Dad understood the ramifications of the order he was
about to give. "It is my decision," he dictated to
his diary, "my decision to send these kids into
battle, my decision that may affect the lives of
innocen[ts]. . . . It is my decision that affects
the husband, the girlfriend, or the wife that is
waiting." He continued, "And yet I know what
I have to do."

I admired the way Dad handled the situation.
He had taken his time. He had explored all options. He had resolved to protect American interests, defend an ally, and promote long-term
peace. He had rallied the world and Congress
to the cause. It was as if his whole life—from
his time in uniform, to his service on Capitol
Hill, to his diplomatic experience—had prepared him for the moment.

As Dad spoke from the Oval Office, the sky
over Baghdad lit up. For the first time in the
history of warfare, the world could watch the
battle unfold live on CNN. I was amazed by
the precision bombs that destroyed military
targets while minimizing civilian loss of life.

Though the air campaign made steady progress, Saddam would not leave Kuwait. It became clear that the only way to liberate the country was to deploy ground troops. Dad gave the order for our forces in Saudi Arabia to cross the border into Kuwait on February 23, 1991. At a church service the next morning, Dick Cheney passed him a note with the first update. The mission looked like a major success. The troops had cut through barbed wire and minefields at the border and begun the drive up the highway toward Kuwait City.

What followed over the ensuing days was astounding. Coalition forces routed Saddam Hussein's military. Thousands of Iraqi soldiers laid down their arms and surrendered. Exactly a hundred hours after Dad sent ground troops into Kuwait, the Gulf War was over. "Kuwait is liberated. Iraq's army is defeated. Our military objectives are met," Dad said from the Oval Office. "We declared that the aggression against Kuwait would not stand. And tonight, America and the world have kept their word."

Dad announced that the Coalition forces would immediately cease active combat operations. All told, 148 Americans were killed, and 467 were wounded. The predictions of a quagmire requiring tens of thousands of body bags proved untrue. The Vietnam syndrome—the reluctance of America to deploy troops abroad for fear of getting bogged down—had been vanquished.

Saddam Hussein left Kuwait, but he retained power in Iraq. Some had urged Dad to expand the mission to remove Saddam from power, but he refused. Congress and the Coalition had signed on to liberate Kuwait. That was the mission. It was achieved. It was time to bring the troops home. President George H.W. Bush's approval rating reached 89 percent, the highest level that any President had ever recorded to that point.

IN MARCH and April of 1991, Iraqi factions in several parts of the country mounted uprisings against Saddam, only to be crushed brutally by Saddam's ground forces and helicopters and then dumped into mass graves. Over the years, some critics have suggested that the United States should have intervened to stop Saddam from suppressing the rebels, some of whom had been counting on American support. Dad's response has always been that he had no mandate from Congress or from our international partners to intervene militarily.

Intelligence gathered during the Gulf War showed that Saddam's biological, chemical, and nuclear weapons programs were more advanced than the CIA had previously estimated. And as the 1990s progressed, he continued to pose a threat. He defied the UN resolutions requiring that he disarm, disclose, and account for his weapons of mass destruction. He circumvented the sanctions that the UN had imposed without facing any serious punishment. And he routinely violated the no-fly zones that had been created to protect Iraqis in the northern and southern parts of the country. In 1998, Congress passed and President Clinton signed the Iraq Liberation Act, which made the removal of Saddam and the promotion of a democratic Iraq the official policy of the United States.

When I took office in 2001, it seemed that the best way to pursue that policy was to contain Saddam and push for tougher sanctions. The hope was that if we pressured the regime hard enough, it would change. On September 11, 2001, the world changed instead. Al Qaeda terrorists operating out of Afghanistan killed nearly three thousand people on American soil. In the ensuing months, we received a constant stream of chilling intelligence that the terrorists wanted to attack the United States again, this time on a grander scale—including with chemical, biological, or nuclear weapons. Intelligence agencies around the world believed that Saddam Hussein had chemical and biological weapons, as well as a nuclear weapons program. One of our greatest fears was that Saddam would share those capabilities with terrorists. We knew that Saddam had paid the families of Palestinian suicide bombers, used chemical weapons on his own people, invaded two of his neighbors, regularly fired on American planes patrolling the no-fly zone, and remained a sworn enemy of the United States. In short, after the horror of September 11 and the threats we were receiving, Saddam Hussein had to be dealt with. Beginning in early 2002, I mounted a sustained diplomatic campaign, backed up by the threat of military force, to convince Saddam to comply with his international obligations. I was not trying "to finish what my father had begun," as some have suggested. My motivation was to protect the United States of America, as I had sworn an oath to do.

I thought about my father's leadership in the Gulf War. Like Dad, I went to the UN Security Council to increase international pressure on Saddam. By that time, the UN Security Council had already passed sixteen resolutions demanding, among other things, that Saddam disclose, disarm, and account for his chemical, biological, and nuclear weapons programs. Saddam had defied every one of those resolutions. In November 2002, I worked with leaders around the world to pass a unanimous seventeenth resolution that declared Iraq to be in "material breach" of the earlier resolutions but afforded Saddam a "final opportunity to comply" with his obligations or else face "serious consequences." In addition to conducting diplomacy at the UN, my administration assembled a large coalition of like-minded nations to put pressure on Saddam. Like Dad, I went to Congress, where both houses delivered bipartisan votes for a resolution authorizing me to take military action to enforce the UN resolutions and defend the country against the threat posed by Saddam Hussein. The Senate

passed the war authorization resolution by a
vote of 77–23, and the House passed it 296–
133. (Interestingly, some of the same Senators
who spent the 1990s running away from their
vote against the Gulf War spent the 2000s running away from their vote for the Iraq War.) I
also spoke out against Saddam's terrible viola-
tions of human dignity and urged our citizens
and our allies to support our efforts against
Saddam as a matter of human rights. And like
Dad, I worked closely with our military com-
manders to assemble a plan to accomplish our
objective—in this case, removing Saddam's regime from power in Baghdad—decisively and
with minimal loss of innocent life if our diplomatic efforts should fail.

Unfortunately, for the second time in two
decades, Saddam Hussein defied the United
States, our allies, and the United Nations. As
it became increasingly clear that military force
might be the only option to address the threat
from Iraq, I sent intelligence briefers to update
Dad on the situation. (I also sent them to brief
former President Clinton.) I never asked Dad
what I should do. We both knew that this was a
decision that only the President can make. We

did talk about the issue, however. Over Christmas 2002 at Camp David, I gave Dad an update on our strategy.

"You know how tough war is, son, and you've got to try everything you can to avoid war," he said. "But if the man won't comply, you don't have any other choice."

In early 2003, Saddam briefly allowed weapons inspectors into the country, but he would not give them the access they needed to verify that he had complied with his obligations to destroy his weapons of mass destruction. Remembering Dad's pledge to "go the extra mile for peace" in 1991, I made one last diplomatic effort to give Saddam a way out. My administration spoke to leaders in the Middle East about taking Saddam into exile. It was clear that he had no intention of leaving. On March 17, 2003, I gave him a final forty-eight hours to leave the country. Again, he refused. Time and again, Saddam Hussein could have chosen peace. Instead, he chose war.

On March 19, 2003, I gave the order to launch Operation Iraqi Freedom. Later that morning, I wrote a letter to Dad. "I know I have taken the right action and do pray few will lose life," I wrote. "Iraq will be free, the world will be safer. The emotion of the moment has passed and now I wait word on the covert action that is taking place. I know what you went through."

A few hours later, he replied, "Your handwritten note, just received, touched my heart. You are doing the right thing. . . . Remember Robin's words, 'I love you more than tongue can tell.' Well, I do."

The military operation, which had support from more than thirty-five nations, was a rapid success. Within a month, our forces had liberated Baghdad and overthrown Saddam's regime. We worked with a diverse group of allies and Iraqi leaders to meet our objective: a free and representative Iraqi government that would replace Saddam's brutal tyranny, a democracy in the heart of the Middle East, and an ally in the war on terror. For a variety of reasons, the mission proved to be more difficult than we expected. First, we never found the stockpiles of weapons of mass destruction that intelligence agencies around the world believed that Saddam had. (We did, however, find evidence that he still had the capacity to make chemical

and biological weapons and that he intended to
restart his nuclear program after the sanctions
were lifted.)

Second, after the rapid and successful liberation of Iraq, a violent insurgency broke out.
The insurgents were fueled in part by internal
ethnic strife that Saddam had cultivated for decades and in part by Iran and Syria, both of
which had incentives to meddle in Iraq as a way
to prevent the development of a democracy that
would be an ally of the free world. The most
dangerous and unexpected force behind the insurgency, however, was al Qaeda. In the years
after the removal of Saddam and after being
routed in Afghanistan, al Qaeda chose to make
a stand against the United States in Iraq. Al
Qaeda's leaders openly talked about developing
a base of operations in Iraq from which they
could mount international terrorist attacks.
And al Qaeda's leaders announced a strategy
to stoke sectarian violence in Iraq by murder-
ing innocent Iraqi Shia as a way to create chaos
that they could exploit. Despite the determined
efforts of our military, al Qaeda and its allies
in Iraq executed that strategy with frightening
brutality and terrifying success.

In 2007, I decided that our strategy in Iraq had to change. I launched a troop surge designed to help Iraq's new democratic government defeat the terrorists and insurgents. Thanks to historic efforts by our military, intelligence officers, and diplomats, the surge was a success. After several months of tough fighting, al Qaeda was defeated in Iraq and the Iraqis were able to reclaim their country.

Regrettably, because of subsequent developments and decisions, an al Qaeda–inspired organization called the Islamic State of Iraq and Syria was able to gain strength in Syria, cross the border into Iraq, wreak havoc on Iraq's fragile democracy, and attempt to set up a base for terrorist operations. Iraq's future is uncertain as I write this in 2014. For the sake of our security and the Iraqi people, I hope we will do what it takes to defeat ISIS and allow Iraq's democratic government a chance to succeed. One thing is certain: The Iraqi people, the United States, and the world are better off without Saddam Hussein in power. I believe the decision that Dad made in 1991 was correct—and I believe the same is true of the decision I made a dozen years later.

*   *   *

IN JUST OVER two years as President, George Bush had skillfully managed American policy regarding the democratic movements in Eastern Europe, the liberation of Panama, and the removal of Saddam Hussein from Kuwait. His foreign policy record would compare favorably with that of any modern President. Then history handed him one more challenge: the collapse of the Soviet Union.

In a short period of time, the Soviet Union had gone from a rival superpower to a crumbling empire. Mikhail Gorbachev had shown restraint when the nations of Central and Eastern Europe rebelled against communism, but nobody knew how the Kremlin would react when republics within the Soviet Union demanded their independence.

Dad's strategy was to develop his friendship with Gorbachev while privately urging him to allow the Soviet Union to unwind peacefully. The strategy paid off in early 1991 when Gorbachev agreed to allow a free election for President of the Russian Federation. The voters elected a charismatic reformer named Boris Yeltsin.

Dad's patient approach encountered some opposition. His speech in Kiev, Ukraine, stressing the importance of a gradual transition to democracy was derided as "Chicken Kiev." George Bush brushed off the criticism. He was confident that the freedom movements would succeed as long as they were not violently suppressed. And he believed that encouraging Gorbachev—not provoking the Soviet hard-liners—was the best way to avoid a crackdown.

The threats posed by hard-liners in the Kremlin became clear in August 1991. We were in Maine with Dad when Brent Scowcroft informed him that Soviet officials opposed to Gorbachev's policies and reforms had mounted a coup. They had put Gorbachev under arrest at his vacation house in the Crimea. Dad tried to call Gorbachev, but no one knew how to reach him. It looked like his friend had lost his battle to the old guard. Then, in a memorable scene, Boris Yeltsin climbed atop a tank and urged the leaders of the coup to back down. Eventually they did, and Gorbachev returned to power. Dad called Yeltsin to thank him and encourage him to stay strong in the face of the hard-liners. Although Gorbachev survived, the Soviet Union had irrevocably changed.

On December 7, 1991, Mother and Dad traveled to Hawaii to commemorate the fiftieth anniversary of Pearl Harbor. It was an emotional day for him, bringing back memories of his service in the war and his comrades who had given their lives. At the memorial honoring the USS **Arizona**, on which more than 1,100 American sailors died, Dad observed a moment of silence at the exact time when the Japanese bombers had first appeared. He and Mother met with survivors and dropped flowers into the water to honor the lost. In his speech, he stressed remembrance and forgiveness. "I have no rancor in my heart towards Germany or Japan," he said. "And I hope, in spite of the loss, that you have none in yours. This is no time for recrimination. World War II is over. It is history. We won. We crushed totalitarianism, and when that was done we helped our enemies give birth to democracies."

The next day, he received a call from Boris Yeltsin, who informed him that the Presidents of the remaining Soviet republics had voted to dissolve the Soviet Union. That meant that Mikhail Gorbachev would no longer have a job.

On Christmas Day, Gorbachev signed the paperwork disbanding the Soviet Union. The flag that had flown over the Kremlin for decades was lowered. Before he left office, Gorbachev placed his final call.

Gorbachev told Dad that he was about to make a statement resigning his position and that he had on his desk a decree disbanding the USSR. Gorbachev thanked the President for the support he had given him, and Dad assured him that history would remember the courageous choices he had made. Then they exchanged the final words ever spoken between a Soviet leader and an American President.

"At this special time of year and at this historic time, we salute you and thank you for what you have done for world peace. Thank you very much," Dad said.

"Thank you, George," Gorbachev said. "I am saying good-bye and shaking your hands."

With the conclusion of that call came one of the most stunning diplomatic achievements in history: a peaceful end to the Cold War.

*   *   *

WITH THE DISTANCE of time, the end of the Cold War can seem inevitable. Yet for the generation of Americans who grew up in a world of air-raid drills and fallout shelters and the Cuban Missile Crisis, it seemed that the Cold War would never end—let alone without a shot being fired. Yet beneath the imposing facade, the suffocating ideology of communism could not compete with the human desire for freedom. Ronald Reagan recognized this before most others, and his determination to defeat the Soviet Union rightly earns him credit as the architect of America's victory in the Cold War. Likewise, Mikhail Gorbachev understood that the Soviet Union had to reform in order to survive. He ultimately failed in that mission. Yet his courageous decision to let his country dissolve without resorting to violence makes him, as the Cold War historian John Lewis Gaddis put it, "the most deserving recipient ever of the Nobel Peace Prize."

I don't believe Gorbachev could have endured without a partner in the United States.

As the August 1991 coup revealed, he faced intense opposition within his own government. Had the United States handled the collapse of communism differently—by gloating over its victory or antagonizing the Soviet hard-liners— Gorbachev might not have been able to resist pressure to intervene violently. Worse, he might have been overthrown by a Soviet leader determined to go down in a hail of nuclear missiles. In some ways, the death throes of the Soviet empire represented one of the most dangerous periods of the Cold War.

Thankfully, the United States had a President suited to the moment. Within months of taking office, George Bush had the vision to recognize Gorbachev's potential, the diplomatic savvy to help him, the humility to avoid provocation, and the strength of character to stand up to pressure from critics. The President who guided the Cold War to a peaceful end was the same decent, humble, thoughtful man that I have known all my life. It's no exaggeration to say that the lessons that Dorothy Walker Bush taught her son a lifetime earlier— win with grace, don't brag, think of the other guy—directly contributed to the peace of the world. Not too many mothers can say that.

Future historians will no doubt give George Bush credit for his leadership in ending the Cold War. At the time, however, his success had an unexpected cost. By removing the main foreign policy issues from the agenda of the 1992 election, he erased his greatest strength. In one of the most dramatic turnarounds in political history, George Bush went from an admired leader with approval ratings in the high eighties to a man without a job.

THE HARDEST YEAR

O N HALLOWEEN 1991, a massive storm pounded the Maine coastline. Winds gusting up to seventy-five miles per hour and thirty-foot waves caused more than two hundred million dollars in property damage. Amid the destruction was my parents' beloved home at Walker's Point. The Wave, a small guest cottage, was ripped off its foundations. My parents' house was severely damaged when giant boulders were swept through the living room. Couches floated out to sea. As Dad put it in a letter to a friend, Kennebunkport had endured a "truly historic pounding." To some local residents, the Halloween nor'easter of 1991 became known as "the perfect storm."

The storm that struck Walker's Point was a harbinger of the tumultuous year ahead for

George Bush. Just a few months earlier, his decisive handling of the Gulf War and the collapse of communism in Eastern Europe had
earned him historically high approval ratings.
Yet the economy was in recession, and the
American people were frustrated. In less than a
year, Dad's approval ratings collapsed by more
than forty points. He faced a primary challenger, a billionaire independent, and a Democratic Party determined to retake the White
House after twelve years in the political wilderness. For all who loved George Bush, 1992 was
a painful year.

ALTHOUGH FOREIGN POLICY dominated
his presidency, George Bush came to the White
House with a serious domestic agenda: to improve education, reduce crime, encourage volunteerism, and stimulate economic growth by
keeping taxes low.

Those plans quickly collided with the realities
of a struggling economy. The economy had been
growing steadily since the recession that Ronald
Reagan had confronted in the early 1980s. But
rising inflation, combined with the savings and

loan crisis, slowed economic growth to a near halt by early 1990. Before long, the country was in recession. The budget deficit ballooned to more than two hundred billion dollars, nearly 4 percent of gross domestic product. Economic advisers warned that the deficit could drag the economy into an even deeper recession.

The White House strategy was to invigorate the economy by lowering the deficit through spending cuts. The economic policy team hoped that a lower deficit would drive down interest rates and restore consumer confidence, which in turn would stimulate economic growth. In 1990, however, Democrats controlled both houses of Congress, and they wanted to reduce the deficit by raising taxes rather than cutting spending. After months of negotiation with leaders from both parties, Dad accepted a budget compromise: In exchange for major spending reductions, he would accept some revenue increases. That was what President Reagan had done in 1982, when he agreed to a tax increase as part of a deficit reduction bill. There was a big difference between 1982 and 1990, however. Unlike Ronald Reagan, George Bush had said, "Read my lips: no new taxes."

Congress considered the compromise in the fall of 1990. Republicans, led by Congressman Newt Gingrich of Georgia—who at one point had supported the compromise—revolted and failed to pass the bill. Without a spending bill in place, the government shut down briefly. The Democrats took the opportunity to demand personal income tax hikes in addition to other revenue increases. (As we have learned over the years, the American people expect their government to function, and a shutdown led by Republicans always strengthens the Democrats' hand.) By that point, Dad had deployed troops to Saudi Arabia, where they were preparing to remove Saddam Hussein from Kuwait. He felt that he could not afford a budget crisis at home while he was managing a national security crisis abroad. And he believed that reducing the deficit was critical to restarting the economy. He agreed to the revised deal, including the tax increases proposed by the Democrats.

From an economic perspective, the budget bill made some sense. It imposed spending discipline by setting firm caps on discretionary spending and requiring additional government spending on programs like Medicare and Social Security to be offset by cuts in other areas. For every dollar in revenue increases that Dad accepted, the Democratic Congress agreed to two dollars in spending cuts.

From a political perspective, however, the budget agreement was a disaster. Dad's decision to break his "no new taxes" pledge fractured the Republican Party. The White House did a poor job of communicating the rationale behind the deficit deal. It seemed to me that there was not a full-scale effort to defend the deal. I'm not sure why. Perhaps senior advisers did not want to attract any more attention to Dad's broken pledge. If so, that was shortsighted.

In retrospect, the White House should have conducted a full-throated public relations campaign to explain the budget decision. By taking the issue to the people, a President can build up public support and change minds in Washington. Unfortunately, George Bush did not do that for the budget agreement of 1990, and the bitterness that resulted from his broken pledge damaged his standing within his party.

Ultimately, many economists would later credit Dad's decision with laying the foundation for the explosive economic growth of the

1990s. Sadly for President George Bush, the positive economic news did not appear until right after the 1992 election.

THE DEFICIT REDUCTION deal obscured many other domestic accomplishments of Dad's presidency. He fulfilled a campaign promise by signing the Americans with Disabilities Act, a landmark piece of legislation that has enabled millions of Americans with physical disabilities to participate more fully in society. I saw the positive impact of the law firsthand. When I was comanaging partner of the Texas Rangers, we designed the new Ballpark in Arlington to include wheelchair ramps and handicap-accessible seating so that all fans could cheer on the Rangers. Dad also signed the Civil Rights Act of 1991—a fitting complement to the open-housing bill that he supported in 1968—which allowed greater access to courts for victims of racial discrimination without endorsing quotas. And he signed the Clean Air Act Amendments of 1990, the most significant environmental legislation in two decades. The bill applied market forces to reduce the problem of acid rain in the most economically efficient way possible. And it worked. In 2002, the **Economist** magazine called the bill "the greatest green success story of the past decade."

In one of his most satisfying personal achievements, he issued an executive order establishing a program to recognize and encourage volunteer organizations. Adopting a line from his inaugural address, he called the initiative Points of Light. Every day, the White House recognized a volunteer who had done something to improve his or her community with a Daily Point of Light Award. By the end of the Bush administration, more than a thousand points of light had been recognized. Dad didn't stop there. When he left office, he turned the Points of Light initiative into a private organization, now chaired by my brother Neil, that continues to encourage volunteerism. In 2013, President Barack Obama invited Dad to the White House to present the five-thousandth Point of Light Award to a couple from Iowa who started an organization to provide food and water to children in need.

Like Presidents before him, Dad also had an opportunity to influence the third branch of government, the judiciary. He replaced Supreme Court Justices William Brennan and Thurgood Marshall, two of the most liberal Justices of the twentieth century, with David Souter and Clarence Thomas. Souter, a former New Hampshire Supreme Court Justice recommended by John Sununu and Senator Warren Rudman, unexpectedly turned out to be almost as liberal as Brennan and Marshall. Clarence Thomas, an African-American who had grown up in rural poverty in Pin Point, Georgia, before working his way through Holy Cross College and Yale Law School, emerged as one of the most consistent and principled Justices of the Supreme Court.

To join the Court, Justice Thomas endured one of the most unfair confirmation proceedings in the history of the Senate. The focus of the hearings quickly turned away from his legal qualifications and judicial opinions to vicious personal smears. Democrats in the Senate called a parade of witnesses to impugn the nominee's character with lurid details about alleged sexual harassment—a shameful display that Clarence Thomas rightly described as a "high-tech lynching." During the hearing, the pressure to withdraw the nomination was enormous. I knew George Bush would never abandon a good man like Clarence Thomas. I remember talking to him after watching the coverage of the hearings on TV.

"This Thomas stuff is getting pretty nasty," I said.

"You know what, son," he said, "the worse they treat him, the more determined I am to get him confirmed."

Dad meant what he said. After a lot of lobbying and hard work, the Senate confirmed Justice Thomas fifty-two to forty-eight, with eleven Democrats voting in his favor.

Watching my father's experience with Supreme Court nominations proved beneficial when I had the opportunity to appoint new Justices. I learned that it is essential for a President to fully vet nominees. Early in my presidency, I directed my counsel's office to research potential Supreme Court nominees. When Justice Sandra Day O'Connor announced her resignation in 2005, I invited five jurists for one-on-one interviews at the White House Residence. I had reviewed their judicial philosophies; what I really wanted to learn was their character and whether their philosophy would change with time. While all the candidates were outstanding, I was especially impressed by Judge John Roberts, a generous and humble man who had argued dozens of cases before the Supreme Court and was widely considered one of the best lawyers of his generation. I first nominated John for Justice O'Connor's seat and later resubmitted his nomination for Chief Justice Rehnquist's seat after the Chief Justice died. For Justice O'Connor's seat, I chose Sam Alito, a soft-spoken and brilliant judge whose love of the law was matched only by his passion for the Philadelphia Phillies. Both men have done me proud during their time on the Court.

DURING DAD'S first term, most people assumed that he would run for reelection. He loved the job, and he was excelling at it. Yet the decision was not automatic. His primary concern was the impact that another campaign would have on our family. One reason was my brother Neil. Neil had served on the board of directors of the Silverado Banking Savings and Loan. Like hundreds of other savings and loan associations, Silverado had overextended its lending, become insolvent when interest rates increased, and required federal taxpayer money to repay depositors. The media and Dad's political adversaries depicted Neil as the "poster boy" for the savings and loan crisis. He appeared before a congressional committee to answer hostile questions. The Federal Deposit Insurance Corporation opened an investigation and eventually filed civil charges (which were later settled out of court).

Dad was crushed. He ached for his middle son. As he later wrote, it killed him to see Neil singled out because he was the President's son. George Bush was willing to take all the heat that came with being President. But when his job affected his children, that was a different story. One day when he and I were fishing in Maine, he told me out of the blue, "Son, I'm thinking about not running again."

"Why, Dad?" I asked.

"Because of what Neil is going through," he said.

"I know it's tough," I said, "but you've still got work to do and the country needs you."

He didn't answer. It was clear that he was

seriously considering giving it all up to ease the pain on his son.

I got a taste of Neil's struggles one day at the gym in Dallas. I overheard somebody say, "There's the President's son—he's about to get indicted." I was hot. I walked over to the guy and blurted, "I'm not about to get indicted, and neither is my brother, and I'd appreciate it if you'd get your facts right instead of spreading gossip." The stranger was taken aback. He stammered an apology. My personal encounter with the Silverado crisis was fleeting. For Neil, it felt like it lasted for an eternity.

I remembered Neil's experience years later when I was deciding whether to run for President. I was very reluctant to expose my family, especially our daughters, to the kind of treatment that Neil had received. Ultimately, like Dad, I decided that our family was strong enough to endure the scrutiny. The presidency attracts a spotlight, and one of the toughest things for any President is to watch that spotlight shine harshly on the people you love.

Dad had another reason for hesitating to run for reelection: his health. In 1989, Mother had been diagnosed with Graves' disease, a thyroid condition that can cause weight loss and serious eye problems. Two years later, Dad started experiencing an irregular heartbeat and exhaustion. When Laura and I came for a state dinner with the Queen of England in May 1991, I was shocked to see Dad looking so tired and worn. He never complained, but I could tell that he was suffering. It was the first time in my life that my father had ever looked old. Strangely, doctors concluded that he also had Graves' disease. They did their best to treat the illness, but it took time for him to adjust to the medication. It seemed like he never had quite the same energy level again. That was a serious problem for someone serving as President and running for reelection. Yet George Bush was a competitor. As he had explained in his 1988 convention speech, he saw the presidency as a mission— and he was determined to complete it.

Around the summer of 1991, I started to worry about the reelection campaign. The American people were focused on the economy. And in the middle of a recession, that was not a good issue for the sitting President—especially one who had angered his own party by breaking his most memorable promise.

In addition to the economy, I worried about the political mood of the country. Between his eight years as Vice President and four years as President, George Bush had been in the public spotlight for a long time. The American people would naturally be looking for a fresh face. The demographics of America were shifting. As baby boomers in their thirties and forties became more politically active, leaders from the World War II generation started to seem increasingly out-of-date. Even among Bush supporters, the energy level and enthusiasm was not nearly as high as it had been in 1988.

To convince the country that he deserved another four years, Dad would need an active, forward-looking message. Tragically, his top strategist, Lee Atwater, had died of brain cancer in 1991. No one of Lee's talent had stepped forward to guide the reelection campaign. The perils of the political landscape became clear in November 1991 when Dick Thornburgh, Dad's former Attorney General and a popular former Governor of Pennsylvania, unexpectedly lost a Senate race in Pennsylvania. In retrospect, that should have been an alarm bell about the dangers that were ahead for George Bush.

The last thing any family member should do is burden the President with complaints or concerns, but in the early fall of 1991, I told Dad that I was worried about the reelection effort. I knew that he shared my misgivings when he asked me to take on a sensitive assignment. He wanted me to analyze how to improve the functioning of the White House and to make recommendations about how to structure the 1992 campaign. He sent a letter to all his senior advisers telling them to meet with me and share their candid thoughts. At first I was startled that he had asked me to take on such an important project. Then I was deeply touched by his confidence in me.

I took the job seriously. Several times I traveled from Dallas to Washington to interview all of the top White House and campaign officials. What became clear is that many senior advisers felt disconnected from the President. They felt that the President was isolated and that the lack of access to him was weakening morale. The consensus of the interviews was that Dad should change the way the White House was operating, starting with the Chief of Staff.

In late November 1991, Mother, Dad, and

I had dinner in the family dining room of the White House. Over the first course, a nice soup, I gave him a summary of the interviews that I had conducted. Dad took it all in and didn't say much during the main course. Finally, during dessert, he said that he agreed with the conclusion that the White House needed to be reorganized and that he needed to find a new Chief of Staff. Then he asked, "Who do you think should tell John Sununu?"

I was surprised by the question. "Why don't you talk to him?" I asked.

He said, "I'd rather it be someone else." We ran down a list of possible names, none of whom he wanted to handle it.

Finally, in spite of my misgivings about the awkwardness of a President's son delivering such a message, I said, "Dad, look, if no one else can do it, I can talk to Sununu anytime you'd like."

To my amazement, after a long pause, he said, "Fine."

Over the years, there has been widespread speculation about my conversation with John Sununu. I merely told John he should go see the President, have a heart-to-heart discussion, and give him the opportunity to make a change if the President so desired. I don't know what transpired after that, but I do know that a few days later John went to talk to Dad at Camp David. Shortly after Thanksgiving 1991, John Sununu—an able man and a loyal friend to George Bush—stepped down as Chief of Staff.

I've always wondered why Dad didn't approach his Chief of Staff himself. I've never asked him. The experience taught me a lesson. When I became Governor and President, I resolved to either make personnel changes myself or to have a close confidant (not a family member) who could speak on my behalf make them. When I decided to reorganize my White House five years into my presidency, I told my dear friend and Chief of Staff Andy Card that I felt it was time for a change. And when I decided to replace Secretary of the Treasury Paul O'Neill and Secretary of Defense Don Rumsfeld, I asked my Vice President, Dick Cheney, to deliver the message.

At that same White House dinner, Dad and I began to discuss how to organize the 1992 campaign. Unlike in 1988, I did not plan to be in Washington for the 1992 campaign. I was busy with the Rangers back in Texas. I suggested to

Dad that he ask Jim Baker, who had been with Dad in every one of his national campaigns, to leave his post as Secretary of State and run the 1992 campaign. Dad was reluctant to ask his friend to leave the State Department and step back into the political arena. I understood his decision, but with Atwater gone and Baker off the political playing field, my concerns about the reelection intensified.

THE YEAR 1992 did not get off to an auspicious beginning for George Bush. He started the year with a long trip through Asia, where he was negotiating several important trade agreements. The final stop was Japan. After a day of meetings, he and Mother attended a banquet with Prime Minister Kiichi Miyazawa. Dad hadn't been feeling well all day, but he was too polite to cancel on his host. Everything went fine until about halfway through the meal, when nausea overtook him. His head drooped and he passed out, falling sideways from his chair and vomiting on the Prime Minister. The Secret Service raced over, as did Mother with a napkin. Dad quickly regained consciousness.

"Why don't you just roll me under the table and you can go on with the banquet?" he cracked.

He went back to his hotel while Mother stayed and delivered Dad's toast. The incident made international news—and provided plenty of fodder for late-night comedy skits.

There was nothing funny about the problem brewing back in New Hampshire. In December 1991, the political commentator and TV show host Patrick J. Buchanan had announced that he was challenging Dad in the New Hampshire Republican primary. Buchanan had never held any elected office and seemed to be running in part to boost his TV ratings. A few months earlier, it had seemed inconceivable that any Republican would challenge George Bush. Buchanan's entry in the race showed how badly Dad's position among Republicans had slipped. Polls in early 1992 showed that Buchanan could pick up more than 30 percent of New Hampshire Republicans—a significant protest vote. I had seen protest candidates run in New Hampshire before: Eugene McCarthy in 1968, Ronald Reagan in 1976, and Ted Kennedy in 1980. Every time, the incumbent was significantly wounded.

Buchanan's basic message was that George Bush had betrayed the conservative legacy of Ronald Reagan—a legacy that Republican politicians continue to invoke today, even though some of them overlook the details of Ronald Reagan's record. He attacked the President not only for breaking his "no new taxes" pledge but also for signing the civil rights bill.

Buchanan described the contrast with Dad in his announcement speech. "He is a globalist and we are nationalists. He believes in some **pax universalis;** we believe in the old republic. He would put America's wealth and power at the service of some vague new world order. We will put America first." Buchanan opposed the Gulf War, which he saw as a sellout to "the Israeli defense ministry and its amen corner in the United States." The message echoed the isolationist position of the America First Committee, which opposed American involvement in World War II. It also reminded me of the Texas far-right movement that I had encountered in the 1960s and 1970s, and it was a forerunner of today's Tea Party. And yet, one out of every three Republicans in New Hampshire was supporting Buchanan.

After initially ignoring the primary challenge, Dad's political advisers decided that the President should go to New Hampshire to counter Buchanan's attacks and reassure Republican voters. At one town hall, he delivered an underwhelming line to New Hampshire voters: "Message: I care." No doubt he did care, a lot. And he laid out a proposal for modest tax reductions that would help ease some of the pain. Beyond that, Dad was banking on what his economic advisers had assured him of—that the economy was growing and that jobs reports would improve soon. So far, the results had not appeared. On primary night, Buchanan garnered more than 37 percent, which the media spun as a repudiation of George Bush.

Buchanan stayed in the race for several months, filling the airwaves with attacks on the President. He eventually dropped out and endorsed Dad, but his challenge revealed that the Republican Party was fractured. The experience illustrated one of the key rules of political campaigning: the importance of consolidating the base. It was easy for me to do that in 2000, when Republicans of all stripes were hungry to reclaim the White House after eight years. In 2004, I reached out early to key leaders and managed to tamp down any concerns from disgruntled factions of the party. Pat Buchanan prevented George Bush from doing that in 1992. And to make matters worse, Buchanan's success energized independents, one of whom was about to enter the presidential race.

ON THE SURFACE, H. Ross Perot and George Bush had some things in common. Like Dad, Perot was a Navy veteran and a Texas businessman. The son of a cotton broker in Texarkana, Perot had graduated from the Naval Academy and gone to work for IBM. He eventually launched his own company, Electronic Data Systems, which became a pioneer in the computer industry and made Perot a rich man. Dad and Perot knew each other from the Texas business community. From Dad's perspective, they got along well. Evidently Perot respected Dad at one time, because he had asked Dad if he would be interested in running a Perot-backed oil company after he left government at the beginning of the Carter administration.

Over the years, something obviously went wrong in their relationship. Dad believed that a problem arose over Ross Perot's belief that American prisoners of war had been left behind in Vietnam. When the Defense Department reported to President Reagan that there was no evidence of living POWs, Perot—who disagreed with that assessment—opened his own discussions with the Vietnamese government. The President decided that Perot's trips had to stop and asked his national security team how to handle the situation.

"I know Ross from Texas," Dad volunteered, "and I'd be glad to convey the message to him."

Perot was convinced that there was a conspiracy to abandon the POWs. After his conversation with Dad, he concluded that George Bush was part of the conspiracy. As Dad would later put it, "Perot shot the messenger."

On February 20, 1992—two days after Pat Buchanan's strong showing in the New Hampshire primary—Perot announced on Larry King's CNN call-in show that he would run for President if grassroots supporters registered him on the presidential ballots of all fifty states. At the time, that seemed like a long shot. Within weeks, however, Perot announced that the Home Shopping Network had been hired to manage the thousands of calls an hour that he was receiving urging him to enter the race.

Perot's agenda had some elements that appealed to both sides of the political aisle. He believed in cutting the deficit and reducing government waste. He espoused a populist protectionist message to safeguard American businesses from foreign competition. He was pro-choice and opposed the Gulf War; he also called for slowing the growth in Social Security benefits to balance the budget and called for an expansion of the war on drugs. His unifying theme was antiestablishment and anti-incumbent. And nobody embodied the political establishment more than the incumbent, President George Bush.

The campaign's first reaction to Perot was somewhat dismissive. To those who had known Perot for many years, it seemed inconceivable that he could survive on the national political stage. I was worried. Perot had lots of money and had tapped into populist discontent with

Washington. The media was thrilled to have a colorful new personality to cover and initially lavished praise on Perot. I monitored his progress from my office building in Dallas, which overlooked a Perot campaign headquarters. Day after day, I watched people in BMWs and SUVs line up to collect yard signs and bumper stickers. It was like watching the disintegration of a political base in slow motion.

By the summer of 1992, the campaign had no choice but to take Perot seriously. Like Pat Buchanan before him, Perot made relentless attacks on Dad and the Washington establishment that were taking a toll. Then, all of sudden, Perot announced that he was withdrawing from the race. His explanation was difficult to understand. First he said that he did not want to deadlock the Electoral College and force the election to be resolved by the House of Representatives. Later, he would claim (with no evidence) that the real reason he had dropped out was that Dad's campaign had threatened to ruin his daughter's wedding. I was amazed that this man was being taken seriously as a presidential candidate. I had also learned not to underestimate Ross Perot. I predicted to friends after Perot's withdrawal, "He'll be back."

IN 1988, Dad had run against history in the form of the Van Buren factor. In 1992, he was trying to do something unprecedented. No two-term Vice President who succeeded to the presidency had ever been elected to two full terms of his own. John Adams came close, but Thomas Jefferson got in the way. Two centuries later, George Bush ran into William Jefferson Clinton.

Governor Bill Clinton of Arkansas was not an obvious choice for the Democrats. In 1991, with Dad riding high in polls after the Gulf War, several of the front-running candidates— Governor Mario Cuomo of New York and Senator Bill Bradley of New Jersey—had decided not to run. Clinton, who was forty-five years old (one month my junior), entered a wide-open Democratic field. Clinton had a charming personality and was a superb campaigner who had been elected Governor five times. He was considered one of his party's brightest policy minds, and he espoused a "third way" of politics that steered a middle ground between traditional liberalism and conservatism. I remember Dad telling me that he had been impressed by the Arkansas Governor at a White House–sponsored education summit.

Clinton had a compelling life story. His father had been killed in a car accident three months before he was born. Raised by his mother, he had worked his way out of small-town Arkansas to Georgetown University, a Rhodes Scholarship, and Yale Law School. In a detail that no campaign scriptwriter could invent, his hometown was called Hope.

The man from Hope also had a lot to overcome. He was seen by some as undisciplined, and he was dogged by rumors about personal indiscretions. He received less than 3 percent of the vote in the Iowa caucuses, and in New Hampshire the media reported allegations of an affair with a former TV news reporter in Arkansas. Clinton responded with a high-profile interview on **60 Minutes** immediately following the Super Bowl. He acknowledged making mistakes, and his wife, Hillary, fully defended her husband and their marriage. Shortly thereafter, Clinton shocked the political world by finishing second in New Hampshire behind the heavy favorite, Senator Paul Tsongas of Massachusetts. In his speech after the New Hampshire primary, Clinton proclaimed himself "the Comeback Kid." And he was. He swept the Southern primaries and outlasted Paul Tsongas and California Governor Jerry Brown to clinch the Democratic nomination.

As the race unfolded, it became clear that Bill Clinton would be a formidable opponent. He understood the importance of clear and simple campaign themes. One of those themes was change. After eight years of Reagan-Bush and four years of Bush-Quayle, Clinton knew that voters were ready for fresh faces. He also recognized the generational changes reshaping the electorate. Clinton cultivated his image, playing his saxophone on late-night TV with Arsenio Hall and appearing with college students on MTV. Clinton doubled down on the change theme by selecting as his running mate Senator Al Gore Jr. of Tennessee, a fellow baby boomer. The message was clear: Their generation's time had arrived.

Clinton and Gore stressed a second theme:

the economy. Bill Clinton recognized that if the election was about foreign policy, he had little chance to beat George Bush. He correctly sensed that Dad was vulnerable on the economy. His campaign adopted the slogan "It's the Economy, Stupid." He accused Dad of being out of touch and even managed to turn Dad's foreign policy successes against him by suggesting that he hadn't done enough on domestic issues. For all of Clinton's lack of discipline in some areas of his life, he was relentlessly disciplined about his campaign message.

Bill Clinton also benefited from a friendly press corps. With their baby boomer background, more liberal views, and Ivy League lawyer credentials, the Clintons fit the mold of many of the baby boomer reporters. In time, of course, the press would turn on Clinton. In the 1992 campaign, however, it seemed to me that some news outlets allowed their zeal for change to undermine their high standards of journalistic objectivity. (The pattern would later repeat with another exciting candidate promising change, Barack Obama.)

A classic example of the media's hostility toward George Bush came in February 1992, when Dad visited a grocery store convention in Florida. Among other products, Dad looked at a new version of an electronic grocery scanner. When he complimented his hosts on their new technology, one reporter concocted the story that he had never seen a grocery scanner before. "This career politician, who has lived the cloistered life of a top Washington bureaucrat for decades, is having trouble presenting himself to the electorate as a man in touch with middle-class life," the **New York Times** reported. It later came out that the reporter who wrote that "firsthand" account wasn't even at the grocery store convention.

The Democratic National Convention in July 1992 provided a perfect opportunity for Clinton and Gore to showcase their campaign before a national audience. The convention was carefully orchestrated to highlight the theme of change, all the way down to the Fleetwood Mac lyrics that played after Clinton's speech, "Don't stop thinking about tomorrow." The message worked. The Democrats had gone into New York roughly in a dead heat with Dad and Dan Quayle. They came out with a twenty-four-point lead.

*   *   *

AFTER THE Democratic convention, there was general despondency among Bush supporters. I too was concerned, but I had not lost hope. I had seen Dad overcome Michael Dukakis's lead in 1988. And I believed that he would benefit from the fact that the 1992 campaign was finally down to a two-man race. After months of withering attacks by Buchanan, Perot, and Clinton, Dad would be able to draw a favorable contrast with his opponent on the crucial issues of leadership, experience, and competence. Starting at his convention, he would revitalize his campaign by debunking the perception that he was out of touch and clarifying where he wanted to lead the country.

One way to demonstrate that he had revitalized his campaign was to change its leadership. In August, Dad brought Jim Baker back to the White House, where he would serve as Chief of Staff and coordinate the fall campaign. I know it was tough for Jim to leave a job he loved, Secretary of State, but he was loyal to his friend.

One area where Dad decided not to make a change was with his running mate. Dan Quayle had served the President faithfully, and Dad felt comfortable with his VP. Although Dad recognized that picking a new running mate had the potential to shake up the race, he felt that a change of that magnitude in an election year would look desperate and embarrass his friend. The Bush-Quayle ticket stayed intact.

With Baker back at the helm, Dad and his advisers developed a campaign strategy for the fall. Unfortunately, the first thing they needed to do was consolidate support from the base of the Republican Party—a basic responsibility that should have been fulfilled months earlier but had been delayed by the challenges from Buchanan and Perot. To do that, the campaign largely returned to the playbook from 1988, when Dad had successfully emphasized values that Republicans cared about. Dan Quayle had made major headlines earlier in the campaign when he criticized Hollywood for diminishing the importance of families. Most memorably, he denounced the popular TV show **Murphy Brown** for featuring "a character who supposedly epitomizes today's intelligent, highly paid professional woman, mocking the importance of fathers by bearing a child alone and calling

it just another 'lifestyle choice.'" While sparring with a fictional character struck me as a little awkward, Quayle had an important point:
Hollywood was out of touch with the values
that mattered to most Americans. George Bush
and Dan Quayle were not.

The best opportunity to unite the party
against Clinton came at the Republican National Convention in Houston. The convention
emphasized the importance of Dad's family
values. Jeb's teenage son George P. delivered
a great speech supporting his grandfather,
whom he called "the greatest man [he had]
ever known," and concluded by leading the
audience in a chant of "Viva Bush!" Mother
spoke movingly about the man she had married almost fifty years earlier. "When George
and I headed west after World War II, we already had our first child," she said. "George
was a veteran. He was a college graduate, and
he had a job here in Texas. And we eventually
settled in Midland, a small, decent community
where neighbors helped each other, a wonderful place to bring up a family, and it still is.
In many ways these were the best years of our
lives." As she put it, "George's days in the fields

were dusty with long hours and hard work, but no matter when he got home, he always had time to throw a ball or listen to the kids." She summed up with, "You know, to us, family means putting your arms around each other and being there." Mother was a strong political asset for George Bush. She was a plain speaker who loved her husband and appealed to many Americans with her bluntness and quick wit.

Some of the other speakers discussed family values in a different tone. In a further attempt to unite the base, the convention organizers had agreed to let Pat Buchanan deliver a prime-time speech. Buchanan offered a strong endorsement of Dad, calling on his "Buchanan Brigades" to "come home and stand beside George Bush." But he also proclaimed that a "religious war" was raging for the soul of the nation, defended the "Judeo-Christian values and beliefs upon which America was founded," and accused Hillary Clinton of trying to impose an agenda of "radical feminism." While it might have helped with some elements of the base, Buchanan's speech did not convey a kinder and gentler Republican Party. (Because the convention was running late, Buchanan's speech bumped former President Ronald Reagan's strong endorsement of Dad—the last speech of President Reagan's public career—out of prime time.)

In his speech on the final night of the convention, Dad had a chance to close the gap with Clinton. As in the 1988 speech, he sought to remind the voters why his experience, integrity, and vision for the future made him the right man for the job. Unlike the 1988 speech, which was completed well in advance so that Dad had plenty of time to rehearse, the 1992 speech was the result of a chaotic process. I remember being shocked when I walked into a conference room at the Houstonian Hotel and saw senior Bush campaign aides scrambling to finish a first draft of the convention speech three days before it was to be delivered. The speech process symbolized one of the flaws of Dad's 1992 campaign: It was reacting, not leading.

Dad started his speech by talking about Iraq and the Cold War, and then pivoted to the economy. "When the Berlin Wall fell," he joked, "I half expected to see a headline, 'Wall Falls, Three Border Guards Lose Jobs.' And underneath, it probably says, 'Clinton Blames

Bush.'" In the key line of the speech, Dad said that he regretted his decision to accept the tax increase that the Democrats had demanded in the budget compromise. He proposed a new round of spending reductions and tax cuts in the year ahead. Unlike the 1988 speech, which soared and presented a positive vision, the 1992 speech was defensive and relatively flat. Nevertheless, there was a traditional polling bounce after the convention. The Bush-Quayle ticket trailed Clinton-Gore by ten points. Although the Bush comeback had begun, it still had a steep hill to climb.

THE UPHILL CLIMB became steeper when Ross Perot announced that he would return to the race on October 1. Perot's reentry meant that he would share the stage at the presidential debates and put his anti-incumbent TV ads back on the airwaves. Just when Dad had started gaining ground, he had to resume fighting a two-front war.

Perot's return wasn't the only setback. In late August, Hurricane Andrew struck the Florida and Louisiana coasts, causing some twenty-five billion dollars in damage and leaving tens of thousands of people homeless. Dad immediately issued a major disaster declaration, which allowed the affected states to receive federal disaster aid. But, as in any large-scale relief effort, it took time for the resources to reach those in need. Dad traveled to Florida to show his commitment, sent troops to help man relief stations, and deployed Secretary of Transportation Andy Card to personally oversee the operation. That didn't stop Bill Clinton, Democratic officials in Florida, or the media from castigating the federal government's "slow response." The criticism echoed the theme that George Bush was out of touch or didn't care. Of course, when it comes to delivering ice and trailers, there is only so much that the President can do. That was a lesson that I would learn years later in my own encounter with the politics of natural disasters after Hurricane Katrina in 2005. It was frustrating to see critics and opponents exploit the difficult task of dealing with nature's wrath for political gain.

When he returned to the campaign trail, Dad pressed ahead with his focus on values. He criticized Clinton's positions on social issues like abortion and denounced his conduct during the Vietnam War, which included avoiding the draft and protesting on foreign soil during his year at Oxford. Nevertheless, he had trouble gaining traction. Bill Clinton was no Michael Dukakis. While he supported most of the traditional Democratic platform, he was also in favor of the death penalty, welfare reform, the North American Free Trade Agreement, and a middle-class tax cut (although after he took office, the middle-class tax cut he promised turned into a tax increase). It was hard to portray him as a left-wing liberal. Just as important, Clinton rarely let an attack go unanswered. And his answers always came back to his two overriding themes: change and the economy.

In the fall of 1992, many in the campaign were banking on the presidential debates to change the dynamics of the race. That was not a good sign. Presidential debates are easy to lose but hard to win. I thought the first debate, held in St. Louis, was essentially a draw. Ross Perot got off the best line of the night when he ended an answer on his deficit reduction plan by saying, "If there's a fairer way, I'm all ears." (Perot's ears were a prominent feature.)

The second debate, in Richmond, was the first presidential debate to adopt a town hall format. Most of the questions came from members of the live studio audience. Instead of standing behind podiums, the candidates had chairs and were encouraged to roam the stage. Once again, I did not attend the debate. But on TV, it seemed that Dad was uncomfortable in the new format. He struggled with an awkwardly worded question about how the national debt had affected him personally. He stayed relatively anchored to his chair as he gave a defensive answer. Clinton, by contrast, sauntered across the stage, looked the questioner in the eye, and spelled out his economic message. The most memorable moment of the night came when Perot was giving a long-winded answer and the cameras caught Dad checking his watch. The image that came across to most voters was one of boredom. (Al Gore did not learn a lesson from Dad's mistake, because he "lost" a debate in 2000 as a result of his loud sighing during my answers. Of course, I didn't learn the lesson either, since I "lost" a 2004 debate because I was grimacing during John Kerry's answers. It is a sign of the shallowness of the presidential debate process that their most memorable moments have centered not on issues but on gestures or quips.)

By the third debate, the story line was set. Clinton was the front-runner, Perot remained a curiosity, and George Bush was in serious trouble. His diary entries show that he had started to contemplate defeat by mid-October. He wrote, "If we should lose, there's great happiness over the horizon—but it will be a very painful process—not for losing but letting people down." Despite his doubts, George Bush was not a quitter. He would finish strong. In the last month of the campaign, he finally got some good economic news. The third-quarter estimates showed that the economy had grown by 2.7 percent, the strongest quarter in two years. The polls started to narrow. Dad was making progress head-to-head against Clinton, and Perot supporters were beginning to have second thoughts. With a week to go, many polls were close to the margin of error. The momentum was on Dad's side.

Then came one final blow. On the Friday before the election, Special Prosecutor Lawrence Walsh announced an indictment against

Caspar Weinberger, President Reagan's Secretary of Defense, for making false statements to Congress related to the Iran-Contra investigation. On the day the story broke, Dad was scheduled to appear on Larry King's talk show. Instead of focusing solely on the positive economic news, Dad had to rehash Iran-Contra. And then there were the call-ins. "We have a call from Little Rock," Larry King announced, "from George Stephanopoulos." If there was any doubt about the media's preferences in the 1992 campaign, it was resolved when Larry King's producers aired a call-in question from Bill Clinton's communications director. A polite Stephanopoulos proceeded to hammer Dad about Iran-Contra. That was a fitting capstone to the campaign. From Buchanan to Perot to Hurricane Andrew to Perot (again) and now to Iran-Contra, Dad had faced one distraction after the next. He might have been able to overcome any one of those in isolation. But together they were like that perfect storm that battered Walker's Point on Halloween 1991.

* * *

MONDAY, NOVEMBER 2, 1992, was the last day of the last campaign of George Bush's public career. I accompanied him on Air Force One as he barnstormed from one battleground state to the next. I tried to stay upbeat, but I had a sinking feeling that this good man would go down in defeat. Dad's favorite country music group, the Oak Ridge Boys, joined him on the plane. On the descent into one of our last stops, Dad and the campaign team gathered to hear the Oaks, as Dad called them, sing "Amazing Grace." By the end of the song, all of us were wiping our tears. I remember thinking that the song—a mainstay at funerals—was a way to help us get our hearts ready for bad news.

On Election Day, George Bush was physically spent. He seemed relieved that the campaign was over. And, characteristically, he was optimistic about his prospects. After voting in Houston, he and Mother camped out at the Houstonian Hotel, where our extended family had gathered. When campaign manager Bob Teeter called me with the first round of exit polls, I knew that it was going to be a tough night. When he called back with the second round, I knew that it was over. I went to Mother and Dad's hotel suite. They were the only two in the room.

"How's it going, son?" he asked cheerfully.

"Not so good," I said gently. "The exit polls are in, and it looks like you're going to lose."

He became very quiet. It seemed like he was steeling himself for the disappointment ahead. He had done his best. He had given it his all. But this was not meant to be. After his decades of public service, eight years as Vice President, and four years as President, the American people had rejected George Bush. Of all the elections he had lost, there was no question that this one hurt the most.

As always, Dad was gracious. He called Clinton shortly after the polls closed on the West Coast, conceded defeat, and gave a warm speech thanking his supporters and congratulating the President-elect. When the tally was complete, Bill Clinton won 43 percent of the vote. Dad took almost 38 percent, while Ross Perot claimed 19 percent. In all, nearly twenty million people had voted for Perot. There is no way to know how those twenty million people would have voted in a two-man race. I be-

lieved then, and I still believe today, that if Ross
Perot had not been on the ballot, George Bush
would have won the 1992 election. I know that
Dad felt the same way. He is not a man to hold
grudges. Yet when asked about Perot in a docu-
mentary aired in 2012, Dad said, "I think he
cost me the election and I don't like him." (Interestingly, despite the 1992 campaign, I went
on to become good friends with Ross Perot's
son, Ross Jr., and with Bill Clinton.)

Of course, Perot alone was not to blame.
After twelve years of George Bush as President and Vice President, the American people
were ready for a change. The baby boom generation increasingly dominated the electorate,
and Bill Clinton epitomized the fresh face that
many voters sought. And then there was the
economy. Bill Clinton was wrong when he said
that George Bush didn't get it or didn't care.
Dad understood the economic anxiety facing
the country. He had taken action to address it.
And in 1993, the Commerce Department revised its estimates for the prior year. It turned
out that the economy grew in all four quarters
of 1992, including a growth rate of 5.7 percent
in the pivotal final quarter, when the election

was held. That growth laid the foundation for the economic boom of the 1990s, which was largely credited to Bill Clinton. In one of the ironies of history, Bill Clinton passed on to me an economy that appeared strong but was actually heading into recession. The lesson was that timing is an important part of politics, and by the time the facts about the economy came in, time had run out for George H.W. Bush.

JUST OVER TWO WEEKS after his defeat, Dad flew to Greenwich, Connecticut. He was still down about the election, and now he faced more bad news. His beloved mother, Dorothy Walker Bush, had entered her final hours. For almost all of her ninety-one years, my grandmother had been an active, vigorous, seemingly ageless woman. She swam and played golf well into her eighties. She never lost her competitive edge, her abiding faith, or her capacity to love. Dad and my sister Dorothy, my grandmother's namesake, sat quietly by her bedside while she slept. At one point his mother asked him to read to her from her Bible. As he opened the well-worn book, a bundle of papers tumbled out.

They were letters that he had written her more than fifty years earlier. She had saved them all that time in her Bible, and every day she had prayed for her son. He prayed with her for the last time, said his good-bye, and flew back to the White House. A few hours later, she died. That night he wrote in his diary, "Mum, I hope you know how much we all love you and care. Tonight she is at rest in God's loving arms and with Dad."

Amid his grief and disappointment, George Bush was determined to make the most of his final days in office. Characteristically, he wanted to use his power to help others. When the Secretary General of the United Nations, Boutros Boutros-Ghali, asked the United States to help address a starvation crisis in Somalia, Dad agreed. He sent U.S. Marines to the war-torn East African nation to help secure infrastructure and allow food shipments to enter the country. In early January, Dad traveled to Somalia to visit the service members carrying out the mission. He was a devoted Commander-in-Chief, and he wanted to use his last trip abroad as President to thank the troops.

Dad was not the only one disappointed

by his defeat. In the weeks after the election, members of the White House staff were despondent. In hopes of lifting their spirits, he decided to invite a surprise guest. Throughout his presidency, he had been portrayed on **Saturday Night Live** by the comedian Dana Carvey, who had honed an impression of Dad that exaggerated his speech patterns, hand gestures, and reputation for "prudence." To the comedian's astonishment, Dad called him a few weeks after the election and invited him and his wife, Paula, to stay in the Lincoln Bedroom and then appear at a White House event. The staff was told to gather for an important message from the President. As "Hail to the Chief" played, Dana Carvey walked into the East Room, took the podium, and regaled the audience with his trademark routine. Among other jokes, he created a scene of Dad informing the Secret Service that he planned to go jogging in the nude. The room roared with laughter. The idea was vintage George Bush: He was thinking of others, laughing at himself, and bringing joy to people who were hurting.

I too was hurting. It stung to see a good man rejected by the voters. As a way to move past the election, I decided to run the Houston marathon the next January. During the eighteen-mile training runs, I was able to begin dealing with the pain of defeat. I also found a sense of liberation after Dad left the White House. I no longer had Secret Service protection, and I was able to drive my Lincoln Town Car on the streets of Dallas for the first time in four years. I did so for two years, until I was elected Governor. I haven't driven a car on any street since 1995.

MOTHER AND DAD hosted the whole family for Christmas at Camp David in 1992. It was a bittersweet trip. We enjoyed the beautiful setting, and we all assumed that this would be the last time that we stayed at Camp David. Dad did his best to stay upbeat and never complained. In a letter to his brother, he recalled the story of a runner in the Olympics who limped across the finish line far behind the winners. He remembered the runner saying, "My country didn't send me all this way to start the race. They sent me here to finish it." Dad felt the same way. "I didn't finish the course," he wrote, "and I will always regret that."

We all reminded him that he had a lot to be proud of. He had accomplished more in one term than many Presidents had in two. History would remember him as the liberator of Kuwait and the President who oversaw the peaceful end of the Cold War. In some ways, he was like Winston Churchill, who had been tossed out of office in 1945 just months after prevailing in World War II. The British voters felt that Churchill had completed his mission and that they wanted someone else for the next phase. Ultimately, that's what happened to George Bush in 1992. In Britain, the people regretted their decision and returned Churchill to office. That would not be the case for Dad. Yet his defeat in 1992 opened up new possibilities for others, including Jeb and me. And while it seemed hard to believe at the time, that Christmas at Camp David would not be the Bush family's last.

THE AFTERLIFE

> Now, I no longer pursue happiness . . . I have
> found happiness. I no longer pursue it, for it is
> mine.
>
> **George H.W. Bush, August 2001**

O N JANUARY 21, 1993, George H.W. Bush
woke up at a rental house in Houston. For
the first time in twelve years, he had no morning intelligence briefing and no packed schedule
to review. Everyone who has ever had the privi-
lege of living in the White House confronts an
adjustment after leaving—a transition to what
Laura once called "the afterlife."

The transition was especially tough on Dad
because his departure was premature. The sting
of defeat lingered long past Bill Clinton's inauguration. For the most part, Dad did not let

his disappointment show. He had been raised to lose with grace, and he detested self-pity. When Bill and Hillary Clinton arrived at the White House on Inauguration Day, Mother and Dad received them with genuine kindness and warmth. Years later, I asked him how he found the strength to conduct himself that way. "I had no choice," he said. But the truth of the matter is that he did have a choice. He could have chosen to be bitter or resentful. Instead, as he wrote in a letter that he left for President Clinton on the Oval Office desk, he was rooting hard for his successor.

The adjustment to private life did not come naturally to Dad. My father was sixty-eight years old, with the energy of a man half that age. It seemed that his earlier health issues had abated. He had spent his entire life pushing himself from one mission to the next. For the past four years, he had held the most mentally stimulating, challenging, and exhilarating job in the world. For the past thirty years, he'd poured all his energy into different pursuits. Then, all of a sudden, he had nothing to do. As I would later put it, leaving the presidency feels like going from a hundred miles per hour to about five.

In Houston, Dad would arrive at his new office at seven a.m. and spend most of the day shuffling through mail. He made phone calls to raise money for his presidential library. He hit the paid speaking circuit, a pursuit that he jokingly called "white-collar crime."

One benefit of involuntary retirement was that Mother and Dad got to take some leisurely trips. Shortly after he left office, they went on a commercial cruise on one of the **Love Boat** ships. Every time they left their cabin they were mobbed by starstruck shipmates. Dad was particularly amused when he walked out of the sauna naked one day and a man blurted out, "Do you mind if I take a photo?" On the positive side, it was nice to know that he still had a fan base. As a follow-up to that trip a few years later, Dad planned a surprise fiftieth-wedding-anniversary party for Mother at the Grand Ole Opry in Nashville. As Mother said, "Your father has a way of planning events without seeking my approval."

Dad also spent some time writing. He decided to coauthor a book about his foreign policy with Brent Scowcroft. The decision to write a joint book was revealing. No President had ever split his byline with an aide. But Dad wanted to share credit with his friend. He also wanted to avoid a memoir that was focused on himself. I suspect that the disappointment about his defeat played a role as well. At that point, he may not have been able to summon up the energy to write a book that had an unhappy political ending. He never did write a presidential memoir.

Although the speeches and writing filled George Bush's time and bank account, they did little to fill the void of intensity and excitement left by his departure from the presidency. And they didn't heal the pain left by his defeat. To make matters worse, Dad's beloved dog Ranger died a few months after he returned home to Houston. Shortly thereafter, Dad and James Baker visited President François Mitterrand in Paris. At the beginning of his presidency, relations between French and American leaders had been frosty. That started to change when Dad invited the French President to Kennebunkport. The personal diplomacy paid off, and the two leaders became close friends. At the dinner in France in 1993, Mitterrand offered a toast to Dad and to their warm relations. When George Bush stood up to return the toast, tears flowed. The moment had reminded him how much he loved the presidency. I think the outpouring of emotion that day—and on other occasions soon after he left the White House—reflected a sense of despondency. I felt a letdown when I left office, and I am sure that other Presidents have as well. For Dad, the pain of rejection made the feeling worse.

For her part, Mother seemed to handle the challenge more smoothly—and with her usual bluntness. Shortly after the election, she announced to the family, "Well, now that's behind us. It's time to move on." She did. She stayed busy planning the construction of their new house in Houston. She started work on a memoir, which eventually became a bestseller. And she bought a Mercury Sable station wagon and drove herself for the first time since the late 1970s. As Dad joked, the most dangerous place in America was on the roads in their neighborhood.

Mother even did some cooking. I was the recipient of one of her first meals the night before the Houston marathon, which I ran four days after my parents returned from Washington. To carbo-load for the race, I asked Mother to make pasta. She generously agreed. She boiled the water successfully. In went the noodles. Then she tried to put a lid on the boiling pot, which sent the water and spaghetti spraying out. As Dad observed, the dish was pretty good, as long as you like your pasta rare. The next day, my parents came to cheer me on during the marathon. As I ran past them, Dad yelled out, "That's my boy!" Mother tried a different form of encouragement. "Keep moving, George," she shouted. "There are some fat people ahead of you."

IN THE SUMMER of 1993, I called my parents with some news: "I'm going to run for Governor of Texas."

Mother's response was swift. "You can't win against such a popular opponent," she blurted.

Dad was quiet. I was not surprised that Dad did not have much to say. Throughout my life, he never tried to steer me in one direction or another. His approach to parenting was to instill values, set an example, and support us in whatever we chose to do.

In spite of his silence on the matter, George Bush had a big influence on my decision to run for Governor. Through his words and his life, he had taught all of his children the value of public service. By helping him over the years, I had learned a lot about campaigns. And by watching his presidency, I had learned that good policy is good politics, not the other way around. I had developed strong convictions about policy changes needed in Texas, especially in the areas of education, tort reform, welfare, and juvenile justice. The only question was whether the timing was right.

Dad's defeat partially helped answer that question. Had he been reelected in 1992, I would not have run for Governor in 1994. I was running against a popular incumbent, and as the son of the President it would have been distracting to answer questions about whether I agreed with every decision that his administration made.

I knew there was a chance that I would not succeed. As I saw it, I could either run and lose, in which case some people would say, "What a lousy candidate." Or I could run and win, in which case some people would say, "What a lousy Governor." But none of that matters if you have the unconditional love of a man you admire. And I admire George H.W. Bush above anyone else.

I wasn't the only one inspired by George Bush. Around that same time, my brother Jeb announced that he was running for Governor of Florida. Jeb and I both felt—and Dad agreed—that he should not play a public role in our campaigns. It was important that the voters see us for what we were: our own men. Dad never intervened or offered unsolicited advice, but it was clear that he was following our races closely. From time to time I would check in with him, and he would always find a way to compliment a recent campaign performance or cheer me up after a lousy editorial. It struck me that our roles had been reversed. After years of my supporting him in the political arena, he was supporting me.

I think my campaign and Jeb's campaign in 1994 played an important role in helping Dad adjust to the new chapter of his life. Just as his father had done after he retired from the Senate in 1964, he embraced his new position as a source of encouragement for the next generation. And he found something positive about his defeat in 1992—it had given rise to the political careers of two people whom he had raised and loves.

On election night 1994, I won the Governor's race in Texas. Jeb lost a close race to Democratic Governor Lawton Chiles. When I called Dad to tell him that I was about to go deliver my victory speech, he told me how happy he was. But I could tell that he was preoccupied with Jeb's defeat. "The joy is in Texas," Dad told reporters, "but our hearts are in Florida." To some, his reaction was surprising. Not to me. It was typical of George Bush to focus on the person who was hurting.

On the morning of my inauguration as Governor—almost exactly two years after Mother and Dad left the White House— Mother brought me an envelope. Inside were a handwritten card and two small metal objects:

Dear George,
    These cufflinks are my most treasured possession. They were given to me by Mum and

Dad on June 9, that day in 1943 when I got my
Navy wings at Corpus Christi. I want you to
have them now; for, in a sense, though you won
your Air Force wings flying those jets, you are
again "getting your wings" as you take the oath
of office as our Governor. . . .

You have given us more than we ever could
have deserved. You have sacrificed for us. You
have given us your unwavering loyalty and devotion. Now it is our turn.

Dad's note moved me deeply. I knew how
much the cuff links—and their connection to
his father—meant to him. By passing on the
cuff links, he was passing on the love and support that he had received from his dad. When
it came time for the swearing in, Laura held a
family Bible, and Barbara and Jenna stood beside me. My parents were seated behind me. I
was not surprised when I later saw a photo cap-
turing the moment: As I took the oath of office,
Dad was wiping away a tear.

A FEW YEARS later, I received a different kind
of note from Dad. "Dear Kids," he wrote. "Okay,

so you might think I have lost it. I plan to make a parachute jump. So there!" I can't say that I saw that one coming from my seventy-two-year-old father. Dad's last parachute jump had come in 1944, when he bailed out of his flaming TBM Avenger amid Japanese anti-aircraft fire. That day he had hit his head on the plane and pulled the rip cord too early. He joked that he wanted an opportunity to correct his form. But what he really wanted was closure—to repeat the experience of jumping from a plane on his own terms.

Mother was not so sure. Her first response was to tell Dad and everyone else that she thought he was crazy. In spite of her seeming reluctance, she knew how important the jump was to him. She was happy that he was going to pursue his dream. Dad asked the Golden Knights, the Army's elite parachute squad, to jump with him. Colin Powell asked Dad if he was serious about his plan. "It's the talk of the Pentagon," Powell said, before mounting a cross-examination: Had Dad considered the risks? Were his knees and ankles in good shape? What about the wind? Apparently the Army brass was not keen on risking a skydiving accident involving the former Commander-in-Chief. They didn't know what they were up against: George Bush had a mission, and he was not turning back.

At the Governor's office one day, I received a call from Dad to inform me that the jump would take place at the Army base in Yuma, Arizona, on March 25, 1997. I congratulated him on making his dream a reality. "Just don't tell anyone about your eighteen-year-old girl-friend," I joked.

On the big day, Dad donned what he called his "Elvis suit"—white helmet and white gloves—and took the solo plunge (without any Golden Knights strapped to his back) from about twelve thousand feet. This time there was no contact between his head and the plane. Thanks to the fine training that he had received from the Golden Knights, he pulled the rip cord at the right time and floated safely to earth. Mother was there for the landing. As Dad later described it, "I was down. It had gone well. I had lived a dream. Bar hugged me and smiled. All was well with the world."

As it turned out, that parachute jump was not his last. He jumped again to celebrate his seventy-fifth, eightieth, eighty-fifth, and ninetieth birthdays. His adventures sent a signal to Americans of his generation: Getting older shouldn't stand in the way of staying active or trying new things. You might be a little slower or a little grayer, but life is rich enough that you can always find new areas to explore and new ways to push yourself. I like to think that I learned from Dad's example when I picked up a paintbrush for the first time at age sixty-six.

Two of Dad's parachute jumps came at his presidential library, which opened at Texas A&M in November 1997. Library dedications are one of the few occasions that bring together the sitting and former Presidents. All the members of the club were represented that day: President Clinton, who was coming off his reelection victory over Bob Dole in 1996, and former Presidents Carter and Ford. Lady Bird Johnson and Nancy Reagan came on behalf of their husbands. Given that President Reagan had announced a few years earlier that he was suffering from Alzheimer's disease, he did not attend.

As the President of Dad's library foundation, Jeb served as the master of ceremonies. As the sitting Governor of Texas, I had the honor of delivering the welcoming address. I took the opportunity to summarize the way I view my father's legacy, both as a President and as a man:

> President Bush was a man who entered the political arena and left with his integrity intact. President Bush was a leader who stared tyranny in the face and never blinked. George Bush was a great President of the United States of America, because he is first and foremost a great man—a man who through it all knew exactly what is most important in life: faith and family. Through four years of world crises and enormous demands on his time, a phone call from me or one of my brothers and sister never went unanswered. The world knows George Bush as a master of personal diplomacy. We know George Bush as the world's best dad.

Dad's speech was vintage George Bush. He thanked President Clinton, who "saw to it that [he had] a wonderful private life." He apologized if his presidential library violated his mother's rule against bragging. He didn't try to burnish his legacy, saying only that the archives housed there would allow future generations to sort it out for themselves. And he closed by saying, "Now that my political days are over, I can honestly say that the three most rewarding titles bestowed upon me are the three that I've got left—a husband, a father, and a granddad. . . . I don't know if Lou Gehrig, my great idol, said it first, but I do know that he said it best—today I feel like the luckiest person in the world."

AS THE YEARS passed and the sting of defeat subsided, Dad fully embraced his new life. Nothing gave him greater joy than being at Walker's Point with his family. He loved to organize tennis matches, pitch horseshoes, play speed golf at Cape Arundel (scoring was based on a combination of strokes and time), and entertain a constant stream of family and visitors. Perhaps his favorite thing to do was fire up his Mercury-powered Fountain speedboat, the **Fidelity**, and race through the water with the throttle at full blast. At age seventy-nine, he sent an e-mail to his grandchildren boasting that he had topped sixty miles per hour. "I felt about 19 years old," he wrote. While he followed politics closely, he was content to stay out of the arena. He liked to describe his role in the words of a Mandarin adage: "Stand on sidelines hands in sleeves."

Although Dad was retired from government, he was not finished serving. He gave his time and his name to causes that mattered to him, just as he had all his life. He served as Chairman of the Board of Visitors at the MD Anderson Cancer Center in Houston, a widely respected cancer hospital. He founded the Bush School of Government and Public Service at Texas A&M, and he loved to drop into classrooms as a surprise guest lecturer. He supported military charities and visited troops around the world. Mother continued to serve as well, creating the Barbara Bush Foundation for Family Literacy and reading books to children every summer at the Maine Medical Center in Portland. Throughout their lives, George and Barbara Bush have been two bright points of light.

Mother and Dad have traveled widely in their retirement. Dad loved to fly-fish, and he visited some of the world's greatest spots: Islamorada, Florida, with his friend Ted Williams; Canada with his grandson Jeb Jr.; and the river Test in England. He kept the family golf tradition alive by serving as the honorary Chairman of The First Tee and attending Ryder Cup and Presidents Cup matches. Occasionally he used his status as a former President to get himself invited to great golf courses like Augusta National or Pine Valley. And he loved to assemble interesting foursomes, such as the time that he and Jeb played with Arnold Palmer and Joe DiMaggio.

In November 1998, Mother and Dad took one of their most meaningful trips when they chartered a plane to Florida to be with Jeb on election night of his second race for Governor. He ran a great campaign and won 55 percent of the vote. For the first time in more than two decades, brothers served together as Governors. Mother liked to point out that one in eight Americans lived in a state governed by one of her sons. Dad expressed his pride a little more quietly. On the day before Jeb's election, he wrote, "People will call to congratulate us, but they will never begin to know the true depth of my feeling toward my sons. It will be what life is really all about for me right now."

I too was thrilled that Jeb won. In our early

years, our seven-year age separation seemed to matter, but as we got older, we became not only brothers but friends. He is a man of conviction with a great deal of inner strength. I was confident that the people of Florida would benefit from his leadership—and I was right. He was a strong and accomplished Governor.

AFTER MY 1998 reelection as Governor, Dad predicted that speculation about a presidential campaign would follow. He was sure right. Prospective advisers, fund-raisers, and organizers all over the country urged me to enter the race. As I told **Washington Post** reporter David Broder, I felt like a cork in a raging river. I was determined not to get swept away. I would make the decision for the right reasons and on my own terms.

More than any presidential candidate in recent history (with the exception of Hillary Clinton), I knew exactly what I was getting myself into. For all the so-called burdens of the presidency, I knew how much Dad had loved the job—the honor of leading a great country and the opportunity to make decisions that would change history. After my experience as Governor, I felt that I could handle the work. I understood the scrutiny that my family would face, and I was concerned about our daughters. But I had learned from my father's experience that it was possible to serve as President and leave office with your family stronger than before.

Mother's example also gave me confidence. One of her great contributions to my father's political career was ensuring that he never had to worry about whether she could handle the pressure of the presidency and at the same time hold our family together. That confidence is liberating. I was blessed that Laura gave me the same peace of mind.

Finally, I believed, as Dad did, in living life to the fullest—in pushing yourself to your limits and working hard for the causes in which you believe. I believed strongly that America needed a new direction on issues like education, taxes, and military readiness. And I believed that I could help provide the leadership that the American people sought.

I never felt the need to ask Dad for a direct opinion on whether I should run. I knew he would support whatever choice I made. And I knew from watching him my whole life that he believed everyone has a duty to serve. After a lot of soul-searching, I decided to give it a shot. I announced my candidacy on June 12, 1999 (coincidentally, my father's seventy-fifth birthday).

I was aware that there would be inevitable comparisons between Dad and me, some good and some not. He had assured me that I should feel free to criticize any of his decisions without fear of offending him. As he wrote in a 1998 letter to Jeb and me, "At some point both of you may want to say, 'Well, I don't agree with my Dad on that point' or 'Frankly I think Dad was wrong on that.' Do it. Chart your own course, not just on the issues but on defining yourselves. No one will ever question your love of family—your devotion to your parents."

When reporters would ask how my father would affect the race, I joked that I had inherited half of his friends and all of his enemies. The truth was that he didn't have many enemies, and I was able to pick up many of his friends. I had no qualms about Dad's friends supporting me. I was running against a sitting

Vice President at a time when the country appeared to be secure and the economy appeared to be strong. And as it turned out, I needed every vote I could get.

On election night, Mother and Dad led a huge convoy of family to Austin. A celebration began late in the evening when Vice President Gore called to concede the election. He then called back a little later to retract his concession. My lead in the pivotal state of Florida was less than a thousand votes—too close to call. A multiweek recount began. I asked Jim Baker to lead my legal team in Florida, while Laura and I retreated to our ranch in Crawford, Texas, to await my fate. Dad on the other hand was obsessed by the news. He constantly called Karl Rove and Jim Baker for updates. He called me frequently too. I could tell by the tone of his voice that he was worried. "Dad, I'm at peace," I said. "Stop watching TV."

Eventually, the legal dispute worked its way to the Supreme Court. On December 12, 2000, thirty-five days after the election, the Court delivered its judgment. By a vote of seven to two, the Justices determined that Florida's haphazard recount process violated the equal protection clause of the Constitution. And by a vote of five to four, they concluded that Florida could not complete a fair recount in time to meet the deadline for the Electoral College. The electoral count stood; I had won. After receiving the news that I had been elected President, the first phone call I made was to Mother and Dad. They were thrilled.

The next day, I addressed the nation from the Texas state capitol. As Mother and Dad watched the speech on television from bed at their home in Houston, the reality of the moment hit them. Dad later wrote, "I saw a couple of shots of George and Laura holding hands. I saw in his posture, in the way he walked in his smile the same mannerisms and expressions we have known ever since he was a little boy." He continued, "As the camera focused on George and Laura walking into the chamber my body was literally wracked with uncontrollable sobs. It just happened. No warning, no thinking that this might be emotional for a mother or dad to get through—just an eruption from deep within me where my body literally shook. Barbara cried, too. We held hands. Just before he began to speak we saw in George's eyes the emotion he was feeling. We know it so well. He did not 'lose it,' but he was clearly moved and his mother and father knew it for fact certain."

Shortly before the moment that so moved Dad, Vice President Gore had delivered a gracious speech conceding the election. That prompted an unexpected phone call. George H.W. Bush called Al Gore to congratulate him on his strong campaign and courageous speech. "I've lost a few times myself," Dad told him, "and I know how you feel."

ONLY TWO TIMES in American history has a President been sworn in with both his parents on hand to witness the moment. The first came in 1961, when Joseph and Rose Kennedy watched their son take the oath of office from Chief Justice Earl Warren. The second came in 2001, when my parents attended my inauguration. I was comforted to know that Mother and Dad were sitting behind me as Chief Justice Rehnquist swore me in as President.

After the swearing in, a luncheon in the Capitol, and the traditional inaugural parade down Pennsylvania Avenue, I went to the Oval

Office for the first time as President. Dad had gone upstairs to the White House residence to take a warm bath and thaw out from the frigid parade, but when the ushers told him that the President was waiting for him in the Oval Office, he hopped out, put on a suit, and came down. A few minutes later, the door swung open and he walked in. We spent a few minutes together just soaking in the moment. Over the next eight years, I would have many memorable meetings in the Oval Office. None compared to standing in the office with my father on my first day.

I made it clear that Mother and Dad had an open invitation to stay at the White House anytime. Laura and I were very happy that they came to Washington frequently, including on September 10, 2001, for a board meeting of a national cancer coalition that they had helped found. That day I flew to Florida, where I had an education event scheduled at a Sarasota school the following morning. Mother and Dad left Washington early on September 11 for a speaking engagement in Minnesota. Later that morning, America suffered the worst terrorist attack in our history—the first major assault on our home soil since the Pearl Harbor attack in 1941.

I knew Mother and Dad would be worried about me. As I was working my way back to Washington, I placed several calls to them from aboard Air Force One. When we finally connected, I asked where they were. "At a motel in Brookfield, Wisconsin," came the response from Mother. "What in the world are you doing there?" I asked. "Son, you grounded our plane," Mother said. Some things never change. Her quip was a light moment on a dark day.

Three days after the September 11 attacks, Laura and I attended a church service at the National Cathedral. Former Presidents Clinton, Carter, and Ford were there, along with Supreme Court Justices, Members of Congress, and—most important to me—Laura and my parents. "Just three days removed from these events, Americans do not yet have the distance of history," I said. "But our responsibility to history is already clear: to answer these attacks and rid the world of evil. War has been waged against us by stealth and deceit and murder. This nation is peaceful, but fierce when stirred to anger. This conflict was begun on the timing and terms of others. It will end in a way, and at an hour, of our choosing."

Delivering that speech without breaking down was challenging. Many people in the cathedral had tears streaming down their cheeks, including some military personnel. My strategy was not to look at Laura or my parents, because I knew that seeing them would push me over the edge. Fortunately, I made it to the end of my speech and returned to my pew. The former Presidents and their families were seated in chronological order, but Dad had asked Bill Clinton if he would be willing to switch places so that Mother and Dad could sit next to Laura and me. Bill had graciously agreed. Just after I sat down, Dad reached over Laura and gently squeezed my arm. My emotions were raw, and his simple, loving gesture brought me comfort, encouragement, and strength.

MOTHER AND DAD made many other visits to the White House over the years. One of the most enjoyable came in January 2005, when Laura and I hosted a party to celebrate their sixtieth wedding anniversary. The whole family came for a black-tie dinner filled with loving toasts and lots of laughter. After their fifty-fourth anniversary, my parents had passed John and Abigail Adams to claim the title of longest-married presidential couple. They are now just a few months away from extending their record to seventy years. In typical style, Dad wrote me a gracious note after the party. "I guess it's fair to say that at 80½ years old I have been to a lot of wonderful events; but, for us, none can compare with the gala. . . . Young and old, relatives and non-relatives, sophisticates and the unwashed, all had the time of their lives. Thanks so very much from the bottom of my achy breaky heart."

Dad and I spoke frequently throughout my presidency, although not necessarily about the topics that some people have assumed. In the limo after a State of the Union address or another big speech, I would often get a call from the White House operator: "Mr. President, your father is on the line." Dad would offer an encouraging and comforting word. I did not use e-mail during my presidency, but Dad would often forward a corny joke or one-liner to my senior aides, knowing that they would bring it into the Oval Office to brighten my day. For example, in 2007, he sent this along: "An eighty-year-old man was arrested for shoplifting. When he went before the judge he asked him what he stole. He replied, 'A can of peaches.' The judge asked how many peaches were in the can. 'Six,' he replied. 'Then I will give you six days in jail,' the judge said. Then the man's wife spoke up: 'He stole a can of peas too!'" George Bush understood the pressure of the presidency and the power of laughter to ease stress. His humor was often just what I needed.

My father and I did talk business from time to time. One common topic was personnel decisions. When I was considering options for my vice presidential nominee, I called to ask his advice about his former Secretary of Defense Dick Cheney. Without hesitating, he said, "Dick would be a great choice. He would give you candid and solid advice. And you'd never have to worry about him going behind your back." He was exactly right, and for eight years I was glad to have Vice President Cheney by my side.

Shortly after my election, I called Dad about another former member of his national security team, former Joint Chiefs Chairman Colin Powell. I was considering Colin for Secretary of State, my first Cabinet selection. "Colin is highly respected around the world," Dad said. "He would be a terrific Secretary of State."

Years later, when I was considering a change in Secretary of Defense, I called to ask his opinion on Bob Gates, his former Deputy National Security Adviser and CIA Director who was then serving as President of Texas A&M.

"Dad, I am considering Bob Gates to be Secretary of Defense," I said. "Do you have any thoughts?"

"I do," he said. "I have the highest respect for Bob Gates, and I think he would do a superb job.

"Do you think he'll do it?" he added.

"The indications are that he will," I said.

"Losing him would be a big loss for A&M but a big gain for the country," Dad said.

He was right. Bob Gates did a fine job as Secretary of Defense. And President Obama kept him on after he took office, making Bob the only Secretary of Defense to serve two Presidents of different parties.

During my presidency, Dad and I didn't talk

much about policy. He understood better than anyone that the President is surrounded by experts with in-depth information about the key issues. If I had asked for his advice on a policy matter, he would have said, "Send your briefers so that I know what I'm talking about." He knew that I had plenty of outside opinions. As the father of the President, he could provide something different: the love and support I needed to handle the pressure of the job.

One area that interested Dad was my relations with foreign leaders. Throughout his career, he had been a master of personal diplomacy—of getting to know people and earning their trust. I had witnessed how effective his approach had been. I held hundreds of face-to-face meetings (and made many more phone calls) with my key counterparts around the world. I invited fellow world leaders not only to the White House but also to Camp David, our ranch in Crawford, and Walker's Point.

In early 2007, I called Dad and asked him if he would invite President Vladimir Putin of Russia to Walker's Point. I felt that it would be a perfect place to discuss the missile defense

systems that we were planning to build in Poland and the Czech Republic.

Dad was thrilled about the idea. "Just let me
know what you need, son," he said.

When Putin arrived on July 1, 2007, Dad
met his plane at the airport in New Hampshire and accompanied him on the helicopter
ride to Walker's Point. Then he took both of us
for a speedboat ride. Although initially startled
by the idea of an eighty-three-year-old former
President driving the boat at top speed, Putin
loved the ride. (His interpreter looked like he
was about to fly out the back of the boat.) The
next morning, we had a long conversation about
missile defenses, in which we found some common ground. We then went fishing. Fittingly,
Putin was the only one who caught anything.

AS THE 2004 election approached, I naturally
thought back to my father's defeat in 1992. In
some ways, I was in an ominously similar position. Like him, my first term had included
approval ratings around 90 percent: after September 11 in my case, and after the Gulf War

in his. Those numbers declined over time, and my race against the Democratic nominee— Senator John Kerry of Massachusetts—looked close. On election night, the whole family gathered at the White House. I think Dad may have been more anxious this time than he was four years earlier. He remembered the agony of 1992, and he did not want me to endure the same pain. At the end of election night, I had a solid lead, but Kerry had not yet conceded. Early the next morning, Mother and Dad left for Houston. Later that morning, I got a call from John Kerry, who graciously conceded the election. I became the first President to win a majority of the popular vote since Dad in 1988. When I called to give him the good news, his reaction was more relief than excitement. The wound from 1992 healed a little more.

ON THE DAY after Christmas in 2004, a massive tsunami in the Indian Ocean devastated several Asian countries. The waves, one hundred feet high in some places, wiped away huge stretches of coastline and killed more than two hundred thousand people. I deployed American naval assets to help with the relief efforts. I decided to ask Dad and Bill Clinton to lead a private fund-raising campaign. I believed that a fund-raising drive led by these two former rivals would send an important signal about America's commitment to those suffering from the disaster.

I called Dad and Clinton to tell them about my idea. Both readily agreed to serve, and they raised an impressive amount of money for the relief effort. As part of their efforts, Dad and Clinton took a lengthy trip to the scene of the devastation. They had seen each other at official events over the years, but they didn't really know each other. That changed on their trip to Asia. Their military plane had only one bed, and Clinton generously let George Bush sleep on it every night. Dad appreciated Clinton's consideration. Like many, he marveled at Clinton's boundless energy and genuine interest in people. Outside the pressure cooker of a political campaign, it was hard not to like the man. The friendship that flourished between the two of them was something that I did not expect.

After Hurricanes Katrina and Rita struck the gulf coast in 2005, I decided to deploy the

odd couple again. Once again, they answered
the call, making multiple visits to the region
and filming public service announcements to
raise awareness about the needs of the victims.
Their bipartisan appeal inspired more than a
hundred million dollars in private donations.
When Hurricane Ike struck in 2008, I called
Presidents 41 and 42 into action for a third
time. Once again, they did a terrific job.

The friendship they formed through their
shared service has endured. Bill Clinton visits
my parents regularly in Maine. Over time, it
became clear that Clinton treated Dad as a sort
of father figure, perhaps because Clinton never
knew his father. Mother took to calling Clinton her long-lost fifth son—or, as Marvin put
it, "a brother from another mother." Clinton
embraced the image and started calling himself
the black sheep of the Bush family. He joked
that Barbara Bush would do anything to claim
another President in the family. In retrospect,
I am not surprised about the relationship that
developed between George Bush and Bill Clinton. Dad is a gracious man who always found
a way to see the best in others. Even the most
painful moment of his political career was not

an obstacle to befriending the man who defeated him.

When my second term ended in 2009, I was
fortunate to become the first President to leave
office with both parents alive. For one of my
final Oval Office meetings, I welcomed the
three living former Presidents—Bill Clinton,
Dad, and Jimmy Carter—and the incoming
President, Barack Obama. While we had our
differences on policy issues, we all enjoyed the
opportunity to sit together in the office that we
shared and to impart some advice to the new-
est member of the club. The President-elect
was gracious, and I noticed that he was particularly deferential to Dad. It was clear that he
genuinely respected and admired George Bush.
Two years later, President Obama awarded him
the Presidential Medal of Freedom, the highest
civilian honor that the President can bestow.
After recounting Dad's accomplishments, President Obama said, "His life is a testament that
public service is a noble calling."

In an era characterized by bitter partisanship, George Bush set an example as a man who
put civility and decency ahead of the ugliness
of politics. When powerful Democratic Con-

gressman Dan Rostenkowski was convicted and sent to prison for his role in the House post office scandal, most of his Washington colleagues abandoned him. Not George Bush. He and Rosty had known each other since they served together on the House Ways and Means Committee in the 1960s. Dad called Rosty in prison, hoping to lift his spirits and helping him pass the time. And it probably helped Rosty's standing a little bit that the warden knew the former President could call at any moment.

Earlier this year, President Obama (who is not popular in Texas) stopped in Houston for a political fund-raiser on the way to an event celebrating the civil rights legacy of Lyndon Johnson. When he came down the steps of Air Force One, George H.W. Bush was waiting on the tarmac in his wheelchair. "When the President comes to your hometown," he said, "you show up and welcome him."

Dad set an example in other ways. He continued to play golf, fish, and take long walks well into his eighties. As he said in an interview after a parachute jump on his eighty-fifth birthday, "Just because you're an old guy, you don't have to sit around drooling in the corner.

Get out and do something. Get out and enjoy life."

Around 2010, Dad's athletic body started to fail him. He was diagnosed with parkinsonism, a condition similar to Parkinson's disease that affects his ability to move his lower body. He can no longer exercise like he loved to do. Eventually he could no longer walk and had to use a wheelchair. Still, he lives joyfully. Sitting in his wheelchair, he realized that his socks were among the most visible parts of his wardrobe. So he started wearing brightly colored socks. His favorites are red, white, and blues. Even though it is a struggle for him to climb in and out of his wheelchair, he accepts invitations to public events. After all, he is the President who signed the Americans with Disabilities Act. He continues his prolific correspondence and constantly entertains people in Houston and especially at Walker's Point. As always, he has a special place in his heart for those who were suffering. When he learned that one of his Secret Service agents had a two-year-old son undergoing treatment for leukemia, my eighty-nine-year-old father shaved his head in solidarity with the boy.

Dad does not do things like that to get attention. He is just living out the values that have defined his whole life. One of his favorite quotes is: "Preach the Gospel at all times; if necessary, use words." Over time, people began to take notice, and there was an outpouring of public affection for Dad. I am so pleased that George Bush's accomplishments and character are receiving the recognition that they deserve—and that he is able to see it. Numerous institutions have named things in his honor: Houston's George Bush Intercontinental Airport, the George Bush Center for Intelligence in Langley, Virginia (the CIA headquarters), the President George Bush Turnpike in Dallas, and—perhaps his favorite—the USS **George H.W. Bush,** a Nimitz-class aircraft carrier.

AS DEVOTED AS he has always been to public service, what matters most to George H.W. Bush is his family. When he said that he no longer pursued happiness because he had found happiness, it was his family that he had in mind. He is especially affectionate with his grandchildren and great-grandchildren. He devotes enormous time and energy to developing a relationship with each of them, smothering them in a blanket of love. He sends cards or e-mails about their part in the school play or game-winning hit in Little League. And in Maine during the summers, he always loves when they arrive.

In November 2012, Dad checked into Houston Methodist hospital with a bad cough. When Laura and I went to visit a few days later, he was wearing a brace around his abdomen and obviously suffering serious pain. "How you feeling, Dad?" I asked. He smiled. "It's not the cough that carries you off; it's the coffin you go off in," he quipped. In typical fashion, he lifted our spirits.

His condition worsened in early December. The brutal, hacking cough turned to pneumonia. I called him often. I wanted to hear his voice and gauge his strength. At the end of every phone call, I said, "I love you." He would always reply, "I love you more."

Fearing the worst, our family surrounded Dad. My brother Neil sat for hours at his bedside reading aloud to him. Jeb, Marvin, and Doro visited with their families. Laura and I made another trip to the hospital in December. This time we brought Barbara and Jenna, who was five months pregnant. Before we went in, I told everyone not to cry. I did not want Dad to sense our despair. As we entered the room, he could barely open his eyes and his voice was weak.

"Hi, George, how are you? And there's Laura. Hi, beautiful." He lay back contently as Barbara and Jenna rubbed his head. Then he reached out and gently put his hand on Jenna's pregnant belly.

"There's death," he said, "and there's new life." We all left the room sobbing.

Long ago, Lieutenant George Bush had narrowly escaped death in the Pacific. For the next seventy years, he made the most of the life God had spared. He and my mother raised and loved six children. He served his fellow citizens at the highest level, striving above all to advance the cause of peace. He has lived a life of faith, devoted to his family. In the winter of 2012, when he was still in a weakened state, I reminded him that my presidential library was scheduled to open the following April.

"I'll be there, son," he said.

Sure enough, when, on a beautiful sunny day in Dallas, the current and former Presidents gathered at SMU, George H.W. Bush was there. He had battled through the illness and regained his strength. He was in his wheelchair sitting tall. When it was his turn to speak, his voice was strong. "It's a great pleasure to be here to honor our son, our oldest son," he said, trying hard to control his emotions. "This is very special for Barbara and me. . . . We're glad to be here. God bless America, and thank you very much." The crowd gave him a standing ovation. I cherished the moment, which a few months earlier had seemed like an unlikely dream. Then he turned to me.

"Too long?" he asked with a twinkle in his eye.

"Perfect, Dad," I said.

ACKNOWLEDGMENTS

ONE OF MY FATHER'S LESSONS is to share credit, and I am fortunate to have many people to thank for their help with this book. The list starts, of course, with its subject, George Herbert Walker Bush. By the time I started work on this project, my father's memory had faded. Aside from an occasional flash of recall, he did not contribute to the research or writing. But his lifelong collection of letters and diaries proved an invaluable resource. I frequently found myself chuckling or wiping a tear.

I asked Mother a lot of questions for this book. She provided some facts and many opinions. She retains a dazzling memory of her nearly seventy years as Mrs. Barbara Bush, and her wit has not dulled a bit. She holds a place

415

in history shared only by Abigail Adams, and she is worthy of a book of her own. I don't plan to write it, but I will say this: My mother influenced me as much as my father did. Every day of my life, I have been grateful for her devotion, her humor, and her love.

I am not the first of George Bush's children to write a biography of him. My sister Dorothy authored a fine book called **My Father, My President** that provided ideas and inspiration. My brother Marvin read the manuscript of this book, and it turns out that Marv is a fine editor. Some of the deepest insights come from him. My brothers Neil and Jeb provided stories, even though Jeb has a few other things on his mind these days. And my father's siblings—my aunt Nancy, uncle Jonathan, and uncle Bucky— all took time to talk to me about this project. (Unfortunately, my uncle Prescott passed away in 2010.) I appreciate the memories they shared and the kindness they have shown to me throughout my life.

Like everything in my life, this book is better because my wife and daughters were involved. Laura, Barbara, and Jenna answered questions, volunteered ideas, and provided constant love and support—as did my son-in-law, Henry, and my granddaughter, Mila, who joined our lives on April 13, 2013 (about two months shy of her great-grandfather's eighty-ninth birthday). As Dad says often, family is what matters most. That makes me a very lucky man.

I was also lucky to have help on this project from many people outside my family, starting with my dear friend Chris Michel. Chris has one of the great minds in our country, and I sincerely thank him.

I also thank Bob Barnett. In the world of political publishing, there's Bob Barnett—and then there's everyone else. I am grateful for his humor, his advice, and his patience (which always comes more easily when you're billing by the hour). Bob is more than an agent; he is a friend.

When I started writing this book, I was unsure when (or even whether) I would publish it. One reason that it made it into print is the tremendous team at Crown Publishers. For the second time in four years, I have been fortunate to work with Maya Mavjee and Tina

Constable. They helped make my last book a bestseller and encouraged me to try for the literary equivalent of reelection. This time, I also benefited from the superb editorial guidance of Mary Choteborsky and Molly Stern. Mary and Molly were unfailingly resourceful, encouraging, and responsive, often on short deadlines. I thank them and everyone else at Crown who helped make this project succeed, including deputy publisher David Drake and audio producer Dan Zitt, as well as the entire design and production team: Emma Berry, Amy Boorstein, Chris Brand, Linnea Knollmueller, Rachel Meier, Aja Pollock, Elizabeth Rendfleisch, and Neil Spitkovsky.

This book benefited from the research and assistance of many others. Emily Kropp Michel tracked down obscure historical data, turned up colorful stories and quotes, and verified countless facts. Two good friends, former Secretary of State Condi Rice and former National Security Adviser Steve Hadley, read the manuscript and offered many valuable suggestions.

Another trusted reader was the incomparable Jean Becker, my father's Chief of Staff for the past twenty years and for all purposes a member of the Bush family. Jean supported this project from day one, and it could not have happened without her. I am grateful to the other members of Dad's current and former staff who answered my calls for help, including Jim McGrath and Coleman Lapointe. And I appreciate the professionals at the George Bush and George W. Bush Presidential Libraries who spent many hours in the archives helping with this project, especially Bob Holzweiss, Debbie Wheeler, and Mary Finch at the 41 Library, and Jodie Steck and Sarah Barca at the 43 Library.

Finally, I thank the team at the Office of George W. Bush, led by my able Chief of Staff Mike Meece, who provided valuable advice on this book. Freddy Ford was not only a fine editor; he also compiled the wonderful photo section while serving as my communications director and personal aide. Logan Dryden and Caroline Nugent made important contributions throughout the project, and everyone in the office helped to make the book possible: Brian Cossiboom, Harrison Horowitz, Christina Piasta, Carol White, and Tobi Young, as well as Caroline Hickey and Audrey Akers from Laura's staff.

When I embarked on this project, I knew that many people like George H.W. Bush. What I did not fully understand was how many people adore him. My greatest challenge has been to capture the profound impact that my father has had on my life and the lives of many others. Following the advice that his mother gave him, I have strived to do my best. I hope the result is a good book; I know it's a great story.

INDEX

Abraham Lincoln, USS, 33
Adams, Abigail, 399
Adams, John, xi, 16, 164, 349, 399
Adams, John Quincy, xi, 16
Afghanistan, 145, 206, 282, 310, 315
Agee, Philip, 175
Agnew, Spiro, 161
Ailes, Roger, 245–46
Alaska International Air, 162
Alfalfa Club, 21
Alibi Club, 138, 140
Alito, Sam, 333
Allen, Ethan, 56
Allen, Woody, 271

Allison, Jimmy, 121
All Veteran Group, 4
al-Qaeda, 218, 300, 309–10, 315–16
America First Committee, 343
American Civil Liberties Union (ACLU), 267
Americans for Bush, 269
Americans with Disabilities Act, 329, 409
Anderson, John, 191
Andover, Mass., 22–24, 25, 31, 42, 98, 109, 120
Andrews Air Force Base, 132, 210, 215

Andropov, Yuri, 219
Apawamis Club, 25
Apollo 8, 138
Arab League, 301
Arizona, USS, 33, 319
Arlington National
    Cemetery, 209
Ashley, Lud, 53–54
Atwater, Lee, 233–34,
    235–37, 241, 252,
    254, 337, 341
Austin, Tex., 109, 213,
    393
Aziz, Tariq, 304

Baghdad, 306, 314
Baker, Howard, 191
Baker, James A., III,
    191–92, 204, 211,
    219, 257–58, 265,
    277, 302, 304, 341,
    354, 376, 393
Baker, Mary, 192
Baldwin, Raymond, 99
Barbara Bush
    Foundation for
    Family Literacy, 388
Bartlett, Charlie, 123
Bayh, Birch, 263

Becker, Jean, 1
Beijing, 147, 165, 169,
    171, 286, 287
Belknap, USS, 293
Bemiss, Gerry, 56, 181
Bentsen, Lloyd, 134–36,
    256, 272–73
Berlin Wall, 292, 294
Bernstein, Carl, 161
Bethesda Naval
    Hospital, 222
bin Laden, Osama, 218,
    301
Birth Control League,
    100
Black Mountain Boys,
    114
Black September, 148
Blair, Tony, 168
Blount, Red, 184
Borman, Frank, 138
Boutros-Ghali,
    Boutrous, 369
Bradley, Bill, 249
Bradley, James, 47
Brady, James, 213
Brando, Marlon, 91
Breen, Jon, 200
Brennan, William, 331

Brezhnev, Leonid, 219–20
Briscoe, Frank, 118
Broder, David, 390
Brokaw, Tom, 253
Bromfield, Louis, 58
Brown, Jerry, 351
Brown Brothers Harriman, 17, 56, 72, 99
Buchanan, Pat, 342–44, 345, 346, 348, 354, 355, 357, 364
Buckeye Steel, 14
Burning Tree Club, 102
Bush, Barbara (author's daughter), 122, 202, 227, 261, 270, 274, 279, 298, 335, 382, 391, 412
Bush, Barbara Pierce (author's mother), 2, 4, 6, 29–30, 42–43, 45, 46, 50, 51, 52–53, 54, 57, 58, 60–62, 65, 67–68, 76, 78–79, 80–82, 84–85, 96, 110, 113, 114, 121, 134, 142, 145–46, 148, 153, 159, 161, 165, 169, 170, 171–72, 183, 187, 192, 196, 199, 207, 209, 210–11, 223, 232, 236, 241–42, 255, 262, 264, 275–76, 278, 279, 280, 283–84, 297, 305, 319, 335, 338, 341–42, 357, 365, 371, 374, 375, 377–78, 381, 383, 384, 388, 389, 391, 395, 396, 398–99, 404, 406, 412, 413
Bush, Bucky, 74
Bush, Columba, 180, 227, 258
Bush, Doro (author's sister), 16, 85, 96, 120, 146, 196, 245, 259, 286, 368, 411
Bush, Dorothy Walker, 9–13, 15–16, 20, 21–22, 30, 33, 49, 52, 82, 85, 86, 125, 145, 150, 167, 169,

Bush, Dorothy Walker
(**cont.**)
208, 224–25, 281,
322, 368–69, 381,
386
Bush, George H.W., xii,
178–79, 180–82,
386–87, 413
accepted to Yale, 24
as Alfalfa Club
presidential
candidate, 20
athleticism of, 23, 24,
54–56, 124, 167,
192, 203, 222,
228–29, 388–89,
408
as aviator, 1–2, 26,
28–29, 34–36,
37–38, 40–41,
81, 87, 244, 260,
382–83
Barbara's first meeting
with, 25
birth of, 16
book written by, 376
budget compromise
(1990) and, 326–29,
343, 359

as Chairman of Harris
County Republican
Party, 107–9, 117
character of, 6, 22–24,
49, 122, 201, 219,
261, 275, 410
children's bonding
with, 72–73, 76–77,
357
as China Liaison
Officer, 164–71,
172, 217, 260, 286,
287–88
as CIA director,
171–78, 180, 260
civil rights and,
128–29, 329, 343
Clinton's post-
presidency
relationship with,
405–7
competitiveness of,
203, 204, 336
congressional
campaign (1966) of,
118–19
as congressman, 120,
123–25, 136,
138–42, 244, 260

considered for vice
president, 163
corporate roles of,
182
criticisms of, 113, 144,
156, 173, 201–2,
240, 244, 251, 269,
318, 343, 360
diary of, 306, 363,
369
domestic agenda of,
325
education of, 22–23,
42, 51–54
eighty-fifth birthday
of, 2, 3–4, 408
emotional expression
of, 82, 83, 85, 377,
382, 394–95
engagement of, 29–30
false extramarital
affair rumor about,
241
family as important
to, 6, 73, 120,
223–24, 225–27,
274, 410–11
father's death and,
150–51

father's impact on,
17–19, 21, 101, 104,
150
father's run for Senate
and, 98–101
finances of, 181, 194
on **Finback,** 39–40,
41–42
flight training of,
28–29, 59
foreign policy of, 146,
284–85, 325
friendship as
important to,
53–54, 123, 160,
195
Gorbachev and,
290–94, 302,
317–18, 320–22
Gulf War and,
298–308, 311,
403–4
and GWB's
congressional
campaign, 184, 185,
188
on GWB's election
as president,
394–95

Bush, George H.W.
(cont.)
and GWB's
gubernatorial
campaign, 378–81
and GWB's
presidency, 312–14,
395–96, 398–403
as hard worker, 53,
55, 66, 80–81, 123,
125, 195–97, 250
health problems of,
97–98, 336, 374,
409, 411–13
as hesitant about
re-election, 334–35,
337
humility and modesty
of, 6, 11–12, 23, 92,
125, 292
Hurricane Andrew
and, 359, 364
impact of World
War II on, 46–49
independence of,
57, 60
Iran-Contra affair
and, 239, 245–46,
276, 364

job opportunities for,
56–60, 72, 88
judiciary influence of,
330–32
leadership ability of,
22, 97, 175–76
letter and e-mail
writing of, 30,
34–35, 40, 90,
111, 123, 156–57,
158, 225, 227, 230,
232, 288–89, 291,
303–4, 369, 374,
381–82, 392, 399
loyalty and
trustworthiness
of, 212–13, 216,
258
marriage of, 50–51,
77, 84–85
mother's relationship
with, 10–11, 13,
224–25
in move to Houston,
95–96
in move to West
Texas, 60–66
Navy joined by,
25–26, 28–29

ninetieth birthday of,
1–7, 41
in oil industry, 58–60,
67, 68–69, 88–97,
111, 113, 169, 182
open-housing bill and,
129–31, 244, 329
Operation Desert
Storm and, 305–7
Operation Just Cause
and, 295–96
parachute jumps of,
1–7, 16, 38,
383–85, 408
parenting approach
of, 75–77, 121–22,
378–79
perceived weakness of,
156, 201, 244, 247
pneumonia of, 1
as president, 35, 41,
146, 168, 176, 179,
223, 253, 276,
277–308, 317–323,
324–72
presidential run
considered by, 183
presidential campaign
(1980) of, 85,
190–91, 192–93,
195–205, 240, 247
presidential campaign
(1988) of, 11–12,
233–34, 235–75,
337, 349, 354, 355,
358, 359, 404
presidential campaign
(1992) of, 253, 289,
323, 325, 329,
336–38, 341–67,
372, 379, 403–4
presidential
inauguration (1989)
of, 21, 280–84
Quayle selected as
running mate of,
263–67, 354–55
Reagan as good friend
of, 221, 223
in Reagan presidential
campaign (1984),
227–34
as religious, 6, 39, 42,
45, 56, 72, 86, 123,
169, 278–79, 282,
306
as Republican, 18,
106–7, 110

Bush, George H.W.
(**cont.**)
as RNC chairman,
152–53, 156–60,
163, 193, 227–28
Robin's death and,
83–86
Robin's illness and,
79, 80–81, 82–83
senatorial campaign
(1964) of, 109–17,
192, 274
senatorial campaign
(1970) of, 134–37,
192, 256
sense of humor of,
3, 31–32, 74, 149,
204–5, 221, 370,
399–400
sharing by, 21
space program interest
of, 138
staph infection of, 85
tough decisions
made by, 26,
131–32
in transition to
private life, 373–77,
387

as UN Ambassador,
142–49, 151, 164,
172, 173, 217
as underdog, 190–91,
195, 203
as vice president,
206, 208–34,
237–40, 243, 246,
251, 255, 258, 259,
262, 273, 277,
279–80, 290, 337,
346, 366
Vietnam trip of,
126–27, 128, 129,
130
Vietnam War
supported by,
126–27
Walker's Point
purchased by, 182
wartime nickname of,
31–32
on Watergate scandal,
156–57
wedding of, 43
in World War II, 1–2,
30–46, 81, 85, 87,
244, 252, 263, 293,
319, 383

at Yale, 50, 51–55, 64, 228
Bush, George Prescott, 180, 258–59, 356
Bush, George W., xi–xii, 21, 59, 65, 69, 75–76, 77, 94–95, 116, 121–22, 136, 162–63, 170, 208, 278–79, 332–33, 378
as artist, xi, 3, 385
birth of, 51–52
congressional campaign (1978) of, 184–87
criticisms of, 201–2, 242
education of, 22
father's birthday and, 1–7
in father's presidential campaign (1980), 196–97
in father's presidential campaign (1988), 11, 235–37, 241–44, 247, 259, 264–65, 271, 273–74
in father's presidential campaign (1992), 340–41
in father's Senate campaigns, 112, 113–15, 134, 184, 274
as governor, 340, 371, 384, 385–86, 389–90, 391
on grandmother, 12–13
gubernatorial campaign (1994) of, 136, 231, 378–81
gubernatorial inauguration of, 381–82
at Harvard Business School, 155, 170, 183
Hurricane Katrina and, 360, 405
Iraq War and, 312–16
marriage of, 186–87
on Nixon, 141–42, 159
in oil industry, 183, 205, 235

Bush, George W. (**cont.**)
  Operation Iraqi
    Freedom and,
    313–15
  as pilot, 28, 134,
    139–40, 162, 382
  as president, 33, 140,
    145, 168, 176, 190,
    222, 223, 245, 248,
    249, 285, 309–16,
    340, 395–96,
    398–403
  presidential campaign
    (2000) of, 119, 198,
    233, 262, 278–79,
    345, 362, 390–94
  presidential campaign
    (2004) of, 242, 362,
    403–4
  presidential
    inauguration of
    (2001), 21,
    395–96
  presidential
    inauguration of
    (2005), 21
  Robin's death and, 83
  September 11, 2001,
    26, 214, 300,
    309–10, 396–97,
    403
  sports played by,
    76, 92
  as Texas Rangers
    comanaging
    partner, 297, 329,
    340
  troop surge in Iraq
    ordered by, 132
Bush, Georgia Helena
  Walker, 227
Bush, James Smith, 14
Bush, Jeb, 21, 73, 80,
  96, 120, 157, 180,
  196, 227, 234, 259,
  356, 372, 380–81,
  385, 389–90, 392,
  441
Bush, Jenna, 4, 41, 122,
  202, 227, 242, 261,
  270, 274, 279, 298,
  335, 382, 391, 412
Bush, John Ellis (Jeb),
  Jr. 227, 388
Bush, Jonathan, 13, 43
Bush, Laura Welch,
  xi, 2, 77, 186–87,
  188–89, 205, 208,

223, 236, 260, 274, 279, 298, 336, 373, 382, 391, 394, 396, 397, 398, 411–12
Bush, Margaret, 226
Bush, Marshall, 226
Bush, Marvin, 5, 96, 102, 120, 121, 196, 225–26, 245, 259, 271, 406, 411
Bush, Nancy, 155
Bush, Neil Mallon, 89, 96, 120, 185, 196, 259, 298, 330, 333–35, 411
Bush, Obadiah, 57
Bush, Prescott, 13–21, 22, 24, 26–27, 49, 52, 54, 56, 58, 59, 62, 82, 89, 98–105, 110–11, 112, 115, 117, 123, 125, 130, 134, 150–51, 164, 281, 369, 380, 382
Bush, Prescott, Jr., 21, 43
Bush, Robin, 67, 78–86, 150, 192, 226, 314
Bush, Sandra, 227
Bush, S.P., 14, 58

Bush, Walker, 226
Bush Belles, 114
Bush-Overbey, 89–90, 92
Bush School of Government and Public Service, 388
Butchart, Stan, 31

Cahoon, Frank, 117
California, 67–68, 204
Camp David, 151, 233, 295–96, 299, 303, 313, 340, 371–72
Card, Andy, 340, 360
Carpenter, Liz, 133
Carswell Air Force Base, 213
Carter, Jimmy, 177, 178, 180, 184, 195, 196, 206, 210, 212, 229, 346, 385, 397, 407
Carvey, Dana, 370
Carvey, Paula, 370
Central Command, U.S., 299
Central Intelligence Agency (CIA), 171–78, 180, 309, 410

Cepeda, Orlando, 228
C. Fred (cocker spaniel),
    169, 170
Challenger, 219
Chambers, C. Fred, 138
Chambers, Marion, 138
Cheney, Dick, 223, 233,
    262, 285, 300, 307,
    340, 400
Cheney, Lynne, 223
Chernenko, Konstantin,
    219, 220
Chiao Kuan Hua, 167
Chichi Jima, 36, 45, 47
Chiles, Lawton, 381
China, 147, 164–70, 217,
    286–89, 291, 303
Church Committee, 172
Churchill, Winston, 372
Civil Rights Act (1964),
    113, 128–29
Civil Rights Act (1991),
    329
C.K. Bronson, USS, 35
Clean Air Act
    Amendments
    (1990), 330
Clements, Bill, 204
Click, Jim, 208

Clinton, Bill, 177, 178,
    224, 256, 289, 309,
    312, 349–50, 356,
    358, 359, 361–62,
    363, 366–68,
    373–74, 385, 386,
    397, 398, 405–7
Clinton, Chelsea, 224
Clinton, Hillary, 224,
    351, 357, 374, 390
Cold War, 221, 278,
    282, 302, 321, 358,
    372
Columbus, Ohio, 14, 58
Commerce Department,
    U.S., 211, 367
Committee to Re-Elect
    the President
    (CREEP), 153
Communist Party, 147,
    168
Congress, U.S., 99, 105,
    118–19, 158, 172,
    174, 216, 238, 255,
    302, 304–5, 309,
    311, 326–27, 364
    see also House of
    Representatives,
    U.S.; Senate, U.S.

Connally, John, 111, 191, 202

Connecticut, 19, 57, 98–99, 119, 198, 203

Connecticut National Guard, 15

Connor, Bull, 128

Constitution, U.S., 304, 394

Contras, 238–39

Cooke, Terence, 149

Coral Sea, Battle of, 34

Corpus Christi Naval Air Station, 29, 59, 382

Cowden Park, 92

Cox, Jack, 111

Craig, Earle, 74–75

Cramer, Richard Ben, 82

Crane, Phil, 191

Crawford, Tex., xi, 402

Crimea, 318

Cuba, 145, 303

Cuban Missile Crisis, 321

Cub Scouts, 76, 78

Cuomo, Mario, 349

Curley, James Michael, 103

Czechoslovakia, 291

Czech Republic, 403

Dallas, Tex., 63, 348, 371, 410

Darfur, 145

Dart, Justin, 208

Dart, Steve, 208

Davis, Milton, 111

Dedeaux, Rod, 55

Defense Department, U.S., 346

Delahanty, Thomas, 213

Delaney, John, 37–38, 40, 47

Delaney, Mary Jane, 40

Democratic National Committee (DNC), 153, 160

Democratic National Convention, 353–54

Democratic Party, 17, 105, 106, 110, 113–14, 136, 172, 238, 325, 327–28, 353

Deng Xiaoping, 168, 286, 288
Denver, John, 145
Detroit, Mich., 205, 206
DiMaggio, Joe, 389
Dodd, Chris, 104
Dodd, Thomas J., 104
Dole, Bob, 152, 191, 201, 202, 248, 251–52, 264, 385
Dresser Industries, 58, 59, 67, 69, 88
Dukakis, Kitty, 271
Dukakis, Michael, 224, 255–56, 260, 267–70, 271–72, 273, 275, 354, 361
Dulles, Allen, 176
du Pont, Pete, 249

Eagleburger, Lawrence, 288–89
Eagleton, Tom, 151
East Germany, 291, 292
Economist, 330
Edwards, Bill, 39
Ehrlichman, John, 142

Eisenhower, Dwight, 102, 112, 117, 151, 263
Electronic Data Systems, 345
Elizabeth II, Queen of England, 336
Elliott, Mike, 5
Esquire, 237
Europe, 144, 145, 217–18, 290–94, 317–18, 325

Fahd, King of Saudi Arabia, 300, 301
Fair Housing Act, 129, 329
Fang Lizhi, 286
Farm, The (Bromfield), 58
Federal Bureau of Investigation (FBI), 157
Federal Deposit Insurance Corporation, 334
Federal Highway Act, 103
Ferraro, Geraldine, 229–30, 232, 273

Fidelity, 93, 387
Finback, USS, 39–40,
    41–42, 48
Finland, 221, 302
First International
    Bancshares, 182
First Presbyterian
    Church, 72
First United Methodist
    Church, 70
Florida, 184, 217, 219,
    360, 389–90, 393
Flyboys (Bradley), 47
Ford, Gerald, 118, 125,
    161–64, 168, 171,
    173, 174, 176–77,
    180, 188, 191, 204,
    205, 211, 250, 277,
    385, 397
Fort Worth, Tex., 69,
    213, 214, 226
France, 15, 164, 303,
    376
Fund for Limited
    Government, 190

Gaddis, John Lewis, 321
Garner, John Nance, 211
Gates, Bob, 401

Gdansk, 290
Gehrig, Lou, 55, 387
Gelb, Bruce, 23
Geneva, 221, 304
George Bush Center for
    Intelligence, 178,
    410
George Bush
    Intercontinental
    Airport, 410
George Bush
    Presidential Library
    (at Texas A&M),
    195, 215, 375,
    385–86
George H.W. Bush,
    USS, 410
George W. Bush
    Presidential Center,
    412
George Washington
    University Hospital,
    213–14
Gephardt, Dick, 255
Germany, 15, 218, 291,
    292, 319
Gerson, Mike, 262
Gingrich, Newt, 327
Gladney Home, 226

Godfather, The, 146
Goldberg, Arthur, 143
Golden Knights, 383
Gold Rush, 57
Goldwater, Barry, 115, 116
Gorbachev, Mikhail, 220, 282, 287, 290–93, 302, 317–19, 320–22
Gore, Al, Jr., 255, 268, 351, 353, 359, 362, 393, 395
Grab, Lou, 31
Grace-New Haven Hospital, 51
Graham, Billy, 280, 306
Grand Ole Opry, 375
Great Britain, 97, 164, 372
Great Society, 112
Greenwich, Conn., 10–11, 12, 16, 25, 52, 60, 61, 82, 99, 110, 145, 167, 368
Greenwich Country Day School, 22

Greenwich Representative Town Meeting, 18
Gregg, Hugh, 198
Gregg, Judd, 198
Grenada, 304
Gulf of Mexico, 93
Gulf War, 298–308, 311, 312, 325, 347, 403
Gurney, Edward, 184
Guy, Jack, 31

Haig, Alexander, 158, 214, 249
Haldeman, H.R., 142
Hale, Nathan, 20
Hall, Arsenio, 351
Hammerschmidt, John Paul, 125
Hamon, Jake, 169–70
Hamon, Nancy, 169–70
Hampton, Lionel, 175
Hance, Kent, 185, 190
Harriman, Roland "Bunny," 17
Harriman, William Averell, 8, 17

Harris County
    Republican Party,
    107–9
Harrison, William
    Henry, 235
Hart, Gary, 229, 241
Harvard Business
    School, 155, 170
Havel, Václav, 291
Hayden, Michael, 177
Hezbollah, 218, 238
Hinckley, John, 213
Hirohito, Emperor of
    Japan, 284, 301
Hiroshima, 45, 48
Holdridge, John, 166
Horton, Willie, 269
House of
    Representatives,
    U.S., 99, 129, 142,
    151, 184, 237, 312,
    348, 408
  Appropriations
    Committee of, 125
  Ways and Means
    Committee of, 125,
    133–34, 408
Houston, Sam, 31

Houston, Tex., 84,
    95–96, 107, 110, 111,
    117, 118, 119, 120,
    123, 130, 134, 138,
    146, 157, 178, 180,
    186, 192, 204, 243,
    278, 356, 365, 373,
    375, 377, 388, 394,
    404, 408, 409, 410
Houston Astros, 96,
    194, 226
Houstonian Hotel, 275,
    358, 365
Houston Oilers, 96
Hu Jintao, 289
Humphrey, Hubert, 132
Hungary, 290–91
Hunt, H. L., 59
Hurricane Andrew,
    359–60, 364
Hurricane Ike, 406
Hurricane Katrina, 360,
    405
Hurricane Rita, 405
Hussein, Saddam, 127,
    298–99, 301,
    302–8, 309,
    310–15, 317, 327

Iceland, 221
Ideco (International Derrick and Equipment Company), 59
INF Treaty, 282
Iowa, 196–99, 240, 245–50, 253, 330, 350
Iran, 206, 210, 238, 239, 299, 315
Iran-Contra affair, 238–39, 245–46, 276, 364
Iraq, 132, 145, 298–99, 301–2, 305–7, 309, 312–16, 358
Iraqi Liberation Act, 309
Iraq War, 312–16
Iron Curtain, 217
Islamic State of Iraq and Syria (ISIS), 316
Israel, 100, 148–49, 343

Jackson, Jesse, 255
Jacksonville, Fla., 187
Japan, 2, 24, 33–34, 35–36, 39, 44, 47–48, 165, 284–85, 319, 341, 383
Javits, Jacob, 149
Jaworski, Leon, 157
Jefferson, Thomas, 20, 164, 349
Jensen, Jackie, 54
John Birch Society, 108–9
John Paul II, Pope, 290
Johnson, Lady Bird, 133, 385
Johnson, Lyndon Baines, 101, 107, 112, 115–17, 127, 130, 132–33, 136, 144, 256, 408
Johnson Space Center, 138
Jones, Bobby, 14

Kaifu, Toshiki, 301
Kemp, Jack, 249, 264
Kennebunkport, Maine, 2, 7, 8, 9, 12, 16, 63, 324, 376
Kennedy, Bobby, 141
Kennedy, John F., 101, 112, 128, 191, 213,

256, 263, 272–73, 395
Kennedy, Joseph, 395
Kennedy, Rose, 395
Kennedy, Ted, 342–43
Kerry, John, 362, 404
King, Larry, 346, 364
King, Martin Luther, Jr., 128, 141
Kinkaid, 96
Kissinger, Henry, 147, 168, 173
Kohl, Helmut, 301
Koizumi, Junichiro, 285
Korean War, 304
Kremlin, 293, 318, 320
Kuwait, 127, 167, 298–308, 317, 327, 372

Langley, Va., 175, 176, 178, 410
Lawson, Dorie McCullough, xi–xii
Lawson, Tim, xi
Lebanon, 148, 218, 238
LeTourneau, R.G., 93–94
Libya, 145
Liedtke, Bill, 90–95

Liedtke, Hugh, 90–95
Liedtke and Liedtke, 90
Lilly, Eli, 182
Li Peng, 286
Liu Chieh, 148
Lockerbie, 282
Lord, Winston, 286
Louisiana, 359
Love Boat, 375

MacArthur, Douglas, 146
McCain, John, 198
McCall Corporation, 60
McCance, Tom, 72
McCarthy, Eugene, 342
McCarthy, Joseph, 102–3, 130
McCarthy, Timothy, 213
McCullough, David, xi
McDaniel, Wahoo, 71
McGovern, George, 151
Madison, Dolley, 141
Mahon, George, 183–84, 187
Maine, 2–7, 29, 44, 92–93, 198, 222, 298, 318, 324, 334, 406, 411

Maine Medical Center, 388

Major, John, 168

Mallon, Neil, 58, 59, 88–89

Malta, 292–93

Mao Zedong, 147–48, 168

Marines, U.S., 369

Marshall, Thurgood, 128, 331

Martin, Lynn, 230

Mason-Dixon Line, 254

Massachusetts, 101, 196, 198, 203, 268–69

Maxim Gorky, 293

MD Anderson Cancer Center, 84, 388

Medicare, 327

Meese, Ed, 238

Melvin, Don, 37

Memorial Sloan Kettering, 79, 83, 150

Merritt Parkway, 19

Mexico, 189

Meyer, Eugene, 89

Midland, Tex., 22, 63, 64, 69–74, 80, 90, 91, 94–95, 96, 106, 110, 117, 170, 181, 183, 185–86, 188, 189, 356

Mills, Wilbur, 125

Milton, Mass., 16

Minneapolis, Minn., 28

Missouri, USS, 45

Mitterrand, François, 301, 303, 376

Miyazawa, Kiichi, 341

Mondale, Walter, 212, 229, 273

Montgomery, Sonny, 124

Moody Air Force Base, 28, 139

Morris, Robert, 111

Mosbacher, Bob, 192–93

Moscow, 220, 290

Mulroney, Brian, 168

Munich, 148

Murchison, Clint, 59

Murphy Brown, 355

Nadeau, Leo, 37

Nagasaki, 45

Nagy, Imre, 290

NASA, 145

Nashua Telegraph, 200
Natchez, 265
National Governors
    Association, 224
National Guard, 248,
    266
Nationalist Party, 147
National Press Club, 11
National Security
    Council, 239, 299
Naval Observatory, 210,
    215, 255, 270, 280
Navy, U.S., 26, 29–40,
    59, 244, 345
Negroponte, John, 146
New Hampshire, 195,
    198–202, 203, 240,
    249–50, 252, 254,
    342–44, 346, 350,
    351, 403
New Haven, Conn., 50,
    52
New Orleans, La., 258
Newsweek, 241,
    243–44
New York, 149
New York, N.Y., 8, 16,
    57, 79–80, 144,
    150, 205

New York Mets, 181,
    226
New York State, 18, 19,
    80–81
New York Times,
    143–44, 149, 171,
    233, 353
Nicaragua, 238
Nicklaus, Jack, 14
Nixon, Julie, 152
Nixon, Pat, 140
Nixon, Richard, 112,
    118, 132, 133, 137,
    139, 141–42, 147,
    151–52, 154–55,
    156, 158–59, 160,
    162, 163, 168, 177,
    191, 263
Nixon, Tricia, 139–40
Noriega, Manuel,
    294–97
North, Oliver, 239
North American Free
    Trade Agreement
    (NAFTA), 361
North Carolina, 27, 270

Obama, Barack, 177,
    330, 352, 401, 407

O'Connor, Sandra Day, 332–33

Odessa, Tex., 59, 63–64, 69, 70, 187

Olympics (Beijing, 2008), 289

Olympics (Munich, 1972), 148

O'Neill, Jan, 186

O'Neill, Joe, 185–86

O'Neill, Paul, 340

O'Neill, Tip, 222, 226

Operation Desert Storm, 305–7

Operation Iraqi Freedom, 313–15

Operation Just Cause, 295–96

Overbey, John, 89–92

Palestine, 148, 310

Palmer, Arnold, 389

Panama, 294–97, 298, 304, 317

Panama Canal, 294

Pappas, Milt, 228

Pauley, Jane, 199

Peace Corps, 103

Pearl Harbor, 24, 26, 33, 42, 319, 397

Pearson, Drew, 100

Pennzoil, 95

Perot, H. Ross, 182, 346–49, 354, 355, 359–60, 361, 363, 364, 367

Perot, Ross, Jr., 367

Perry, Rick, 184

Pershing, John "Black Jack," 15

Pettis, Jerry, 125

Phillips Academy (Andover), 22–23, 25, 31, 98, 109, 120

Pickle, Jake, 132

Pierce, Barbara, see Bush, Barbara Pierce

Pierce, Martha, 61

Pierce, Marvin, 60

Pierce, Pauline Robinson, 61, 68

Pike Committee, 172

Plimpton, George, 280

Poindexter, John, 239

Points of Light, 330

Poland, 218, 290, 403
Pollard, Ed, 214
Portland, Maine, 224
Portman, Rob, 178
Powell, Alvy, 280
Powell, Colin, 296, 300,
    383, 401
President George Bush
    Turnpike, 410
Price, Bob, 125
Proctor, Mike, 77–78
Putin, Vladimir, 402

Quayle, Dan, 263–67,
    272–73, 351,
    354–55, 356, 359
Quayle, Marilyn, 265

Ranger (dog), 376
Rather, Dan, 245–48
Reagan, Nancy, 223,
    385
Reagan, Ronald, 177,
    188, 191, 197, 199,
    202, 203–4, 206,
    208, 209, 211–13,
    214, 216, 218,
    221–23, 225, 229,

233–34, 237–39,
    243, 257, 258, 262,
    273, 277, 281, 292,
    294, 321, 326, 343,
    346, 351, 358, 364,
    385
Reconstruction, 105
Red Square, 220
Reese, Jim, 187
Rehnquist, William,
    280, 333, 395
Republican National
    Committee (RNC),
    32, 152, 153, 156,
    193
Republican National
    Convention, 205,
    258, 356
Republican Party, 18,
    99, 101, 105–7, 110,
    113, 117, 135, 151,
    155, 159, 237–38,
    327, 342–44
Reykjavik, 221
Rhodes, Don, 193–95
Rice, Condoleezza, 128
Richards, Ann, 231, 256
Richman, Arthur, 226

Roberts, John, 333
Robertson, Pat, 248–49, 254
Robinson, James E., 60
Rockefeller, Nelson, 19, 164
Rockefeller family, 108
Rodgers, June Scobee, 219
Rogers, Kenny, 204–5
Roosevelt, Franklin D., 18, 24, 44, 211, 302
Ross, Donald, 14
Rostenkowski, Dan, 408
Rove, Karl, 193, 393
Rubber Company, U.S., 16
Rudman, Warren, 331
Rumsfeld, Donald, 250, 340
Russia, 402
Russian Federation, 317
Ruth, Babe, 55
Rwanda, 145
Rye, N.Y., 25, 42–43

St. Ann's, 4–5, 12, 15
St. George's, 14

St. Louis, Mo., 8, 13, 15, 57
St. Martin's Episcopal Church, 220, 278
Sam Houston Elementary School, 22, 83
San Jacinto, USS, 30, 31, 33–34, 37, 42, 46, 293
Saturday Night Live, 370
Saturday Night Massacre, 154
Saudi Arabia, 300, 301, 307, 327
Schaap, Dick, 149
Schwarzenegger, Arnold, 7
Schwarzkopf, Norman, 299
Scobee, Dick, 219
Scowcroft, Brent, 277, 288–89, 318, 376
Senate, U.S., 82, 98–104, 109–15, 120, 142, 152, 154, 228, 263–64, 285, 305, 311–12, 332

September 11, 2001
   terrorist attacks, 26,
   214, 300, 309–10,
   397, 403
Shaw, Bernard, 271
Shea Stadium, 145
Shevardnadze, Eduard,
   302
Shivers, Allan, 105, 184,
   189
Silverado Banking
   Savings and Loan,
   333–34
Simmons Hardware, 15
Simpson, Alan, 120
Simpson, Milward, 120
Situation Room, 215
Sixteenth Amendment,
   108
60 Minutes, 350
Smith, Mary Louise,
   197
Smith College, 29
SMU, 413
Social Security, 327–28
Solidarity movement,
   218, 290
Somalia, 369
Souter, David, 331

South Braintree,
   Mass., 16
South Carolina, 203,
   254
South Penn Oil, 95
Soviet Union, 11, 160,
   206, 219–21, 282,
   290–94, 301–2,
   317–23
Sports Illustrated, 280
Stahl, Lesley, 206
Stalin, Joseph, 302
START treaty, 231
State of the Union,
   201
Stedman Products, 16
Steiger, Bill, 125
Stephanopoulos, George,
   364
Stevenson, Adlai, 143
Stewart, Potter, 209
Stimson, Henry, 24
Strauss, Bob, 160
Stuart, Gilbert, 141
Sulzberger, Arthur, 149
Sununu, John, 250, 277,
   331, 339
Super Tuesday, 240–41,
   254

Supreme Court, U.S., 157, 330–32, 333, 393

Syria, 148, 315, 316

Taft, Robert, 101

Taft, William Howard, 54

Taiwan, 147–48, 167

Tauke, Tom, 197

Tea Party, 344

Teeter, Bob, 365

Tenet, George, 178

Texas, 50–51, 54, 58–61, 63–66, 69–72, 81, 87, 94–97, 98, 101, 105–14, 117, 135, 152, 163, 169, 172, 180–89, 203, 254, 274, 276, 298, 340, 343, 345–46, 356–57, 379, 394, 408

Texas, University of, 70, 89

Texas A&M, 70, 215, 385, 388

Texas Air National Guard, 134, 139

Texas and Pacific Railway, 69

Texasgulf Oil, 182

Texas Rangers, 297, 329, 340

Thatcher, Margaret, 217, 301

Thomas, Clarence, 331–32

Thornburgh, Dick, 337

Tiananmen Square, 287–88, 291

Time, 19

TODAY show, 4

Tokyo, 44, 48

Tonkin Gulf, 126

Tower, John, 107, 135, 285

Tracy, Spencer, 200

Truman, Harry, 18, 44

Tsongas, Paul, 351

Turbo (poodle), 52

Tuttle, Holmes, 208

Tuttle, Robert, 208

Tutu, Desmond, 222

Twain, Mark, 253

Twenty-Fifth Amendment, 222

'21' Club, 205

Ukraine, 318
United Nations, 108,
142–49, 164, 167,
217, 302–3, 304,
309, 311–12
General Assembly of,
147–48
Human Rights
Council of, 145
Security Council of,
147, 148, 302, 311
United Negro College
Fund (UNCF), 18,
129
United Service
Organizations
(USO), 18
United States Golf
Association, 18
United States
Information
Agency, 23
United States Liaison
Office (Beijing),
164, 165–67, 170
U.S. Open, 247
of 1926, 14
U.S. Senior Open, 14
Utah, USS, 33

Valdosta, Ga., 28, 139
Van Buren, Martin, 235,
276, 349
Velvet Revolution, 291
Venezuela, 196
Vietnam syndrome,
308
Vietnam War, 126–27,
130, 141, 266, 295,
346, 361
Vincent, Fay, 74
Virginia Beach, 45
Viva Zapata!, 91
Vogue, 61

W.A. Harriman &
Company, 8, 17
Wake Island, 35
Waldorf Astoria, 144,
146, 149, 153
Wałesa, Lech, 218,
290
Walker Cup, 8
Walker, Dorothy, see
Bush, Dorothy
Walker
Walker, George Herbert
"Bert," 7–9, 16, 17,
57, 59, 63, 81, 93

Walker, George Herbert "Herbie", Jr., 56, 89, 91, 181
Walker, John, 79–80
Walker, Lou, 8
Walker, Mary, 181
Walker, Nancy, 13, 30
Walker family, 81
Walker's Point, 3–4, 6–7, 8, 10, 16, 63, 92–93, 145, 182, 224, 255, 298, 301, 324, 364, 387, 402, 409
Wall Street, 18, 51, 57, 72, 87, 91, 99, 110, 165
Walsh, Lawrence, 363
Warner, Margaret, 243
Warren, Earl, 108, 395
Washington, D.C., 11, 20, 120, 124, 137, 139, 143, 153, 165, 207, 208–13, 221, 225, 298, 328, 348
Washington, George, 141, 280
Washington Monument, 209

Washington Post, 89, 161, 240, 390
Watergate scandal, 153–59, 160–62, 172, 228
Webster, William, 177
Weinberger, Caspar, 364
Welch, Harold, 70
Welch, Laura, see Bush, Laura Welch
West, Doug, 38
West Germany, 292
West Texas, 50–51, 58, 60, 63–66, 69–72, 87, 96, 113–14, 165, 276
White, Ted, 37–38, 40, 47
White House, xi, 139, 142, 152–53, 161, 222, 277, 284, 300, 339, 402
Will, George, 240
Williams, Ted, 251, 388
Wold-Chamberlain Naval Air Base, 28
Wolfe, Tom, 29
Woodward, Bob, 161
World War I, 15

World War II, 1–2, 24,
     32–46, 87, 135,
     244, 251–53, 263,
     284, 293, 304, 319,
     337, 343, 356, 372
Wykes, Jim, 34
Wyvell, Dorothy, 78–80

Yale Glee Club, 15
Yale University, 14, 17,
     24, 42, 50, 51–56,
     58, 64, 101, 116,
     228

Yale Whiffenpoofs, 15,
     100
Yarborough, Ralph,
     112, 115, 118, 133,
     134–35
Yeltsin, Boris, 318, 319
Yemen, 303

Zahn, Paula, 47
Zapata Offshore, 93–95,
     97
Zapata Petroleum, 91,
     93